100
DIVING SITES
UNDERWATER PARADISES AROUND THE GLOBE

Parragon
Queen Street House
4 Queen Street
Bath BA1 1HE, UK

ISBN 978-1-4454-0111-9

Original German edition Design:
LKO Verlagsgesellschaft mbH, Cologne;
Production and picture research: Inga Menkhoff, Cologne

English-language edition produced by Cambridge Publishing Management Ltd

Translator: David Darrah-Morgan

Printed in China

Picture credits:

Photos © Paul Munzinger, www.uw-media.de
p. 23 top © Heike Merz, www.nauticteam.com
p. 26/27 © Ingo Vollmer, www.marlin.de
p. 39 © Waltraud Binanzer, www.dietaucher.com
p. 143 top © Craig "Monty" Sheppard, www.bilikiki.com
p. 144 © Helmut Debelius
p. 146 © Horst Ringeisen
p. 147 top © www.moorea-fundive.com
p. 147 bottom © www.bigstockphoto.com
p. 153 bottom & p. 155 top © Courtesy of Tourism Queensland
p. 156 © Gerald Nowak
p. 162/163 © www.underseahunter.com
p. 182 left © Ty Sawyer

Key for the Facts boxes:

❖ **Level of difficulty:** ■ (= easy) – ■■■■■ (= difficult)

❖ **Diversity of coral species:** ■ (= limited) – ■■■■■ (= wide)

❖ **Diversity of fish species:** ■ (= limited) – ■■■■■ (= wide)

❖ **Big fish:** ■ (= few) – ■■■■■ (= many)

❖ **Wrecks:** ■ (= few) – ■■■■■ (= many)

❖ **Caves:** ■ (= few) – ■■■■■ (= many)

❖ **Walls:** ■ (= few) – ■■■■■ (= many)

❖ **Snorkeling:** ■ (= few opportunities) – ■■■■■ (= many opportunities)

100
DIVING SITES
UNDERWATER PARADISES AROUND THE GLOBE

PAUL MUNZINGER

Parragon
Bath · New York · Singapore · Hong Kong · Cologne · Delhi · Melbourne

Contents

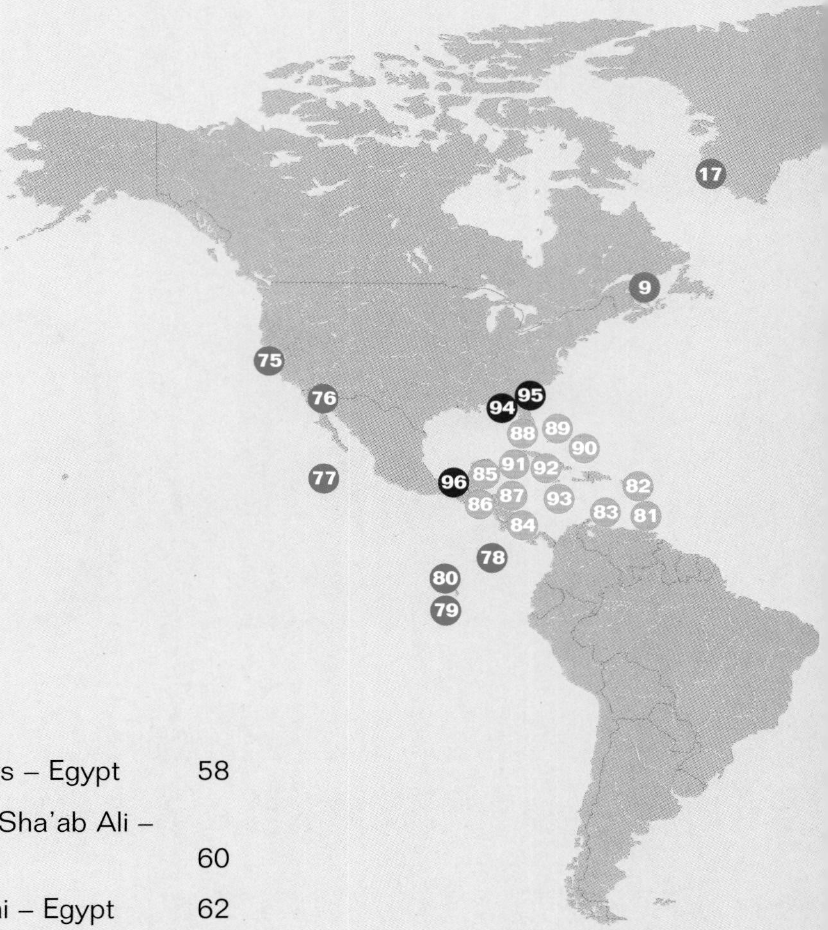

Foreword

Selecting the best dive locations in the world is a difficult task—after all, the oceans cover more than two-thirds of the surface of our planet. The Mediterranean alone covers an area of more than 1,150,000 square miles/3 million square km, and the sea floor there is strewn with numerous wrecks. Indonesia has more than 18,000 islands with wonderful coral-covered walls, the Caribbean numbers thirty-six archipelagos; and have the many atolls and reefs of the entire Pacific ever been counted?

Worldwide, there are many fascinating dive spots that are worth visiting, all of them unique in their own different ways. Wrecks and amphora fields rich in history offer thrilling underwater experiences. Encounters with big fish such as the great white shark are a dream for some, a nightmare for others. Caves and caverns are a source of delight for many, but if you suffer from claustrophobia you would be better off diving along the endless walls or the colorful tropical coral formations.

Various criteria were used to select the best diving areas. For a reef to be chosen as one of the best and most beautiful dive sites in the world, its underwater flora and fauna have to be varied and unusual.

Unfortunately, advancing climate change, together with the associated warming of the oceans, is having deleterious effects on the reefs. Due to coral bleaching and the gradual dying off of the reefs, once-beautiful areas have over time deteriorated into underwater deserts.

Water quality is also of key importance, whether in the bone-chillingly cold ocean north of the Arctic Circle in Greenland, in warm tropical waters, or in the many lakes and rivers that are still undervalued by most divers. Extraordinary things are to be found almost everywhere, and this book shows you exactly where to find them. The spots have been selected to provide as much variety as possible. They are intended to inspire novices and to point out alternative sites for expert divers. Dive with us into the wonders of the oceans, the fantastic world beneath the waves, where unforgettable adventures await you.

Between Europe and Africa in the east and the Americas in the west, the Atlantic, the world's second-largest ocean, stretches from the Arctic to the Antarctic. While the coral life here is less diverse than in some of the other oceans, the range of underwater flora and fauna is very wide. The most popular diving destinations are in one of its adjacent seas, the Mediterranean.

ATLANTIC OCEAN
AND ADJACENT SEAS

MEDITERRANEAN: FRANCE

Îles d'Hyères

THIS ARCHIPELAGO OFF THE CÔTE D'AZUR IS AN UNDERWATER PARADISE THAT IS CONSIDERED THE CRADLE OF RECREATIONAL DIVING. THE AREA ALSO INCLUDES PORT-CROS, A MARINE NATIONAL PARK, AND A VAST SHIPS' GRAVEYARD.

The Côte d'Azur is part of underwater history. It was here, on the French Riviera, in the 1930s that Austrian diving pioneer Hans Hass first put his head beneath the waves, and that his colleague Jacques-Yves Cousteau, in collaboration with Émile Gagnan, developed the first diving regulator.

This section of the coast, which stretches roughly from Marseille to Monte Carlo, features numerous highlights along its entire length and is a real El Dorado for recreational divers. Just 30 miles/50 km east of Toulon, French diving continues to thrive in its heartland, the Îles d'Hyères archipelago.

The three main islands, Porquerolles, Port-Cros, and the Île du Levant, lie east of the Giens Peninsula, where several dive centers have been established. Every morning, dive boats set off from here to more than forty spots around the peninsula and the small island archipelago. The main destinations they head for are the island of Porquerolles and the popular nature conservation area of Port-Cros, which exudes a real Caribbean atmosphere.

The small island of La Gabinière holds a particular attraction: several dozen groupers live around this rock, the Methuselah of them all measuring 5 ft/1.5 m in length. At the dive spot known as Sec de la Gabinière, divers can marvel at dense forests of red gorgonian sea fans, large hake, and fat conger eels.

1 FACTS

- ❖ **Depth:** 50–180 ft/15–55 m
- ❖ **Visibility:** 40–100 ft/12–30 m
- ❖ **Water temperature:** 57–73°F/ 14–23°C
- ❖ **Best time of year:** May–Oct
- ❖ **Level of difficulty:** ■–■■■■■
- ❖ **Diversity of coral species:** ■■■
- ❖ **Diversity of fish species:** ■■■
- ❖ **Big fish:** ■■■
- ❖ **Wrecks:** ■■■■■
- ❖ **Caves:** ■
- ❖ **Walls:** ■■■
- ❖ **Snorkeling:** ■■■, Port-Cros: ■■■■

"Must-see" sites also include the numerous shipwrecks and wrecked aircraft, of course. If the weather plays ball and you have the necessary experience, you should definitely take a look at the shipwrecks *Donator* (maximum depth 170 ft/52 m), well known for its coral, and *Le Grec* (maximum depth 155 ft/47 m). Both freighters fell victim to floating mines at the end of World War II. They lie fairly close together, between Porquerolles and Port-Cros, southeast of the small island of Petit Sarranier, which is also a prime dive site. Further wrecks in the area include the *Conger*, the *Ville de Grasse*, the *Rubis*, the *Michel C*, a Heinkel, and a Mustang.

As impressive as the diving around the Hyères is today, it is hard to imagine that not all that long ago the area looked totally different. At the beginning of the 1980s, the sea was very polluted and overfished. There was nothing left for divers to see, and, to cap it all, everything was very expensive. This led to the mass exodus of divers to the Red Sea. It is still not exactly cheap on the Côte d'Azur today, but thanks not least to stricter laws, the sea is clean again and has plenty to offer underwater.

Opposite page: The stern and deck superstructure of *Le Grec*.

Above: Yellow and red gorgonian sea fans at the Sec du Serranier.

Left: About a dozen groupers live around the small rocky island of La Gabinière.

MEDITERRANEAN: SPAIN

Costa Brava

ALONG THE COSTA BRAVA'S COASTLINE, WHICH IS ABOUT 100 MILES/160 KM LONG, EXCELLENT DIVING SPOTS ABOUND. THE "WILD COAST'S" TWO ENCHANTING MARINE PARKS MAKE THIS AREA THE DIVING MECCA OF THE MEDITERRANEAN.

The Costa Brava stretches from the Spanish/French border at Portbou as far as Blanes and forms part of the autonomous region of Catalonia. The name of this stretch of coastline was coined by the writer Ferran Agulló as far back as 1908. The parts of the coast he described as particularly "wild" were the bizarre rocky cliffs of the Cap de Creus peninsula in the north, some of which are extremely steep, and the coast of the Cap de Begur farther south. Nowadays, these wild places are especially popular with divers. Between the two capes lie former small fishing villages that over the years have developed into tourist centers.

In the north of the Costa Brava, recreational diving is centered around the town of Rosas and the Cap de Creus Natural Park. For connoisseurs, the dive sites at Cap Norfeu, such as El Gat, Trencast, and La Rata, are particularly alluring. These can be reached from the dive centers in Rosas, Cala Joncols, and Cadaqués. La Rata, also known as Massa d'Or, is the unspoken favorite on the entire Costa Brava coast, but due to the often difficult weather conditions can only rarely be visited and then only by very experienced divers. All the northern sites feature forests of gorgonian sea fans, octopuses, spiny lobsters, conger eels, scorpionfish, sea bass, and also precious red corals.

The town of L'Estartit and the protected Islas Medas that lie just offshore are the center for diving in the south. Between here and San Feliu there is a whole range of different top-class dive sites. Since the use of harpoons was banned, the numbers of huge groupers in the waters around the islands have increased, and spiny lobsters are also well protected here. In the caves and caverns it is often still possible to find "red gold" beneath overhangs—but the precious red corals, which can be as large as a hand, are protected by law and must not be touched.

Farther south, off Tamariu, there is a thriving, densely packed colony of what are probably the most impressive gorgonian sea fans in the whole Mediterranean. Anthias and even oarfish dart between the red and yellow fans. In the bay of Tamariu you can find sea horses, pipefish, weevers, sea robins, and snake eels. In bad weather it attracts not only divers, but also large numbers of biologists.

The whole Costa Brava, with its two great dive sites in the north and in the south, has made a substantial contribution to the renaissance of the Mediterranean.

Opposite page: This octopus is cunningly concealing itself from the divers.

Above: A conger eel in the bay of Cala Joncols.

Left: A picture-perfect coral wall in Tamariu.

2 FACTS

- **Depth:** 15–130 ft/5–40 m
- **Visibility:** 30–100 ft/10–30 m
- **Water temperature:** 57–75°F/ 14–24°C
- **Best time of year:** May–Oct
- **Level of difficulty:** ■–■■■
- **Diversity of coral species:** ■■■■
- **Diversity of fish species:** ■■■■
- **Big fish:** ■■■
- **Wrecks:** ■■
- **Caves:** ■■■
- **Walls:** ■■■■
- **Snorkeling:** ■■■■

MEDITERRANEAN: SPAIN

Mallorca

MALLORCA, THE LARGEST ISLAND IN THE BALEARICS, HAS ALMOST THREE DOZEN DIVE CENTERS. MINORCA, IBIZA, AND FORMENTERA ADD ANOTHER 25, MAKING IT A REAL DIVERS' PARADISE.

The Balearics lie in the western Mediterranean, about 55–125 miles/ 90–200 km from the Spanish mainland, and are one of the world's most popular travel destinations. Each year, millions of Europeans travel to these holiday islands, which have far more to offer than just palm-lined beaches and parties. It is thus hardly surprising that a number of international dive centers have set themselves up on this fantastically indented coastline.

The dive sites in the southwest, southeast, and northeast of Mallorca are particularly well known and popular. The island of Sa Dragonera ("dragon island") in the southwestern corner is a protected conservation area and is often recommended by divers as a personal tip. You can reach it quickly from the dive shops around Port Andratx and San Telmo.

Sa Dragonera, the La Mola peninsula, and Cap de Llamp alone contain enough subjects to fill an entire picture book on the flora and fauna of the Mediterranean. The variety of fish species is greatest in the months from April to July. As well as the corals, which lie at a depth of about 130 ft/40 m, there are walls and overhangs that are covered with yellow polyps. Caverns and caves such as K6 and El Catedral, with their magnificent dripstone formations, provide added variety. Divers with caving experience can dive into two air-filled caves to admire the stalactites and stalagmites. Besides having more than forty dive sites well worth visiting, the southwest also has two wrecks: the MS *Goggi III* and the MS *Josephine* should definitely go in your logbook, although they do require a degree of experience.

In the northeast of Mallorca lies Cala Ratjada, with walls 30–125 ft/10–38 m deep, overgrown canyons, and the impressive Jaimes Cathedral, a superlative cave discovered in 1970. Rays, tuna, and barracuda live in these waters, which contain little plankton and are therefore generally very clear.

There are nearly forty more dive sites on the Cala d'Or in the southeast of the island. With everything from reefs to caves, they cater to every diver's taste. Probably no one has ever counted how many top spots there are around the whole island.... But don't forget the neighboring islands, each of which merits a diving holiday in its own right.

Opposite page: A beautifully encrusted anchor at Punta Galinda near Port Andratx.

Top: The painted comber is found in caves and recesses.

Center: The conger eel is generally well hidden and therefore harder to find.

Bottom: When disturbed, the tube anemone retracts into its tube at lightning speed.

3 FACTS

- **Depth:** 15–130 ft/5–40 m
- **Visibility:** 50–115 ft/15–35 m
- **Water temperature:** 57–82°F/ 14–28°C
- **Best time of year:** Mar–Nov
- **Level of difficulty:** ■–■■■■■
- **Diversity of coral species:** ■■■
- **Diversity of fish species:** ■■■■
- **Big fish:** ■■■
- **Wrecks:** ■
- **Caves:** ■■■■■
- **Walls:** ■■■■
- **Snorkeling:** ■■■

MEDITERRANEAN: ITALY

Cala Gonone

ON THE EAST COAST OF SARDINIA, IN THE GULF OF OROSEI, LIES THE SMALL SEASIDE RESORT OF CALA GONONE. THE UNDERWATER CAVERNS AND CAVES THAT ARE FOUND HERE ARE SOME OF THE MOST BEAUTIFUL THE MEDITERRANEAN HAS TO OFFER.

The water here is so clear that when the sea is calm you can even make out the wreck, which sits upright on the sandy sea bed at a depth of 110 ft/34 m, from the surface. The *KT 12* was built in Livorno for the German Navy during World War II to transport vehicles, fuel, and food to north Africa. However, the armed naval vessel was attacked on June 10, 1943 by the English submarine *Safari* and hit across the bow by one of its torpedoes. It sank, and now it lies on the sea floor off Orosei.

Pink anthias, black damselfish, congers, moray eels, and sea bass have since made their home on this artificial reef. It is easy to swim around the deck superstructure, and it is possible to see the wheelhouse and the remains of the ship's cargo, for example some trucks, in one dive. The propeller, the deck gun, and the colorful aft wheel are particularly beautiful. If you want to dive down to the *KT 12*, you should have nitrox in your tank, otherwise you will have to endure tedious decompression stops in open water on the way up.

Directly offshore from the Cala Luna, the most famous beach in the area around Cala Gonone, is the wreck of the former steamer *Nasello*, which was also sunk in 1943. World War II has left a terrible legacy all along the Sardinian coast—a hundred wrecks slumber around the island's coasts. Many of these lie too deep for recreational divers and are thus the preserve of technical divers, sometimes also called tech divers.

4 FACTS

- ❖ **Depth:** 10–130 ft/3–40 m
- ❖ **Visibility:** 65–130 ft/20–40 m
- ❖ **Water temperature:** 57–75°F/14–24°C
- ❖ **Best time of year:** May–Oct
- ❖ **Level of difficulty:** ■–■■■■■
- ❖ **Diversity of coral species:** ■■
- ❖ **Diversity of fish species:** ■■■
- ❖ **Big fish:** ■
- ❖ **Wrecks:** ■■■
- ❖ **Caves:** ■■■■■
- ❖ **Walls:** ■■
- ❖ **Snorkeling:** ■■■■

Besides wrecks, this section of the coast also has caves that are well worth visiting. One of these is the seemingly endless Utopia cave system off Cala Gonone. The passages of the Galeria and Grotta della Ostriche also take you right to the edge of the daylight zone and into the depths of the earth. However, cavern and cave diving courses are a prerequisite for these dives. The Grotta Smeralda, on the other hand, is easy to dive, since you can surface at any time. In general, diving around Cala Gonone is ideal for novice divers, as the sea floor slopes gently away from the coast.

Although Sardinia is the second-largest island in the Mediterranean, there are very few dive centers along its coast. The superb coastline of the Gulf of Orosei, together with the area around Alghero in the northwest of the island, has to be the absolute highlight for any diver. Even internationally renowned cave divers return here again and again because there is still so much left to discover.

Opposite page: A mystical view—the deck gun on the *KT 12*.

Above: After surfacing in the magical Grotta Smeralda.

Below left: A wheel of the *KT 12*, encrusted with new life.

Below right: Not for beginners—diving in the Utopia caves.

MEDITERRANEAN: ITALY

Elba

SINCE THE TIME OF THE POSTWAR ECONOMIC BOOM IN EUROPE, ELBA HAS BEEN CONSIDERED ONE OF THE CLASSIC DIVING DESTINATIONS. EVEN TODAY, THE UNDERWATER TYRRHENIAN SEA IS EXTRAORDINARILY BEAUTIFUL.

The iron ore island of Elba has had a checkered history: Etruscans, Romans, Lombards, and a number of other peoples have occupied the island over the course of the last 2,750 years. One famous person came here against his will—Napoleon. After his failed Russian campaign in 1814, the former ruler of Europe was exiled to Elba, where he enacted laws and reforms that made a major contribution to the island's progress.

In 1996, another law of great importance ensured the protection of large sections of the natural world above and below the water. This had become necessary because, due to overfishing and harpooning, scarcely any big fish remained off the coasts of Elba. The situation changed only after the establishment of the Parco Nazionale Arcipelago Toscano, a national park.

From a bird's-eye view, Corsica's little sister, which lies just 12 miles/20 km from Italy, looks like a giant whale. The island's coastline, which is 108 miles/174 km long, can be divided into the following diving areas: the north around Portoferraio and Cavo, the east around Porto Azurro, the south around Marina di Campo, and the west around Pomonte.

In the north of Elba, off the little lighthouse island of Scoglietto, there are caves, walls covered in gorgonian sea fans, sea bass, and occasionally even sunfish. With a bit of luck you will see shoals of tuna at the nearby Capo d'Enfola. From Marciana Marina you

Opposite page: A wall covered with brilliant red gorgonian sea fans.

Right: A moray eel in menacing pose.

Below: Precious coral, also known as "red coral."

can reach Punto Nasuto, where a legendary statue of Christ stands underwater; and in the bay of Portoferraio, at a depth of about 120 ft/37 m, there are sections of a shot-down "Ju 52." At the northernmost end, at Capo Vita,an anchor as tall as two men, which is said to have come from a papal ship, lies among coral fans.

In the northeast of Elba, off the small island of Palmaiola, you can dive the shallows at Secca del Frate, where the sea bed rises almost to the surface, and which is a good area for nudibranchs. The walls situated to the east of the island at Punta delle Cannelle, just off Porto Azurro at Picchi di Pablo, and around the island of Remaiolo to the southeast, are just as colorfully overgrown.

In the south, there are fantastic coral forests at Capo di Stella. At Secca di Fonza, the highlights are congers, octopuses, and precious corals. The best-known wreck off the coast of Elba is the *Elviscott*. It has been lying off the western tip near Pomonte since 1971, and as it lies at a depth of just 40 ft/13 m, it is also suitable for novices.

There is superb diving about 30 miles/ 50 km to the south of Elba, off the island of Giglio, where you can see lobsters.

5 FACTS

- **Depth:** 30–130 ft/10–40 m
- **Visibility:** 50–100 ft/15–30 m
- **Water temperature:** 55–81°F/ 13–27°C
- **Best time of year:** May–Oct
- **Level of difficulty:** ■–■■■
- **Diversity of coral species:** ■■■
- **Diversity of fish species:** ■■■
- **Big fish:** ■■
- **Wrecks:** ■
- **Caves:** ■
- **Walls:** ■■■■
- **Snorkeling:** ■■■

MEDITERRANEAN: CROATIA

The Kornati

THE KORNATI, THE LARGEST GROUP OF ISLANDS IN THE MEDITERRANEAN, ARE CROATIA'S LARGEST CONTIGUOUS DIVING AREA. THEY ARE STRICTLY PROTECTED, AND THEIR FLORA AND FAUNA REMAIN ALMOST UNTOUCHED. DIVERS HERE ARE IN FOR A REAL SURPRISE.

Divine, secluded islands, surrounded by crystal-clear water—that is how the Kornati advertise themselves, and they are not exaggerating. This unique chain of islands, with its austere charm, is located in the center of the Adriatic and extends over an area 22 miles/35 km in length and 5 miles/8 km in width. The Kornati archipelago is privately owned by some of the inhabitants of the island of Murter.

As early as 1980, most of the territory was designated a national park. Today, 89 of the approximately 150 islands are protected—underwater as well as on land. The largest and longest island is known as Kornat and comprises two-thirds of the park's land area—you can imagine how tiny the other islands, which lie to the southwest, are. They have a combined coastline totaling some 115 miles/185 km and have much to offer, as do the numerous dive spots outside the national park.

There are two official ways into the labyrinth of islands, from which divers start their day trips: the northern one is located 15 nautical miles from Šibenik, near Dugi Otok, a highly praised diving island. It is possible to reach the national park somewhat faster from the dive centers on Murter in the south.

Underwater, divers get their money's worth, particularly at close range: colorful nudibranchs, delicate sea horses, ferocious-looking scorpionfish, shy spiny lobsters, and wily octopuses, to name but a few of the area's inhabitants. There are superb, profusely overgrown walls at the Cathedral as well as at Samograd and Balun. Besides fan corals, various species of sponge are also found here.

As the Kornati are located on one of the most important waterways of the Ancient Greeks and Romans, remnants of amphorae are frequently found on the sea bed. The winds in this area are still notorious today, as a number of recent wrecks bear witness. The showpiece wreck off Murter is the wonderfully overgrown *Francesca di Rimini*, which was laden with munitions for the troops in Africa when it sank in 1944. The deck lies at a depth of about 130 ft/40 m and can therefore only be explored by experienced divers.

Throughout the national park, diving is permitted only for organized groups and in marked zones, and fees are charged.

Opposite page: An amphora field in the Kornati diving area.

Below: Getting close to a Mediterranean jellyfish.

6 FACTS

- **Depth:** 15–215 ft/5–65 m
- **Visibility:** 50–130 ft/15–40 m
- **Water temperature:** 55–75°F/13–24°C
- **Best time of year:** May–Oct
- **Level of difficulty:** ■–■■■■■
- **Diversity of coral species:** ■■■
- **Diversity of fish species:** ■■■
- **Big fish:** ■
- **Wrecks:** ■■
- **Caves:** ■■
- **Walls:** ■■■■
- **Snorkeling:** ■■■

MEDITERRANEAN: MALTA

Malta

MALTA IS THE SMALLEST COUNTRY IN THE EU AND LIES IN THE SOUTHERN MEDITERRANEAN. THE ARCHIPELAGO, CONSISTING OF MALTA, GOZO, AND COMINO, IS A HOT TIP FOR DIVERS WITH AN INTEREST IN CULTURE.

Thanks to its strategic position, the island of Malta has always been popular. The Maltese islands, lying south of Sicily, east of Tunisia, and north of Libya, have been a trading and military center for more than 6,000 years. Carthaginians, Phoenicians, Romans, Arabs, French, British, and others have all come to Malta. Over the years, the Maltese islands have thus become an enormous open-air museum bearing traces of various styles and epochs, underwater as well as on land.

The popularity of Malta, Gozo, and Comino has not waned over the years. This tiny paradise in the Mediterranean attracts tourists from all over Europe. It is an extremely attractive destination for divers due to the very good visibility conditions, pleasant water temperatures and enthralling dive sites.

The very high cliffs continue beneath the surface of the water, making the coast ideal for diving. It is a wonderful experience to hang in the crystal-clear water in front of the drop-offs that plunge down into the blue depths. The flora and fauna there are among the most beautiful in this, the Atlantic's warmer neighboring sea.

What is special about Malta are the numerous tunnels, some of which form giant caves and caverns, such as Billinghurst, Coral, Gudja, L'Ahrax, and St. Mary's Cave, as well as a whole series of shipwrecks. "Battleships" is a game played in real life in Malta and subsidized by the state and the EU, as

7 FACTS

- ❖ **Depth:** 15–140 ft/5–42 m
- ❖ **Visibility:** 65–130 ft/20–40 m
- ❖ **Water temperature:** 59–82°F/ 15–28°C
- ❖ **Best time of year:** May–Oct
- ❖ **Level of difficulty:** ■–■■■■■
- ❖ **Diversity of coral species:** ■
- ❖ **Diversity of fish species:** ■■■■
- ❖ **Big fish:** ■
- ❖ **Wrecks:** ■■■■
- ❖ **Caves:** ■■■■
- ❖ **Walls:** ■■■■
- ❖ **Snorkeling:** ■■■

every sunken ship constitutes a tourist attraction. The most recent highlights rusting on the sea bed are the two Gozo ferries *Imperial Eagle* (lying at about 140 ft/ 42 m) and *Xlendi* (at about 150 ft/45 m).

Other attractions include the 165-ft-long/ 50-m-long *Karwela*, the smaller *Comino Land* shipwreck, and the *Boltenhagen*, a former minesweeper and patrol boat, which now rests near the harbor tug MS *Rozi*. The 390-ft-long/119-m-long oil tanker *Um el Faroud* and other wrecks from World War II are also popular.

Malta has not only almost everything a diver's heart could desire, but also a first-class emergency medical service for divers, which even has a rescue helicopter with a mobile decompression chamber. The leading dive centers here have received numerous awards.

Opposite page: The artistic display of a Mediterranean fan worm.

Above: The wreck of the 165-ft-long/50-m-long *Karwela*.

Left: The painted comber is an archetypal sit-and-wait predator.

Kaş

ABOVE THE WATER, THE PICTURESQUE FISHING VILLAGE OF KAŞ ON THE LYCIAN COAST IS A FAIRLY QUIET PLACE, BUT UNDER THE WATER THERE IS LOTS GOING ON: A DIVING HOLIDAY IN TURKEY IS LIKE A JOURNEY INTO THE PAST.

The village of Kaş, with 5,000 inhabitants, lies on the southern coast of Turkey between the two tourist centers of Dalaman and Antalya. Although the village has so far escaped mass tourism, the charming bay is not entirely deserted in the high season, as there are more than two dozen dive spots here, and the area has often been included in diving magazines' lists of the best dive sites. This is hardly surprising, as the sites are very varied and have an excellent range of fauna as well as many amphora fields. Novices and professionals alike will get their money's worth, and if you like warm, clear water and are interested in culture, this spot on the edge of the Taurus Mountains is the one for you.

Although there aren't that many corals in the sea off Kaş and you will search in vain for larger fish, increasing numbers of tropical fish are arriving from the Red Sea via the Suez Canal. So in these clear and turquoise-colored waters, which are not far behind tropical seas in terms of visibility, you often come across parrotfish, soldierfish, rabbitfish, triggerfish, and cornetfish. These live among huge groupers and schools of amberjacks, barracuda, bream, and tuna, and together with rays, moray eels, and turtles. In the plentiful seagrass meadows you will discover the fishes' nurseries, and even large pen shells are not uncommon.

Fascinating dive sites for looking at Greek and Roman amphorae include Assi Island and the three rocks of Üç Kaya, where there are clay vessels measuring up to 3 ft/1 m in diameter lying on the sea floor. At Çapo Banko, old stone anchors have even been found. But be warned: Turkish laws are very strict, and theft will land you in jail, with no clemency shown.

There are eight wrecks worth visiting in this area. One real gem is an Italian bomber from World War II, which lies at the foot of a diverse and interesting reef at the Flying Fish dive site. Since it lies at a depth of between 180 and 215 ft/55 and 65 m, it is suitable only for very experienced divers. Canyons, chasms, and caves, some of which even have cold fresh water flowing out of them, will fill the diver's cup of happiness to overflowing. The Lycian coast shows the Mediterranean at its best, and no diver should miss it.

Opposite page: Diving on the Turkish coast, you often come across amphorae.

Top: A sea star has taken possession of this amphora.

Center: A dotted sea slug.

Bottom: The slipper lobster has shovel-like protuberances on its head.

8 FACTS

- **Depth:** 15–215 ft/5–65 m
- **Visibility:** 65–130 ft/20–40 m
- **Water temperature:** 64–84°F/18–29°C
- **Best time of year:** Apr–Oct
- **Level of difficulty:** ■–■■■■■
- **Diversity of coral species:** ■
- **Diversity of fish species:** ■■■■
- **Big fish:** ■■■
- **Wrecks:** ■■■
- **Caves:** ■■
- **Walls:** ■■■■
- **Snorkeling:** ■■■■

ATLANTIC: CANADA

Nova Scotia

THANKS TO THE GULF STREAM, THE WATER AROUND NOVA SCOTIA IS NOT NEARLY AS COLD AS MANY IMAGINE. THE UNDERWATER WORLD HERE IN THE NORTH ATLANTIC IS COLORFUL, AND FEATURES LOBSTERS, KELP FORESTS, WRECKS, AND PRECIPITOUS COASTS.

The Nova Scotia peninsula in the east of Canada is washed by the Atlantic Ocean along its 4,700 miles/7,600 km or so of coast, and, together with Cape Breton Island, forms Canada's second-smallest province. Nova Scotia is a byword for unspoiled nature—both on land and underwater. The peninsula lies on the 45th parallel and is therefore at the same latitude as the northern Mediterranean. The temperatures are relatively mild, which means that divers need a thicker suit but not necessarily a dry suit.

From the airport in the capital of Halifax, most divers head directly to the northernmost point of the peninsula,—Janvrin's Island, between the peninsula and Cape Breton Island—which has one of the few dive shops in the area. At first, the underwater scenery in the dive sites that can be reached from here looks very green due to the dense forests of kelp. However, when you take a closer look, it is sometimes just as colorful as in many tropical climes, as corals also thrive in this region, and the fish and crustaceans are anything but monochrome.

The house reef of this picture-perfect diving resort is unusual in that it is a wreck. The *Arrow*, a former oil tanker, sank in 1970 in the middle of Chedabucto Bay and broke in two. The photogenic stern section is 525 ft/160 m long and colonized to a depth of about 40 ft/12 m by kelp forest, in which seals occasionally hunt. A few fin-strokes deeper lies the territory of lobsters, sculpins, and sea bass, and even farther down, fierce wolffish live between the sea anemones. Not far away lies the somewhat more demanding wreck of the Norwegian timber carrier *Gard*, the highest point of which lies about 60 ft/18 m below the surface. Of the many others, the wreck of the fish oil tanker *Baleine* is also particularly worth diving.

Diving expeditions to the southern bay of Fox Island, where soft corals grow from a depth of about 50 ft/15 m, have just as much to recommend them as those to the eastern diving spots. At Forest Cave anglerfish and sea ravens abound, and in the dense kelp forests off Crid lobsters will sometimes wave their claws at you. They are the trademark of Nova Scotia, the largest exporter of lobsters in the world. If you are lucky, you may even see whales and dolphins on your boat trips.

9 FACTS

- **Depth:** 15–130 ft/5–40 m
- **Visibility:** 23–65 ft/7–20 m
- **Water temperature:** 45–64°F/7–18°C
- **Best time of year:** June–Oct
- **Level of difficulty:** ■–■■■
- **Diversity of coral species:** ■
- **Diversity of fish species:** ■■■
- **Big fish:** ■■
- **Wrecks:** ■■■■■
- **Caves:** –
- **Walls:** ■■
- **Snorkeling:** ■

Opposite page: Anemones at the Cape Hogan dive site.

Left: A diver in the top superstructure of the *Arrow*.

Below: A small wolffish in a pipe near the wreck of the *Arrow*.

ATLANTIC: REPUBLIC OF CAPE VERDE

Cape Verde Islands

THE TINY ISLAND STATE OF CAPE VERDE, CONSISTING OF 15 VOLCANIC ISLANDS, LIES OFF THE WEST COAST OF AFRICA. IN THE EARLY 1990s, THE AREA WAS PASSED ON AS A TIP FROM DIVER TO DIVER, BUT IN THE LAST FEW YEARS THE ISLANDS HAVE EXPERIENCED A MINI-BOOM.

An entry in my logbook reads: "July 7, 1992, depth 100 ft/30 m, Sal Island, big nurse sharks, lots of schooling fish, very beautiful." One day later, at Punta Preta on Santiago, was added: "Dull, not much happening, murky." Just three hours later it reads "Great excitement on same island due to old anchor," and later off Fogo, "Absolutely fantastic site with mantas, groupers, whole walls covered in schools of fish."

These entries were made during a cruise at the beginning of the 1990s from the Windward Islands (Barlavento) to the Leeward Islands (Sotavento). It was an expedition-like trip, promising much in the way of unexplored terrain and sheer adventure. The swell here in the mid-Atlantic, about 280 miles/450 km west of the mainland of Africa, is often very strong, and you need to be in good physical condition, not least because of the currents which constantly crop up. However, you will be rewarded with unforgettable experiences and memories.

Off Cidade Velha, the former capital of Cape Verde on the island of Santiago, enormous anchors were being found at that time. The large valley facing the settlement, which is now a small, ordinary fishing village, once served as a natural prison for African slaves who were to be sold in Brazil and the Caribbean. The large number of anchors found underwater today are evidence of numerous pirate raids. Sir Francis Drake himself attacked the town twice. Vasco da Gama and Christopher Columbus also came to the

Opposite page: A diver looking at a gigantic anchor.

Right: A Cape Verde sea horse.

Below: Bristleworms on a sponge.

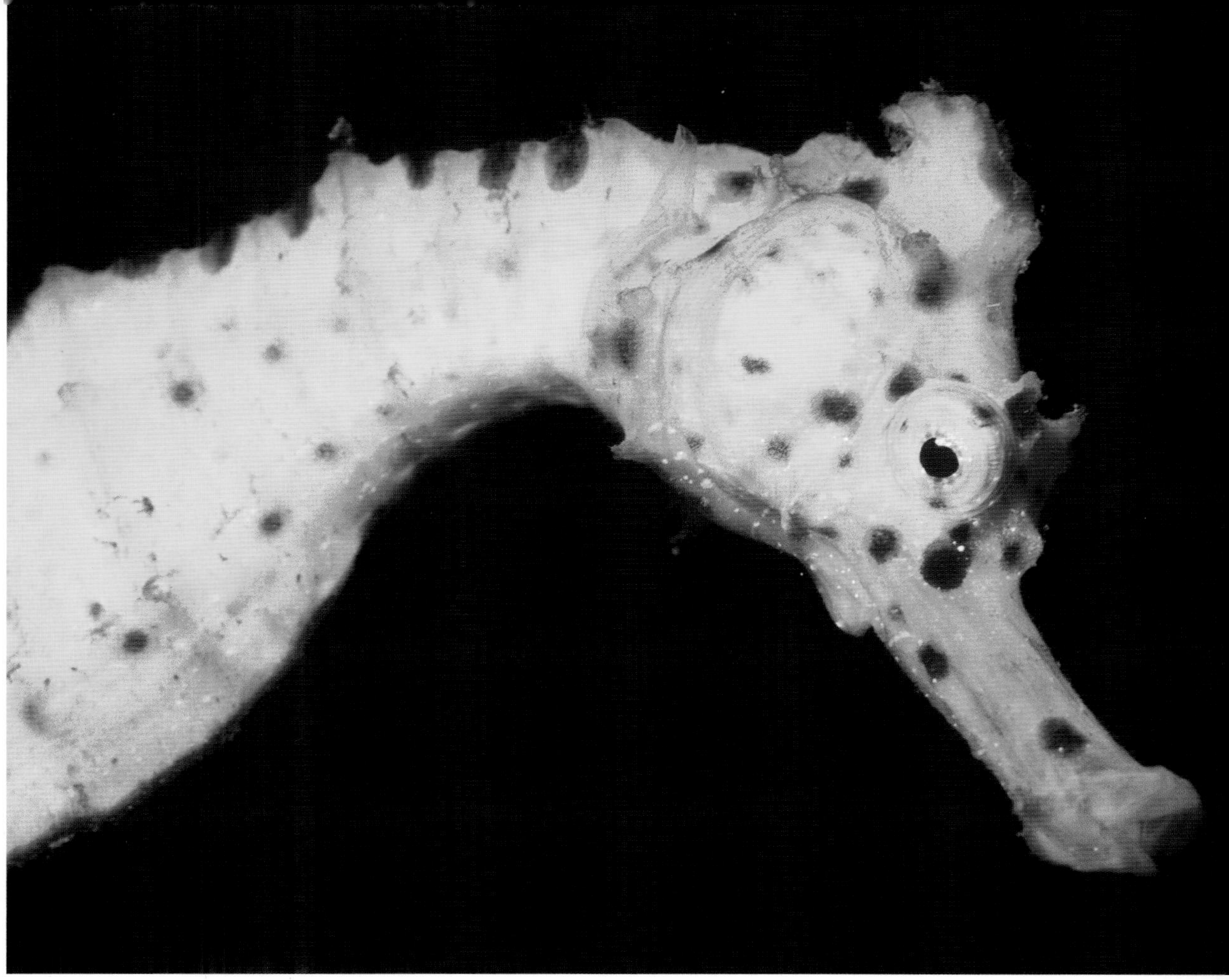

Cape Verde Islands on their early voyages of discovery.

The "mini-boom" means that today there are about a dozen dive shops here. Most of these are located on the island of Sal, due to its proximity to the airport. Santiago, where the current capital, Praia, is located, also has some dive shops as well as gorgeous beaches.

The dive guides now know the underwater landscape of the Cape Verde Islands intimately, so divers certainly get their money's worth. The variety of fishes at the dive sites is enormous, and the fact that warm and cold currents meet here means that the chances of seeing larger fish are very good. This volcanic area also has many underwater caverns, overhangs, canyons, and walls; it is, however, less colorful than other tropical diving sites.

10 FACTS

- **Depth:** 15–165 ft/5–50 m
- **Visibility:** 30–100 ft/10–30 m
- **Water temperature:** 68–82°F/20–28°C
- **Best time of year:** Mar–Nov
- **Level of difficulty:** ■–■■■■■
- **Diversity of coral species:** ■■■
- **Diversity of fish species:** ■■■■
- **Big fish:** ■■
- **Wrecks:** ■■
- **Caves:** ■■■
- **Walls:** ■■■
- **Snorkeling:** ■■

ATLANTIC: PORTUGAL

Madeira

MADEIRA LIES IN THE EASTERN ATLANTIC OCEAN, SOME 600 MILES/1,000 KM SOUTHWEST OF LISBON. IT IS A WELL-KNOWN HIKING DESTINATION, BUT ITS COASTLINE AND MARINE NATIONAL PARK MEAN THAT IT IS ALSO A PARADISE FOR DIVERS.

The wind on Madeira blows mainly from the northeast, bringing moisture and high waves with it. The north coast is therefore not ideal for diving; the south coast is drier, sunnier, and calmer. The shortage of water in this area is managed using irrigation channels called *levadas*. Alongside these run narrow paths that are used as hiking routes.

This colorful volcanic island is characterized by its mountains and steep cliffs. The highest mountain on the island, Pico Ruivo, forms merely the top quarter of a volcanic system, the steep rocky slopes of which continue down below the waves to a depth of about 13,000 ft/4,000 m. The island has very few sandy beaches, but it does have some of the highest sea cliffs in the world.

Most dive centers on Madeira are to be found in the capital Funchal and in Caniço de Baixo, not far from the airport in the east of the island. Diving here is popular largely on account of the Reserva Natural Parcial de Garajau, a marine national park that was established in 1981 on the initiative of a German activist. On this protected section of the coast, there is a hotel complex with a dive center, which has direct access to the sea. Divers can dive the house reef from the shore independently. There are four sites available to them, which have small caves and caverns where fat slipper lobsters live. Underwater, the rocky volcanic landscape provides a large number of clefts and cavities in which many fish and small creatures hide.

Besides colorful sponges and anemones with their amazing symbioses, you can also marvel at moray eels, sea bass, soldierfish, goatfish, bright red parrotfish, barracuda, and rays. The undisputed highlight, however, is the colossal hand-tame giant groupers at Cape Garajau farther south, just five minutes by boat from the hotel dive shop. If you are lucky, you will see a "yellow lemon," an unusual yellow grouper, and also manta rays or even a monk seal.

There are also some dive shops on the island of Porto Santo to the northeast of Madeira. There are a couple of dozen dive spots here, including the wreck of the *Madeirense*, a tuna and barracuda reef, and the cannon site, where several cannons dating from the eighteenth century lie strewn around between the boulders.

The marine fauna and flora around Madeira are a mixture of what divers will be familiar with from more northerly waters, the Mediterranean, and the tropical south Atlantic.

Above: The unique yellow slender grouper.

Left: An Atlantic stingray camouflaging itself in the sand.

11 FACTS

- **Depth:** 10–115 ft/3–35 m
- **Visibility:** 30–100 ft/10–30 m
- **Water temperature:** 64–75°F/ 18–24°C
- **Best time of year:** May–Oct
- **Level of difficulty:** ■–■■■
- **Diversity of coral species:** ■■
- **Diversity of fish species:** ■■■
- **Big fish:** ■■■
- **Wrecks:** ■
- **Caves:** ■■■
- **Walls:** ■■■
- **Snorkeling:** ■■■

ATLANTIC: SPAIN

Tenerife

TENERIFE IS THE LARGEST OF THE CANARY ISLANDS, WHICH BELONG GEOGRAPHICALLY TO AFRICA AND POLITICALLY TO SPAIN. IT HAS BEEN A POPULAR DIVING DESTINATION FOR MORE THAN THIRTY YEARS AND HAS MORE THAN THIRTY DIVE SHOPS.

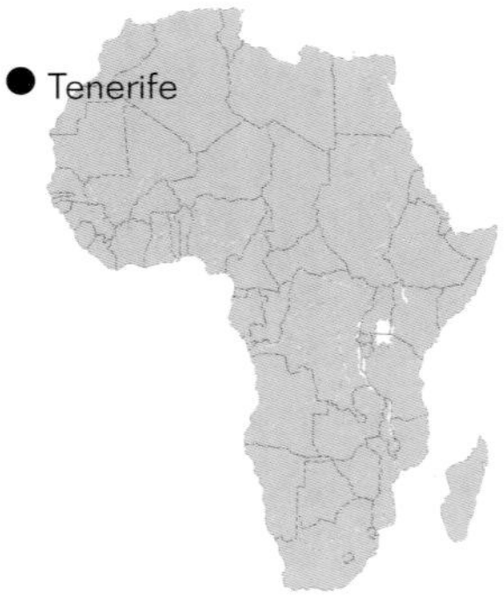

Thanks to their proximity to the Tropic of Cancer, the Canary Islands enjoy a Mediterranean/subtropical climate. It is pleasantly warm the whole year round, so the high season continues for twelve months, and the "islands of eternal spring" don't have to worry about attracting tourists. In order to keep it this way, the International Maritime Organization enacted a law in 2006 stating that ships carrying hazardous freight must make a detour and remain outside a radius of 12 nautical miles. This is intended to prevent ship accidents, which could have catastrophic consequences for the flora and fauna and also for tourism.

Tenerife is an island of contrasts, offering sun, sand, sea, and captivating scenery. Two centuries ago, Alexander von Humboldt described it as a unique natural paradise, encompassing the scenic diversity of an entire continent in an area just 50 miles/80 km long and about 30 miles/50 km wide.

As well as being home to the highest mountain in Spain, Pico del Teide, rising proudly to a height of 12,198 ft/3,718 m from a high volcanic massif, Tenerife also has much to offer below sea level. The large number of dive centers around the island are a clear indication of this.

On the more tranquil western side, slightly away from the tourist centers of the southern Playa Paraíso, there is an internationally renowned dive center under German management, which has been based there since 1980. It lies about 7 miles/12 km to the northwest of Playa de las Américas and has already received a number of awards from the diving community. It is often possible to dive directly from the shore, so beginners can also get their money's worth.

The underwater scenery, like the rest of the island, is shaped by volcanic forces. Divers will find caverns, caves, canyons, and impressive rock formations, some of which are overgrown with sponges and gorgonian sea fans. There are plenty of finned friends, too, including barracuda, rays, sea bass, tuna, trevally, wrasse, parrotfish, cow bream, moray eels, and flatfish. The underwater environment is thus a good mixture of the tropics and the Mediterranean.

Popular dive sites include the 5-Star Reef, where there are lots of rays, the Aquarium, and the Lighthouse. Gorilla Rock is famous for the sea horses that live there, El Puertito for its turtles. By boat it is also possible to reach a variety of wrecks. Sometimes, when the weather allows, there are boat trips out to see the pilot whales that live off the coast, a highlight for all divers.

Opposite page: A pilot whale.

Below left: A moray eel with cleaner shrimp.

Below right: A flamboyant anemone.

12 FACTS

- **Depth:** 35–130 ft/10–40 m
- **Visibility:** 30–100 ft/10–30 m
- **Water temperature:** 64–75°F/18–24°C
- **Best time of year:** Mar–Nov
- **Level of difficulty:** ■–■■■
- **Diversity of coral species:** ■■
- **Diversity of fish species:** ■■■
- **Big fish:** ■■■
- **Wrecks:** ■■
- **Caves:** ■■■
- **Walls:** ■■■
- **Snorkeling:** ■■■

ATLANTIC: SÃO TOMÉ AND PRÍNCIPE

São Tomé

THE SECOND-SMALLEST AFRICAN COUNTRY LIES OFF THE TOURIST TRACK, IN THE GULF OF GUINEA OFF THE COAST OF GABON. ITS DIVE LOCATIONS, WHICH ARE STILL LARGELY UNDEVELOPED, OFFER MUCH TO EXPLORE.

São Tomé is the larger of the two islands in the country of São Tomé and Príncipe, and its southern tip touches the Equator. This island is just 30 miles/50 km long, and tourists seldom venture here. This gives divers a good chance of discovering sites that no one else has ever seen.

The island lies about 125 miles/200 km from the mainland. There are no reefs to protect it, and the water conditions are therefore extremely rough. Divers must brace themselves for waves, currents, and swells.

On São Tomé itself there is a dive base in the eponymous capital. There is another to the south on the island of Rolas, which covers an area of just 1 square mile/3 square km and has about 200 inhabitants. On the main island, Lagoa Azul is one of the best-known dive sites. This "blue lagoon" in the north of the island can be dived only by making an 80-ft/24-m freefall descent through open water. Visibility is very limited by the abundance of plankton, but this also means that there are lots of fish, corals, and sponges.

South of the capital lies Ilheu Santana. At a depth of 100 ft/30 m, shoals of rainbow runners swim around a small reef of gorgonian sea fans, octopuses peer out of crevices, and occasionally you can see turtles, although they are a little shy. One unusual dive goes right through the island, via a tunnel with a maximum depth of 45 ft/14 m, in which there is always the possibility of surfacing.

13 FACTS

- **Depth:** 30–130 ft/10–40 m
- **Visibility:** 15–100 ft/5–30 m
- **Water temperature:** 79–86°F/26–30°C
- **Best time of year:** June–Feb
- **Level of difficulty:** ■■■
- **Diversity of coral species:** ■■■■
- **Diversity of fish species:** ■■■■
- **Big fish:** ■■
- **Wrecks:** ■
- **Caves:** ■■
- **Walls:** ■■
- **Snorkeling** ■

You will search in vain for proper roads on São Tomé, because since the Portuguese colonial rulers left the island in 1975 the infrastructure has gradually deteriorated. If you would like to visit the island of Rolas, you should allow at least three hours for the journey to the departure jetty. The house reef on the southern tip of this manicured hotel island is called Pedra do Hirondino and can only be reached by boat.

Here, you can get a close-up view of pencil urchins, cuttlefish, spider crabs, small gorgonian sea fans, and sea horses. *Pedra do Braga* is another rocky reef lying at a depth of 72 ft/22 m, teeming with schools of fish under overhangs, in crevices, and around an archway covered in corals. Under another overhang, an army of soldierfish stands guard over photogenic yellowmouth morays.

Perhaps the best site of all is called Sete Pedrus. As the name implies, it consists of seven rocky islets lying to the east of Rolas. Here you will find walls with a myriad of fish, bright red reef lobsters, fat moray eels, beautiful corals, turtles, and nurse sharks.

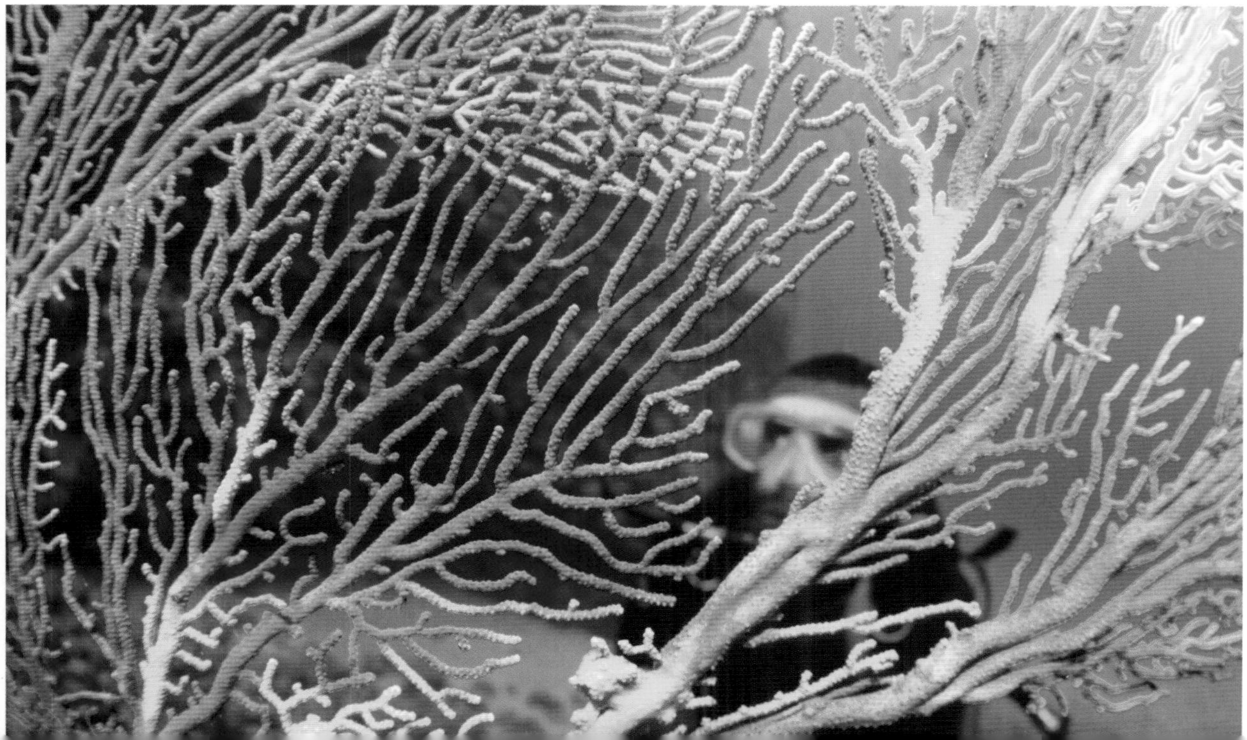

Opposite page: A magnificent reef lobster.

Top: Filigree cleaner shrimps.

Above: A yellowmouth moray, guarded by a shoal of soldierfish.

Left: A beautiful bicolored gorgonian sea fan.

ATLANTIC: SOUTH AFRICA

Cape Town

SOUTH AFRICA IS PARTICULARLY RENOWNED AMONG DIVERS FOR ITS LARGE NUMBER OF SHARKS. HOWEVER, THERE IS FAR MORE TO SEE AT THE SOUTHERN TIP OF AFRICA THAN JUST BIG FISH: ONE OF THE LARGEST ANIMAL MIGRATIONS IN THE WORLD, FOR EXAMPLE.

South Africa offers divers two experiences that are in a class of their own: firstly, an encounter with a great white shark and its smaller relatives, such as sandtiger sharks, tiger sharks, bronze whalers, hammerhead sharks, and cat sharks, which inhabit the waters between Durban and Port Elizabeth; and secondly, the spectacular "sardine run." In May in Port Elizabeth, with a lot of luck on your side, you can observe huge shoals of sardines forming so-called bait balls during one of the largest animal migrations in the world. Dolphins, whales, and sharks propel themselves ferociously into these rotating defensive formations, but most of the small fish are able to survive.

Cape Town itself is relatively unknown as a diving area, although most tourists to South Africa visit it. Nearby, at Cape Agulhas, to the east of the Cape of Good Hope, the Atlantic and Indian oceans meet. Here, at the southernmost tip of Africa, the cold Benguela current and the warm Agulhas current provide for plenty of marine life, and sometimes create quite tumultuous conditions. When the waves are only 3 ft/1 m high, the sea is considered calm and the diving conditions ideal.

Off the Cape, the sea is divided into two diving areas: False Bay and the Atlantic side. When winter reigns in Europe, in South Africa it is summer. In False Bay, the diving is good the whole year round, but the visibility is worse in the summer, whereas in winter waves can reach up to 80 ft/25 m.

The region also holds an unfortunate record: more than 2,000 wrecks lie just off the coast. However, only a few of them can be visited by divers. Besides the wrecks in Smitswinkel Bay, the SAS *Pietermaritzburg*, the *Clan Stuart*, the *Lusitania*, and the *Good Hope*, the colorful reefs are the main attraction. Boulders are encrusted with various fan corals, sponges, anemones, and soft corals. In the upper zone there are kelp forests, in which large numbers of colorful sea urchins and sea stars wander, together with more than 200 different recorded species of nudibranch. Their much speedier companions, the sea lions, often approach divers inquisitively. Smaller species of shark doze in crevices, and beautiful, enormous jellyfish sail by in open water.

The colder Atlantic side is at its quietest during the South African summer (December–March). The attractions for divers are similar to those in False Bay, and you may even encounter dolphins. There is a colony of African penguins in Simonstown, and you can snorkel with seals.

Opposite page: At the wreck of the *Good Hope*, which is luxuriantly overgrown with gorgonian sea fans and anemones.

Above: Giant jellyfish enjoy fishing in murky waters.

Left: South Africa—a rainbow nation even under the water.

14 FACTS

- **Depth:** 15–140 ft/5–42 m
- **Visibility:** 15–80 ft/5–25 m
- **Water temperature:** 50–70°F/10–21°C
- **Best time of year:** May–Feb
- **Level of difficulty:** ■■■
- **Diversity of coral species:** ■■■
- **Diversity of fish species:** ■■■■
- **Big fish:** ■■■■
- **Wrecks:** ■■■■
- **Caves:** ■
- **Walls:** ■■
- **Snorkeling:** ■■

ATLANTIC: SOUTH AFRICA

Gansbaai

YOUR BEST CHANCE OF AN ENCOUNTER WITH A GREAT WHITE SHARK IS OFF THE COAST OF SOUTH AFRICA AT GANSBAAI. HERE THERE IS THE OPPORTUNITY TO "CAGE DIVE"—A DREAM FOR MANY DIVERS, FOR OTHERS A NIGHTMARE.

Gansbaai is in South Africa's Western Cape province and lies about 105 miles/170 km southeast of Cape Town. Until a few years ago it was a sleepy fishing village, but today it makes its living from shark tourism. Many fishermen have long since exchanged their nets for cages. They no longer catch fish, but transport divers in cages into the open sea in order to give them the chance to meet a great white face to face.

Between Dyer Island and Geyser Rock, 5½ miles/8 km from the mainland, is Shark Alley, a channel approximately 300 ft/100 m wide. Great white sharks can be observed here in large numbers all year round. Sharks tend to come and stay here for six to eight weeks at a time. These creatures, which measure up to 26 ft/8 m in length, feed mainly on the seals living on Dyer Island.

The sharks are lured with bait so that diving tourists can watch them feeding from the safety of a cage. Photos showing the great white shark as an aggressive eating machine have made their way around the world, but this behavior has been provoked by large amounts of bait in the water. Actually, these intelligent creatures are rather shy around humans. Many shark conservationists therefore have mixed feelings about cage diving.

15 FACTS

- **Depth:** 3 ft/1 m
- **Visibility:** 5–50 ft/2–15 m
- **Water temperature:** 55–68°F/13–20°C
- **Best time of year:** May–Oct
- **Level of difficulty:** ■
- **Diversity of coral species:** –
- **Diversity of fish species:** –
- **Big fish:** ■■■■■
- **Wrecks:** –
- **Caves:** –
- **Walls:** –
- **Snorkeling:** prohibited

Below left: The great white shark is actually rather shy.

Below right: A glimpse into the feared jaws of the great white shark.

NORTHERN WATERS: SCOTLAND

Scapa Flow

Above: Wreck of the SMS *Cöln*.

AT THE END OF WORLD WAR I, THE GERMAN HIGH SEAS FLEET WAS SCUTTLED IN SCAPA FLOW. ALTHOUGH MANY OF THE WRECKS HAVE NOW BEEN RAISED, THIS NATURAL HARBOR IS A PARADISE FOR WRECK DIVERS.

The famous Orkney Islands are principally known for their Neolithic stone circles and burial sites, which constitute a World Heritage Site. They lie to the north of mainland Scotland, and Scapa Flow is reckoned by divers to be one of Europe's best wreck areas.

At the end of World War I, 74 ships of the German High Seas Fleet were interned at Scapa Flow. Fleet Commander Ludwig von Reuters believed that the peace talks of June 21, 1919 had collapsed, and therefore gave the order to scuttle the fleet, so that the ships would not fall into British hands.

Most of the wrecks have since been raised, and today there are only seven left resting on the sea bed. The 509-ft-long/155-m-long SMS *Cöln* is the most popular among divers, as good diving is also possible inside the vessel. The SMS *Kronprinz Wilhelm*, SMS *Markgraf*, and SMS *König* are huge warships, measuring 580 ft/177 m in length, with large deck guns. They lie at depths between about 110 and 150 ft/33–46 m, but unfortunately the deck sections are upside-down on the sea bed. It is also possible to dive inside parts of the *Karlsruhe* (500 ft/150 m long) and the *Brummer* (460 ft/140 m long).

During World War II, a German U-47 submarine managed to enter the natural harbor and sink a British ship. The British then deliberately sank some blockships in shallow water to act as a barrier: these now provide interesting areas for divers.

16 FACTS

- **Depth:** 30–210 ft/10–63 m
- **Visibility:** 12–50 ft/4–15 m
- **Water temperature:** 46–57°F/8–14°C
- **Best time of year:** May–Aug
- **Level of difficulty:** ■■■–■■■■■
- **Diversity of coral species:** ■
- **Diversity of fish species:** ■■
- **Big fish:** ■
- **Wrecks:** ■■■■■
- **Caves:** –
- **Walls:** –
- **Snorkeling:** –

NORTHERN WATERS: GREENLAND

Sisimiut

COLORFUL, RICH IN SPECIES, CRYSTAL CLEAR, ICE COLD, EXTREME—DIVING IN THE ARCTIC CIRCLE ON GREENLAND'S ICEBERGS IS A SUB-ZERO SENSATION IN A CLASS OF ITS OWN. THOSE DIVING HERE, WHETHER HUMAN OR ANIMAL, NEED A THICK SKIN.

Kalaallit Nunaat, as Greenland is called in its own language, means "land of the people." The name is misleading, as the largest island in the world, at 1,650 miles/2,650 km long and up to 600 miles/1,000 km wide, is the most sparsely populated region in Europe.

There is only one dive center in the whole country, as the plunge into these icy waters is not for everyone. The water temperature is sometimes below 0°C (32°F), your teeth clench on the mouthpiece, the piston in the first stage of the regulator has to work overtime, and even professional divers use up as much air as a novice usually does. Still, diving on and under icebergs is worth all the discomfort and is certainly one of the most memorable experiences a diver will ever have.

The dive center lies on the west coast, in Sisimiut. Not far offshore from the town, a kelp forest with a multitude of colorful inhabitants awaits the diver: huge sun stars, sea cucumbers, sea urchins and nudibranchs live alongside fish such as sculpins, cod, wolffish, and ghostly-looking crabs. Wrecks have even been found there: the *Borgin*, a three-masted schooner, and a Portuguese prison ship.

It is also possible to dive in Disko Bay, offshore from Ilulissat in the north. As sections of taller icebergs can easily break off, responsible dive guides will always choose smaller, rounded icebergs from which to make a descent. The visibility in summer, at

17 FACTS

- **Depth:** 3–130 ft/1–40 m
- **Visibility:** 50–200 ft/15–60 m
- **Water temperature:** 30–45°F/–1 to 7°C
- **Best time of year:** May–Aug
- **Level of difficulty:** ■■■–■■■■■
- **Diversity of coral species:** ■
- **Diversity of fish species:** ■■■■
- **Big fish:** ■■
- **Wrecks:** ■■
- **Caves:** ■
- **Walls:** ■■■■
- **Snorkeling:** ■

a temperature of about 45°F (7°C), is between 30 and 50 ft/10 and 15 m, with each extra degree of cold bringing approximately an extra 15 ft/5 m of clarity. In winter, the visibility increases to an astounding 165 to 200 ft/50 to 60 m.

Only one-eighth of an iceberg is above the surface, with the vast bulk lying underwater. Seeing a panorama of these floating, frozen works of art offers an indescribable and unique experience. The vastness and strangeness of the scene, together with the colors, light, and reflections, cast a spell over the landscape. The stillness that elsewhere reigns beneath the waves is missing—there are cracking and creaking sounds, and somewhere there is always a section of ice breaking off and crashing into the sea.

Opposite page: Iceberg-diving in Greenland—an experience for which a thick skin is needed.

Above: A vibrant sun star.

Left: A spectacular view of a jellyfish.

NORTHERN WATERS: NORWAY

Ålesund

DIVING IN NORWAY IS BECOMING INCREASINGLY POPULAR. THERE IS MUCH TO DISCOVER ALONG ITS 50,000 MILES/80,000 KM OF COAST. OFF ÅLESUND AND THE ISLANDS AROUND IT, IN PARTICULAR, THERE IS—QUITE LITERALLY—TREASURE UNDER THE WATER.

Ålesund lies between the well-known recreational dive centers of Kristiansand in the south of Norway and Narvik in the north. Although this area is situated on the same latitude as Iceland, it has a mild, damp climate and, due to the Gulf Stream, relatively warm water. If you plan to undertake long or deep dives, however, you would be advised to dive in a dry suit.

This smart "Art Nouveau" town has five wrecks sunk off its shores. The most attractive is the *Konsul Karl Fisser*, a German supply vessel that was hit by British bombers during World War II and now lies 115 ft/35 m down. The dive often starts in the open water, where the currents are strong, so you have to dive quickly down through the greenish twilight to a depth of 72 ft/22 m, where the first part of the deck superstructure is located. This 420-ft-long/128-m-long rusting giant has long since been colonized by sponges and sea anemones, and between these teem myriad fish, pollack being the main species that lives here. The 10,000-ton freighter, which is well preserved and sits upright on the sea bed, stands up well in comparison with tropical wrecks.

There is also the opportunity of wall dives at lushly vegetated sites here, as well as exciting drift dives. Huge shoals of fish swim past, jellyfish drift by, and crabs and flatfish such as plaice and flounder hide on the sea floor. The most colorful fish here are the wrasses.

A diving highlight of this area is the offshore island of Runde, a well-known bird paradise. There is an impressive underwater jungle of kelp, up to 13 ft/4 m tall, a meeting place for the local marine creatures. Northern Europe's greatest underwater treasure is also found here: fewer than half of the fourteen chests of gold and silver coins from the *Akerendam*, which sank in 1725, have so far been found. Nonetheless, divers have found many of the ship's cannons. There are marvelous dives to enjoy at the Blue Lagoon, Gardbaen and The Cave, a cave beneath a bird cliff.

Not to be missed is the inland valley of Norangsdalen, where you can dive in the lake to see the ruins of a village, complete with streets and rock gardens. Another delight is the emerald-colored lake at Grotli, near the Geiranger fjord, where even in summer you can dive among small floating icebergs that have broken off the glacier.

Opposite page: A really special experience—diving under the ice in the lake near Grotli.

Above: A brightly colored wrasse.

Left: A diver in the kelp forest.

18 FACTS

- **Depth:** 15–150 ft/5–45 m
- **Visibility:** 30–100 ft/10–30 m
- **Water temperature:** 46–64°F/8–18°C
- **Best time of year:** May–Aug
- **Level of difficulty:** ■–■■■■■
- **Diversity of coral species:** ■■■
- **Diversity of fish species:** ■■■
- **Big fish:** ■■
- **Wrecks:** ■■■
- **Caves:** ■■
- **Walls:** ■■■■
- **Snorkeling:** ■

NORTHERN WATERS: ENGLAND

Lundy

THIS GRANITE ISLAND AT THE ENTRANCE TO THE BRISTOL CHANNEL IS EXPOSED TO ALL KINDS OF WEATHER. IN THE MARINE PROTECTED AREA AROUND LUNDY, DIVERS WILL FIND WRECKS, SEALS, AND BASKING SHARKS.

Lundy is a green island with no roads or cars, famous for its beer, its own stamps, and its castle. It has a population of about thirty, and if you visit as a tourist and want to stay overnight, you must book early to get one of the few beds available. Divers can visit the island from centers in Ilfracombe, to the east in the county of Devon.

The diving season on Lundy is short but spectacular. It is determined by the wind, the waves and the currents, which swirl around this rocky granite island. Lundy measures just 3 miles/5 km long by 550 yd/500 m wide. It lies in a shipping lane, and the oldest recorded shipwrecks there date back to 1793. As well as the frequently seething Atlantic, thick fog also played its part in bringing many a voyage to an unhappy ending on these precipitous cliffs and shallows. More than 200 wrecks have so far been recorded, but only about a dozen are intact to any degree; the rest have been so ravaged by time and the rough seas that only a few remnants are left. The best-known wreck is that of the British warship HMS *Montagu* (23–40 ft/7–12 m deep), which ran aground on May 29, 1906 just off the southern tip of the island.

Lundy is England's crown jewel when it comes to diving. The waters around the island were declared England's first marine nature reserve in 1986. Since that time, the area has been protected and a fishing ban imposed, so fish stocks are increasing year by year.

The underwater world around Lundy is renowned, and not only among English divers, as it has plenty to offer: at Gannet's Rock (50 ft/ 15 m deep) you can watch the masterly acrobatic performances of the inquisitive seals. Around Gull Rock the water teems with brightly colored cuckoo wrasse, and there are dogfish egg sacs anchored to the gorgonian sea fans. Nudibranchs and flatworms graze on the rocks inhabited by anemones, lobsters, and spider crabs.

The two seamounts, Knoll Pins, are adorned with pink and yellow jewel anemones, and patrolled by eels, cod, and pollack. The warm water fostered by the currents has made it possible for more Mediterranean creatures, or even some linked to the tropics, to settle here. Nowhere else in England will you find five different species of coral. In summer, the plankton attracts toothless basking sharks. These fish, the second-largest in the world, come back year after year and are a real attraction.

Opposite page: A seal and a diver sharing a game together.

Above: An inquisitive seal in a kelp forest.

Left: Jewel anemones at the Knoll Pins dive site.

Below: Delusions of grandeur—a small sea star trying to eat a big one.

19 FACTS

- **Depth:** 15–115 ft/5–35 m
- **Visibility:** 10–50 ft/3–15 m
- **Water temperature:** 50–66°F/ 10–19°C
- **Best time of year:** May–Sept
- **Level of difficulty:** ■■■–■■■■■
- **Diversity of coral species:** ■■
- **Diversity of fish species:** ■■■
- **Big fish:** ■■■■
- **Wrecks:** ■■■
- **Caves:** ■■
- **Walls:** ■■■
- **Snorkeling:** ■

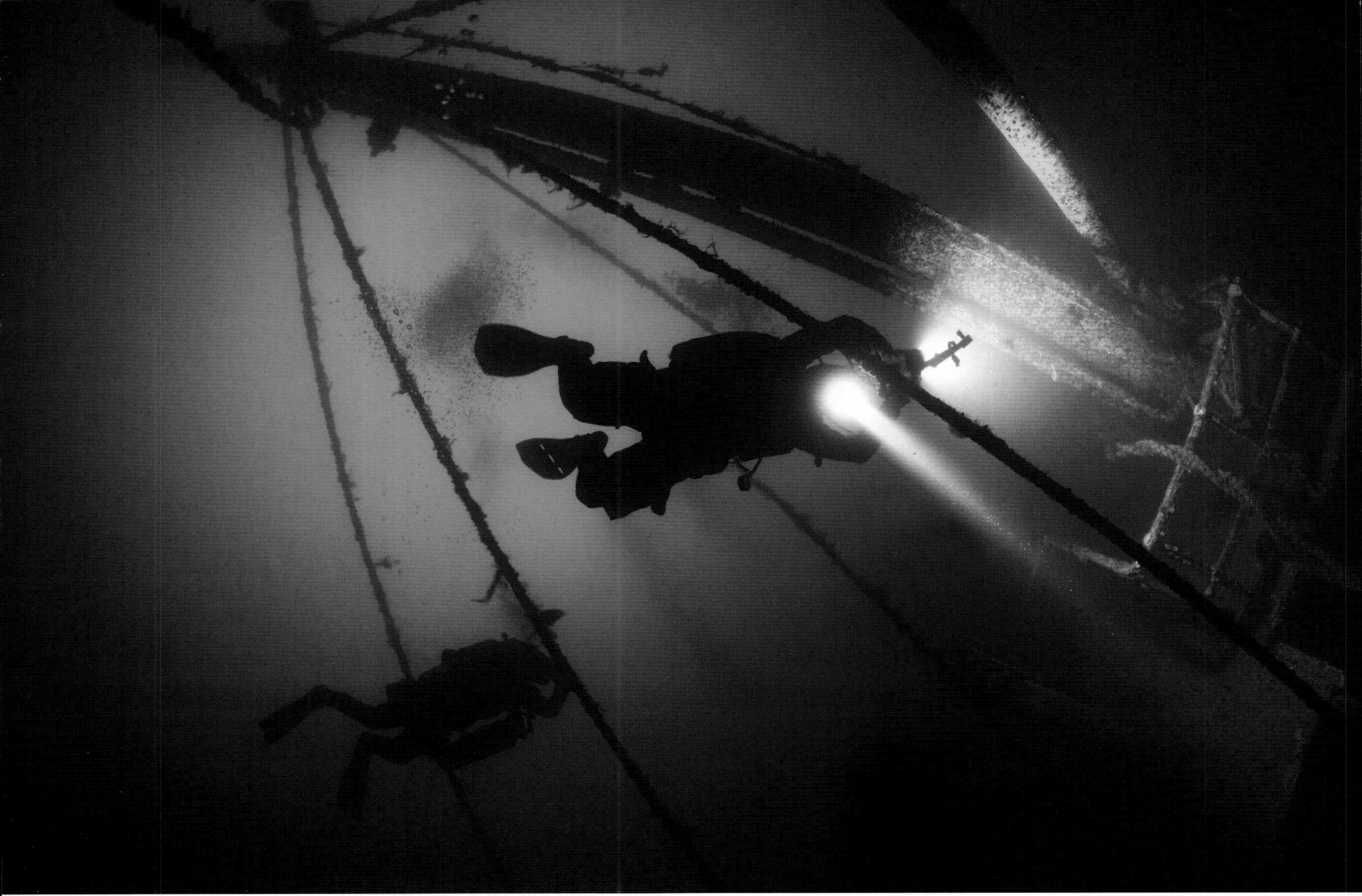

NORTHERN WATERS: FINLAND

Åland

THE WATER IN ÅLAND IS GENERALLY MURKY, IT HAS LITTLE TO OFFER IN THE WAY OF FLORA AND FAUNA, AND IT IS COLD. NONETHELESS, THIS AUTONOMOUS PROVINCE IS EXTREMELY POPULAR WITH DIVERS—EUROPE'S "TRUK LAGOON" HAS THE DUBIOUS HONOR OF HOLDING THE RECORD FOR ACCIDENTS AT SEA AND IS A PARADISE FOR WRECK DIVERS.

It is the year 1918: the *Hindenburg*, an icebreaker and minesweeper of the German Imperial Navy, hits a mine and sinks. This 167-ft-long/51-m-long ship, lying to the west of Åland, is one of the most beautiful wrecks in the area, and has been officially designated a war monument.

Fifteen years later, the 233-ft-long/71-m-long three-masted iron barque *Plus* is sailing from London when the captain makes a disastrous decision in the thick fog and continues in the direction of the harbor of Mariehamn without a pilot: the sailing vessel sinks near the pilot station of Kobba Klintar.

Countless similar stories have played out around the islands in the Baltic Sea. This island realm is part of Finland, according to international law, but linguistically and culturally it belongs to Sweden. It has thus been of great strategic importance throughout history and even today is one of the most difficult areas of the world to navigate.

This "waterland" includes more than 6,500 named islands, and an equal number of nameless rocky islets. More than 600 wrecks lie at rest around this scenic archipelago, and of these 100 have so far been identified and more than 30 can be dived. They are some of the best-preserved wrecks in Europe, even the wooden ships. This is due to the cold, the low salt

20 FACTS

- **Depth:** 15–230 ft/5–70 m
- **Visibility:** 5–65 ft/2–20 m
- **Water temperature:** 37–66°F/ 3–19°C
- **Best time of year:** June–Aug
- **Level of difficulty:** ■■■–■■■■■
- **Diversity of coral species:** –
- **Diversity of fish species:** ■
- **Big fish:** –
- **Wrecks:** ■■■■■
- **Caves:** –
- **Walls:** –
- **Snorkeling:** –

content of the Baltic Sea, and relatively strict laws on preserving wrecks. The *Rotterdam*, a 115-ft-long/ 35-m-long wooden boat dating from the nineteenth century, was found in the fall of 2007 at a depth of 110 ft/34 m.

The only dive center here is at Mariehamn on the main island of Åland. The house wreck there is the *Plus*, which lies at a depth of between 55 and 105 ft/17–32 m. Other wrecks that can be reached from here include the *Hesperus*, a 210-ft-long/ 64-m-long freighter that sank in 1884 (35–140 ft/ 11–42 m deep), the 200-ft-long/60-m-long steamship *L'Espérance* (35–115 ft/11–35 m deep), which sank to the sea floor in 1901, and the steamship *Helge*, dating from 1915. Two years later, the Russian destroyer *Burakov* joined them, followed in 1928 by the 150-ft-long/45-m-long sailing ship *Balder* (215 ft/ 65 m deep) and in 1975 by the Swedish government vessel *Gävle* (150–175 ft/45–54 m deep).

Around Åland, there is good-value diving for everyone. Wreck specialists travel from all over the world to the best ships' graveyard in northern Europe.

Opposite page: Divers examining the mast of the *Gävle*.

Above: The time is up—the clock from the icebreaker *Hindenburg*.

Left: A wheel beneath the wreckage of the *Rotterdam*.

The 1,390-mile/2,240-km-long and approximately 225-mile/360-km-wide strait between northeast Africa and the Arabian Peninsula is a magnet for dive tourists. This is scarcely any wonder, for the biodiversity in these waters is enormous, the myriad reefs are a magical kingdom of color and form, and, being strategically important, the sea has great wrecks for divers to explore. The Red Sea is one of the best diving locations in the world.

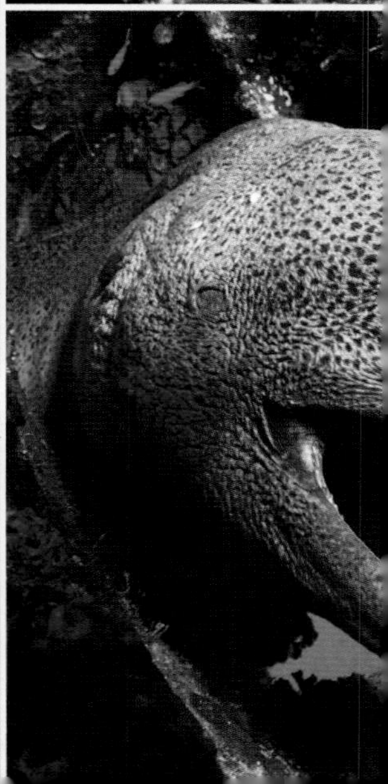

RED SEA

RED SEA: SAUDI ARABIA

Saudi Arabia

AT MORE THAN 1,100 MILES/1,800 KM, THE KINGDOM OF SAUDI ARABIA HAS THE LONGEST COASTLINE OF ANY OF THE COUNTRIES BORDERING ON THE RED SEA. THERE ARE STILL A FEW UNDISCOVERED PLACES HERE.

It is a fact that the most beautiful dive sites in the world are to be found in the Red Sea. However, for a long time divers could only dream about the reefs off Saudi Arabia, as the country was closed to tourism. Recently, though, the kingdom has started to open up. Each year, about 1,200 divers make the journey here. Current facilities do not allow for any more than this number.

While on the other side of the Red Sea, boats crowd around the best reefs and you are seldom alone, these coasts are wonderfully peaceful. It is possible to make a day trip out from Jeddah or from the new (and as yet only) dive resort in the country at Al Lith, which was opened in January 2009 by a diving-enthusiast prince.

A more comfortable and efficient option is to take a longer tour on a cruiser. There are two live-aboards—floating dive resorts—operating off this coast, both of which are also owned by the prince. One offers longer tours of the north, starting out from Jeddah, on which you can dive the wrecks around Yanbu. In this area there are approximately two dozen known shipwrecks, together with a huge number of undiscovered ones. The southern tour has been operating since 2004; it starts out from Al Lith, heading for the Farasan Banks and more southern destinations.

While the reef systems of the northern Farasan Islands are relatively virgin territory, the southern part holds out the promise of genuine expedition diving. Diving a reef where no one has ever been before is a

21 FACTS

- **Depth:** 10–180 ft/3–55 m
- **Visibility:** 50–130 ft/15–40 m
- **Water temperature:** 77–90°F/ 25–32°C
- **Best time of year:** Mar–Nov
- **Level of difficulty:** ■–■■■
- **Diversity of coral species:** ■■■■
- **Diversity of fish species:** ■■■■
- **Big fish:** ■■■
- **Wrecks:** ■■■■
- **Caves:** ■■■
- **Walls:** ■■■■■
- **Snorkeling:** ■■■■

dream that you can fulfill here. However, it is unfortunately the case that even in the "aqua incognita," illegal fishermen have been doing their dirty work and have already decimated the fish stocks.

The topography around many of the unnamed islands and reefs is characterized by steep drop-offs. Interspersed with plateaus and having an ideal diving profile, they are adorned with the finest the Red Sea has to offer. In 2006, the "Hanging Gardens" were discovered: a then unknown species of colonial sea squirts in a multitude of colors hanging from the black coral like lametta. Nearby, there are soft corals growing, and the walls teem with fish. Around Shib Mubarak, an exposed site in the middle of the sea, even larger fish such as manta rays, dolphins, bumphead parrotfish, barracuda, and sharks, ply the waters.

Opposite page: Colonial sea squirts in a variety of colors at the Hanging Gardens.

Above: An iridescent bumphead parrotfish.

Left: Young whitetip sharks playing.

RED SEA: SUDAN

Sudan

DIVING IN SUDAN IS A DREAM THAT IS NOT SO EASY TO REALIZE. FAR FROM THE TOURIST INFRASTRUCTURE, YOU WILL EXPERIENCE REEFS THAT ARE PRACTICALLY UNTOUCHED, ALTHOUGH FOR DECADES THEY HAVE BEEN RANKED AMONG THE BEST IN THE WORLD.

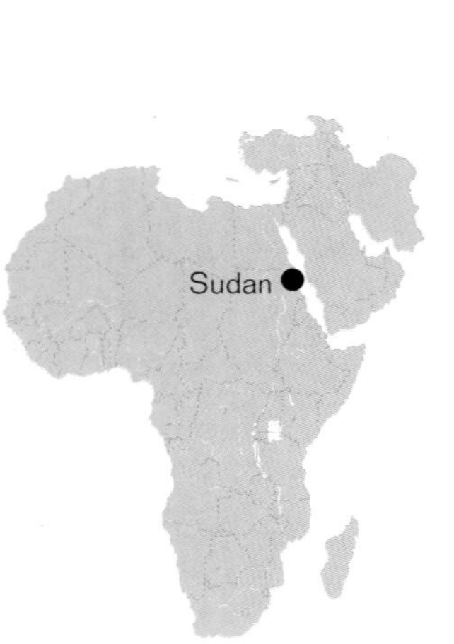

The Sudan is near the top of the wish list for many true diving enthusiasts—and this despite its remoteness, the often-unsettled political situation, and the need to forgo luxury. It is for these reasons that this country on the western side of the Red Sea is still not overrun and is far from the madding underwater crowds found elsewhere.

There are only a handful of safari boats in the area, so the small number of divers are still justified in harboring hopes of seeing big fish on the intact reefs. The journey there is also a minor adventure in itself, whether you travel by cruiser from Egypt or by plane.

The country is still in its infancy where diving is concerned, despite government regulations and early landmark achievements: Hans Hass described the reefs off Port Sudan as early as 1952 in his book *Manta—Teufel im Roten Meer* [*Manta Ray—The Devil in the Red Sea*], and Jacques-Yves Cousteau tried to investigate the possibility of living underwater in his "Precontinent II" project there in 1963. Two aquanauts spent a week below the surface in a habitat near Sha'ab Rumi. You can still visit the settlement, which lies at a depth of between 30 and 90 ft/ 10–27 m, and is now overgrown with corals and sponges, but unfortunately it has suffered greatly from the ravages of time.

Off Port Sudan lies the Wingate Reef, where one of the most famous and beautiful wrecks in the world lies. The freighter *Umbria*, fully laden with munitions, was scuttled in 1940 by its Italian crew so that the highly explosive cargo would not fall into British hands.

Huge shoals of fish circle the northern tip of the legendary Sanganeb Reef. Sharks are still present around the southwest plateau, although there are not as many as before. You can get a better view of these elegant hunters, especially hammerhead sharks, in the north at Angarosh Reef, the name of which translates as "mother of sharks."

In 1977, the cargo ship *Blue Belt* sank at Sha'ab Su'adi, and its cargo of Toyotas can still be visited by divers today. Further great reefs include Abington, Merlo, Protector, and Elba. Off the latter, it is possible to dive the wreck of the freighter *Levanzo*, which sank in 1923.

Opposite page: The former underwater house from Cousteau's "Precontinent II" project.

Right: Red fire sponges on the wreck of the *Umbria*.

Below: Magnificent royal angelfish.

22 FACTS

- **Depth:** 5–165 ft/2–50 m
- **Visibility:** 65–165 ft/20–50 m
- **Water temperature:** 75–88°F/24–31°C
- **Best time of year:** Nov–Mar
- **Level of difficulty:** ■■■
- **Diversity of coral species:** ■■■■
- **Diversity of fish species:** ■■■■
- **Big fish:** ■■■■
- **Wrecks:** ■■■■
- **Caves:** ■■
- **Walls:** ■■■■■
- **Snorkeling:** ■■■■

RED SEA: EGYPT

Deep South

SINCE THE END OF THE 1970s, THE WHOLE OF EGYPT HAS BEEN PARTICULARLY POPULAR WITH EUROPEAN DIVERS. IN THE SOUTH, THE FURY SHOALS AND ST. JOHN'S REEF BECKON, WITH ALL KINDS OF INTERESTING THINGS TO SEE.

Recreational diving in Egypt began in the north of the country, where masses of divers now spend their vacations. The farther south you go, the fewer divers you meet. However, you should not draw any conclusions from this as to the quality of the southern dive sites.

Ras Banas marks the beginning of the area for dive cruises. Classy live-aboards are *de rigueur* for divers here and are the best way of experiencing the fascinating world beneath the waves. Most tours begin from the harbor of Ras Ghalib or from Marsa Alam. The most popular destinations in the deep south are the large expanses of the Fury Shoals north of Ras Banas, and St. John's Reef near the Sudanese border.

The smaller areas of Zabargad and Rocky Island, where the government first permitted diving at the beginning of the 1990s, are also worth a journey—they are located in a marine reserve. Generally, tours of the south are offered all year round, although the best time to go is between May and September, when the Red Sea is at its quietest.

Fury Shoals is a highly diverse environment. The shallows are seen at their best at Sha'ab Claudia. On the western part of the reef there is a coral labyrinth with passages, tunnels, and caves, and an intact hard coral garden. At Dolphin Reef, near Sataya, from the afternoon onwards you can snorkel with dolphins in the reef lagoon where they rest at night. At the protected southern end of Sha'ab Mansour, two

beautifully encrusted coral blocks rise to a height of 40 ft/12 m below the surface, with snappers circling around them and barracuda and trevally hunting a little deeper below.

The second-largest diving area is St. John's Reef, where you could easily spend an entire week without getting bored. Habili Ali is a huge, densely encrusted coral block where you will often encounter hammerhead and silvertip sharks as well as gray reef sharks. Small Habili is a coral pinnacle surrounded by lots of schooling fish. It rises to a height of 13 ft/4 m below the surface and can be circumnavigated several times during the course of a dive. The southernmost reef lies just below the surface of the water and is thus dubbed Dangerous Reef by the Red Sea captains, although boats can anchor safely inside it. Various coral pinnacles teeming with life rise up from the sandy sea bed 80 ft/24 m below.

Northeast of the St. John's group, you will find a variety of spots off the volcanic island of Zabargad: walls on the southeast, coral gardens, and atmospheric canyons. The small Rocky Island is deeply fissured and surrounded by a fringing reef. When the currents are good you can see sharks, barracuda, manta rays, tuna, and trevally at the drop-off.

Above: Soft corals at Rocky Island.

Left: In the system of caverns at St. John's.

23 FACTS

- **Depth:** 15–130 ft/5–40 m
- **Visibility:** 50–130 ft/15–40 m
- **Water temperature:** 72–88°F/ 22–31°C
- **Best time of year:** May–Sept
- **Level of difficulty:** ■–■■■
- **Diversity of coral species:** ■■■■
- **Diversity of fish species:** ■■■■
- **Big fish:** ■■■■
- **Wrecks:** ■■
- **Caves:** ■■■■
- **Walls:** ■■■■■
- **Snorkeling:** ■■■■

Golden Center

IN CENTRAL EGYPT THERE IS A GREAT DEAL TO SEE UNDERWATER: SHARKS, DOLPHINS—AND LOTS OF OTHER DIVERS. SINCE THE OPENING OF MARSA ALAM'S SMALL INTERNATIONAL AIRPORT, INCREASING NUMBERS OF TOURISTS ARE COMING HERE.

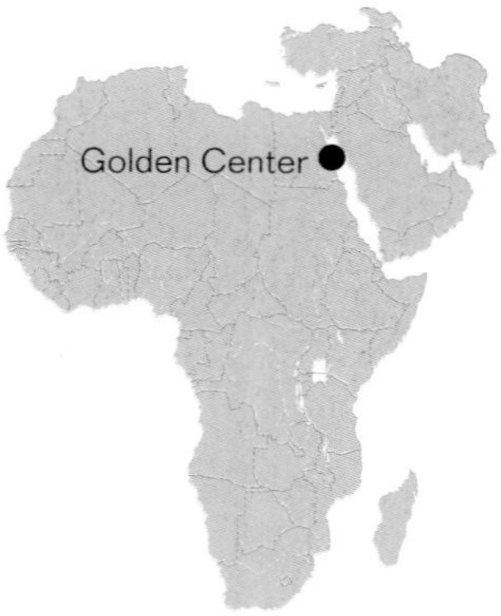

One last look at the instruments, then down we go into the deep blue yonder: We arrive quickly at our maximum depth of 130 ft/40 m and then check our buoyancy, look around, and wait—wait for the hammerhead sharks that cruise around the north end of Daedalus Reef. The end of our non-decompression time is fast approaching, the waiting becomes torture. Suddenly one of the divers starts to gesticulate wildly—he has spotted them. The school passes by slowly and elegantly, and then they disappear from view again. We ascend, making a lengthy safety stop in the open water, but it is impossible to find the reef in the current. Then the dinghy comes and takes us back to the boat. We are all unanimous: that one fleeting first-class moment was worth all the effort.

Until 1999, this exposed island in the middle of the Red Sea was a restricted military zone, but now it is advertised by tour operators as a shark hotspot. As well as hammerhead sharks, you can also see fast-swimming thresher sharks at the southern tip of the island. Divers should keep their eyes peeled here, as spectacular encounters can happen at any time. The same is true at Elphinstone Reef, which lies closer to the shore. It is impossible to miss this site, as it is constantly besieged by dive boats. However, you should not let this put you off, as the underwater world here is extremely attractive. If you want to see big fish, for example the oceanic whitetip shark (*C. longimanus*), the northern plateau is recommended. You dive out with the current to the eastern or western wall with their lovely coral growth.

Dives around Marsa Alam are also highly worthwhile. This former fishing village was a tip passed on by word of mouth for years after the dive sites were opened up at the beginning of the 1990s. When the airport was opened in 2001, there was a run on the place, and a whole string of hotels opened.

One attraction that has contributed to the diving boom is Sha'ab Saamadai. In this lagoon, dolphins mate and rear their young. The government has had to control the influx of visitors and has established protection zones. Now there is a rest area for the dolphins, which is completely cordoned off, with access for divers strictly limited. In Abu Dabab, too, protection measures have been introduced. Divers are now permitted to approach the dugongs and turtles only from the shore.

The area also has much to offer non-divers: Wadi Miya with its temples, prehistoric rock art, and the Wadi El Jimal National Park in the south.

Opposite page, top: A school of dolphins in the Red Sea.

Opposite page, bottom: A school of hammerhead sharks on Daedalus Reef.

Below left: An impressive turtle.

Below right: A dugong in the bay of Abu Dabab.

24 FACTS

- **Depth:** 15–200 ft/5–60 m
- **Visibility:** 50–130 ft/15–40 m
- **Water temperature:** 72–88°F/22–31°C
- **Best time of year:** Apr–Oct
- **Level of difficulty:** ■–■■■■■
- **Diversity of coral species:** ■■■■■
- **Diversity of fish species:** ■■■■
- **Big fish:** ■■■■
- **Wrecks:** ■■
- **Caves:** ■■
- **Walls:** ■■■■■
- **Snorkeling:** ■■■■■

RED SEA: EGYPT

Brother Islands

THESE TWO BARREN ROCKY ISLANDS ARE AMONG THE MOST POPULAR DIVING DESTINATIONS IN THE WORLD. THEY LIE IN A PROTECTED MARINE PARK IN THE MIDDLE OF OPEN WATER, SO THE CONDITIONS ARE NOT THE EASIEST.

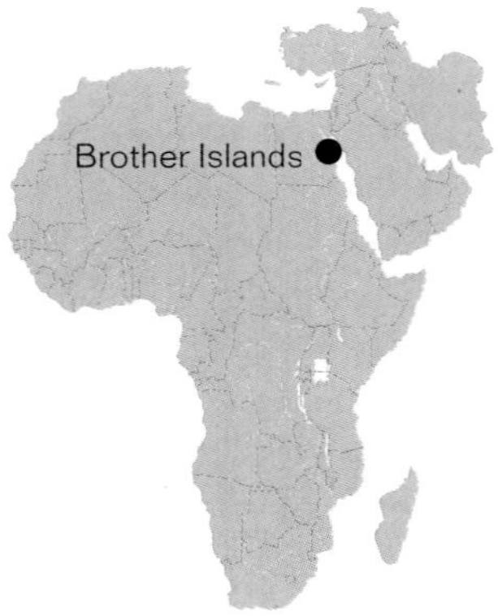

The Brother Islands lie completely isolated in the shipping lane that leads from the Red Sea to the Suez Canal. They are the remains of two volcanic craters and are oases that attract not only divers. The two flat islands, called "El Akhawein" in Arabic, lie about 1 mile/1.5 km apart and, except for the lighthouse keeper, are uninhabited. Diving cruises lasting several days are available, generally starting from Hurghada, but these can sometimes be a little uncomfortable, as high wind and waves are almost the norm.

Catching the right moment is rather a matter of luck. From June to August the winds are lighter and the chances of more or less reasonable conditions are at their best. However, the heat outside the water should not be underestimated, and even in the water the temperature rises to as much as 86°F/30°C, so big fish dive down to the cooler depths.

The "big brother" is the more northerly island, on which there is a lighthouse which was built in 1880 by the British and is still in operation. The island is about 1,320 ft/400 m long and 130 ft/40 m wide. Underwater highlights include the wrecks of the *Numida* (30–300 ft/10–90 m deep) and the *Aida II* (100–200 ft/30–60 m deep) in the windy northwest. These have become blossoming gardens, so it is sometimes difficult to tell where the wreck stops and the reef begins.

You drift from north to south, sometimes in strong currents, past sheer rock faces with an unbelievable variety of corals and fishes. Solitary pelagic fish and group operators patrol in the current, and huge humphead wrasses sometimes approach you. On the southern side, better protected from wind and waves, where the safari boat anchors, you slowly ascend again. The southern plateau, at a depth of about 115 ft/35 m, is not as spectacular as the northern side. Sometimes you can watch thresher sharks being cleaned by small fish.

The smaller island is just as barren above the water surface as its big brother, and underwater it is at least as impressive. On the east wall, in particular, everything the Red Sea has to offer is there in one place. Unfortunately, the dream diving around these two islands can sometimes turn into a nightmare. Diving accidents, mostly caused by the strong currents, have repeatedly given rise to negative headlines.

Opposite page: A fat humphead wrasse off Little Brother Island.

Above: A superbly encrusted wreck—the *Numidia* off Big Brother Island.

Left: Top-class wall-diving around Little Brother Island.

25 FACTS

- **Depth:** 15–260 ft/5–80 m
- **Visibility:** 65–130 ft/20–40 m
- **Water temperature:** 68–86°F/20–30°C
- **Best time of year:** May–Sept
- **Level of difficulty:** ■■■–■■■■■
- **Diversity of coral species:** ■■■■■
- **Diversity of fish species:** ■■■■■
- **Big fish:** ■■■■■
- **Wrecks:** ■■■■
- **Caves:** ■■
- **Walls:** ■■■■■
- **Snorkeling:** ■■■■

RED SEA: EGYPT

Abu Nuhas & Sha'ab Ali

IN THE PAST, THERE HAVE BEEN A NUMBER OF SHIPPING ACCIDENTS AROUND THESE TWO CORAL REEFS AT THE ENTRANCE TO THE GULF OF SUEZ. NOW THE AREA IS FAMOUS FOR ITS WRECKS. THE *THISTLEGORM* IS PROBABLY THE MOST POPULAR WRECK IN THE RED SEA.

In the north of the Red Sea, there are a large number of reefs just below the surface. When the sea is calm, the sun is low, or at dusk, they are barely discernible from above. With wind and waves adding to the problem, collisions were a frequent occurrence before the advent of modern navigational aids. Once the Suez Canal, the most important link between Asia and Europe, opened to shipping in 1869, accidents became more frequent. Nowadays, the Straits of Gubal are the largest ships' graveyard in the Red Sea. Some of the wreckage off the coast of Abu Nuhas is no longer identifiable, so no one knows exactly how many ships lie here.

Just two months after the opening of the canal, the sail and steam ship *Carnatic* ran onto the reef and broke apart. She was laden with wine bottles, copper ingots, and gold, but even at that time, helmet divers were able to salvage the valuable cargo. The ship (at a maximum depth of 90 ft/27 m) is a sight that would delight any diver, from the propeller and the frames encrusted with soft corals and sponges, to the atmosphere in the interior when dancing sunbeams illuminate parts of the wreck.

In the far west, the *Giannis D* lies at the same depth. This Greek timber freighter sank and broke up in 1983. The stern lies on the port side and is particularly well preserved: you can dive into the superstructure—a delight for wreck lovers. If you want to venture deeper inside, there are three essentials you must remember—air, line, and light.

26 FACTS

- **Depth:** 15–100 ft/5–30 m
- **Visibility:** 50–130 ft/15–40 m
- **Water temperature:** 68–86°F/ 20–30°C
- **Best time of year:** Apr–Oct
- **Level of difficulty:** ■–■■■
- **Diversity of coral species:** ■■■
- **Diversity of fish species:** ■■■
- **Big fish:** ■■
- **Wrecks:** ■■■■■
- **Caves:** –
- **Walls:** –
- **Snorkeling:** ■■

On its way to Jeddah in 1981, the 330-ft-long/100-m-long *Chrisoula K*, laden with tiles, ran aground on the northeast of the reef. You can still just make out the cargo in the fore holds, but the stern section is in much better condition. This wreck, like many others, can readily be recognized from the surface. Another artificial reef is formed by the *Kimon* M, lying to the east at a depth of between 40 and 105 ft/12 and 32 m.

The most popular of all the wrecks has been sitting upright off Sha'ab Ali in the north since 1941—the *Thistlegorm*, a British supply vessel. This wreck has attained almost cult status among divers. Fully laden with munitions, trucks, and motorcycles, it was attacked by a German Heinkel bomber and sank after a huge explosion. A large part of the cargo is still preserved today, but unfortunately the heavy diving traffic and souvenir hunters have taken their toll. These wrecks can be accessed from the dive centers in Sharm-el-Sheikh and Hurghada.

Opposite page: A diver in front of the wreck of the *Giannis D.*

Above: Sponges and corals growing on the wreck of the *Carnatic.*

Left: An English motorcycle in the hold of the *Thistlegorm.*

RED SEA: EGYPT

Southern Sinai

RAS MOHAMMED NATIONAL PARK AT THE SOUTHERN TIP OF THE SINAI PENINSULA IS THE EPITOME OF SUPERLATIVE DIVING. THERE ARE SEVERAL TOP DIVE SPOTS HERE, AS WELL AS COLORFUL WALLS LEADING DOWN TO UNFATHOMABLE DEPTHS.

To describe Ras Mohammed as a dive site is not strictly accurate, as there are actually several sites here, tightly packed together. This area is seen as the classic of the Red Sea and has lost hardly any of its appeal, despite the fact that it has been dived hundreds of thousands of times. All the great names in diving—pioneers, scientists, filmmakers, and photographers—have been here and have been amazed.

The special feature of all the dive sites in the national park here is the immense, colorful walls, possibly the most beautiful in the Red Sea. They seem to fall away into infinity and are frequently given names such as "The Abyss," "Eiger North Face of the Seas," or "Deep Hole." In some places they drop away to 2,500 ft/750 m or so, and you can really feel the depth of water below you.

At Ras Mohammed, it is possible to admire three dive sites in the space of one dive. You jump off the boat in Anemone City, dive along the wall, keeping it on your right shoulder at a depth of 65 ft/20 m and holding a course of 150 degrees across the blue depths of the trench. When the current hits Shark Reef, it generally divides. You must keep the reef on your right, as otherwise you will be taken lower. The depths between 65 and 100 ft/20 and 30 m are the best: Off the wall there are shoals of snappers, barracuda swim to and fro, occasionally you will see sharks, and a photogenic school of batfish are permanent residents. If the current is not too strong, you can, finning gently, even dive into these shoals. However, you should not let all these fish distract you entirely from the wall: Soft corals flourish there in abundance and are really eye-catching, and there are also large and small sea bass everywhere.

The boat waits for you at Yolanda Reef. When you see the toilet bowls that formed part of the cargo of the *Yolanda* strewn on the sea bed, it is time to think about ascending safely and sending up a marker buoy, as there are dinghies everywhere collecting their guests.

Other names to bear in mind are Ras Za'atar and Shark Observatory. Each site at Ras Mohammed is an experience in itself, and everywhere you are likely at any moment to come across rarities such as sharks, barracuda, trevally, or, with luck, even a whale shark.

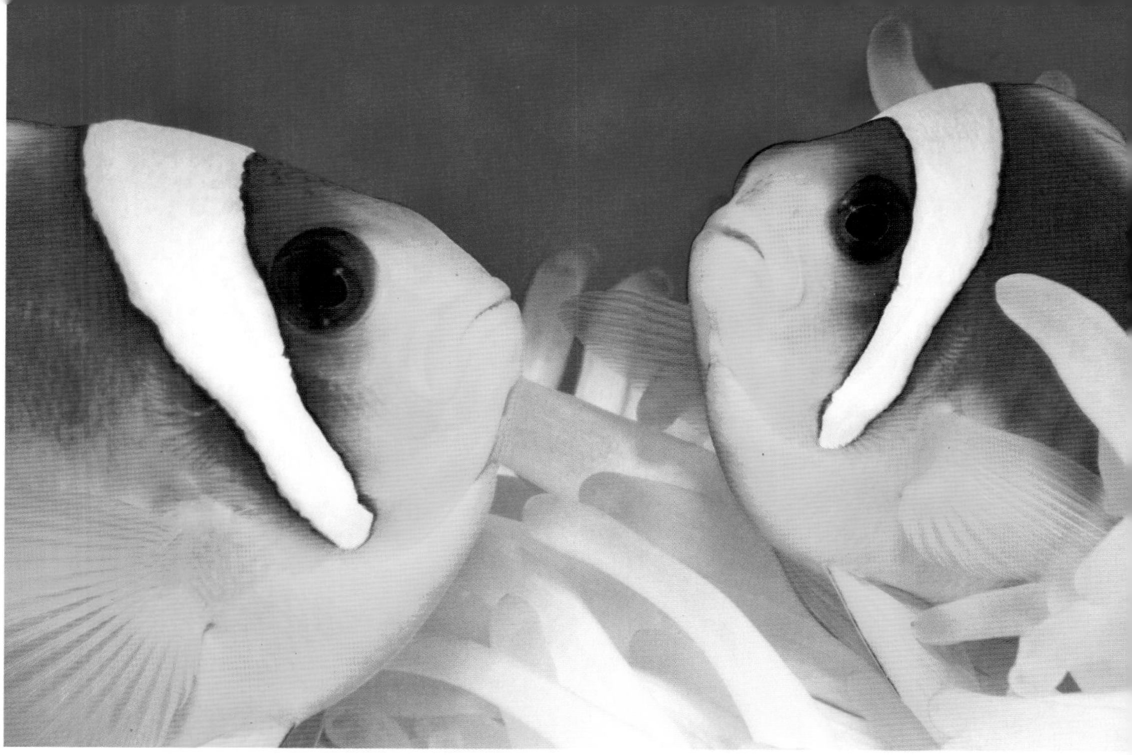

Opposite page: Batfish at Ras Mohammed.

Above: Clown fish, widely recognized, especially since the release of the movie, *Finding Nemo*.

Left: Diving through blue water in the trench at Ras Mohammed—an unforgettable experience.

27 FACTS

- **Depth:** 5–130 ft/2–40 m
- **Visibility:** 50–130 ft/15–40 m
- **Water temperature:** 68–86°F/20–30°C
- **Best time of year:** Apr–Oct
- **Level of difficulty:** ■–■■■■■
- **Diversity of coral species:** ■■■■■
- **Diversity of fish species:** ■■■■
- **Big fish:** ■■■■
- **Wrecks:** ■■■
- **Caves:** ■■■
- **Walls:** ■■■■■
- **Snorkeling:** ■■■■■

RED SEA: EGYPT

Tiran Reefs

IN THE STRAITS OF TIRAN, WHICH LINK THE RED SEA TO THE GULF OF AQABA, THERE ARE FOUR EXCEPTIONAL REEFS. DIVERS HAVE BEEN ABLE TO REACH THIS DREAM DESTINATION BY BOAT SINCE THE 1970s.

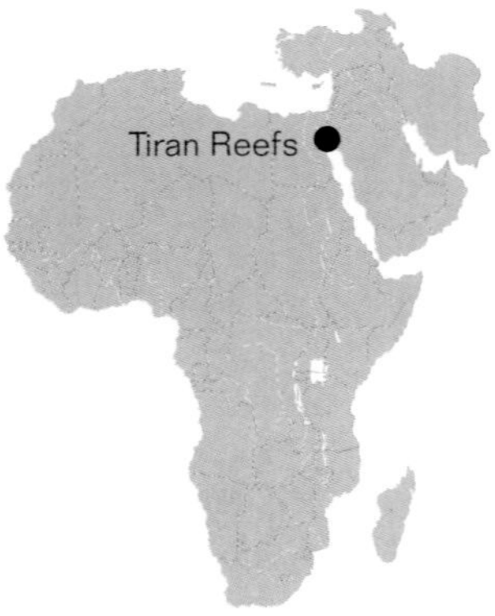

Opposite page: A giant lettuce coral on Jackson Reef.

Top: Large gorgonian sea fan, illuminated to spectacular effect.

Center: Picasso triggerfish with beautiful markings.

Bottom: Bluespotted stingrays are commonly encountered in the Red Sea.

28 FACTS

- **Depth:** 5–200 ft/2–60 m
- **Visibility:** 50–130 ft/15–40 m
- **Water temperature:** 66–84°F/19–29°C
- **Best time of year:** Mar–Oct
- **Level of difficulty:** ■–■■■
- **Diversity of coral species:** ■■■■■
- **Diversity of fish species:** ■■■■■
- **Big fish:** ■■■■
- **Wrecks:** ■
- **Caves:** ■
- **Walls:** ■■■■■
- **Snorkeling:** ■■■■■

The former Bedouin settlement of Sharm-el-Sheikh is today almost universally known. A few huts have been transformed into a mini-Las Vegas with hotel blocks. The construction boom shows no sign of abating, not least because of the many can't-miss dive sites that can be reached from here, such as the reefs in the Straits of Tiran, lying at the southern end of the Gulf of Aqaba.

The four platform reefs are located where the sea in the eastern arm bordering the Sinai Peninsula rises from a depth of 6,500 ft/2,000 m. They lie on a saddle in the exact center of the narrow strait and are named after English cartographers: Gordon, Thomas, Woodhouse, and Jackson.

The first reef, coming from the south, is Gordon Reef. It is the largest of the Tiran reefs and is easily identifiable by the wreck of the *Louilla*, a ship that ran aground in 1981. You anchor to the south, where the currents are not as strong. To the southwest, you will find a plateau and the Amphitheater, followed by a wall with large gorgonian sea fans. To the east, in a coral garden, lie ancient encrusted oil jars, and the oil that has leaked from them and solidified has created bizarre shapes.

The next reef, Thomas Reef, is small and somewhat unpredictable. Here, drift dives are the order of the day. While the tide is turning, conditions are calm and you can dive around the reef and enjoy the diversity of species that is a feature of this, the smallest of the four reefs. There are whitetip and reef sharks, barracuda, rays, turtles, and triggerfish. The bushy black corals and the fan corals are indications of the current, which often prevails.

The long and narrow Woodhouse Reef gives little protection for ships to anchor, and you normally drift very rapidly past its colorful east wall. To the north, it is joined by a saddle to the most spectacular of the four reefs, Jackson Reef. This spot is often referred to by dive guides as "the washing machine" due to the turbulence that frequently reigns underwater, and you should only venture here if the conditions are ideal.

Jackson Reef offers the most beautiful flora and fauna, which are able to flourish really well here on the sites exposed to the current. In the summer, it is possible to encounter scalloped hammerhead sharks on the north side around the wreck of the *Lara*.

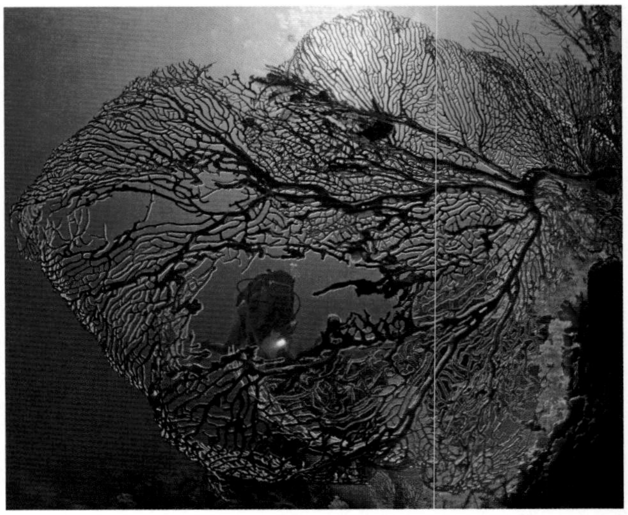

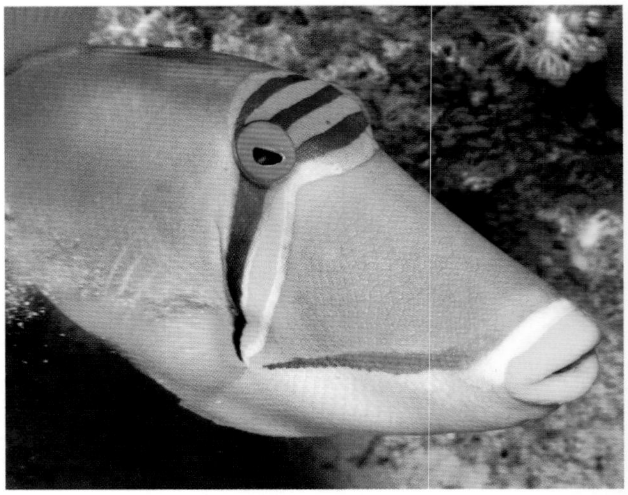

RED SEA: EGYPT

Dahab

THIS LOCATION IN THE SOUTH OF THE SINAI PENINSULA ENCOMPASSES MORE THAN THIRTY DIVE SITES WITHIN ITS BOUNDARIES, ALMOST ALL OF WHICH CAN BE DIVED FROM THE SHORE. THE MYSTERIOUS BLUE HOLE IS WORLD FAMOUS.

Dahab lies on the deepest and widest point of the Gulf of Aqaba, north of the popular resort of Sharm-el-Sheikh. This former fishing village is now a lively tourist center, but with its numerous beaches, it is also suitable for visiting divers seeking peace and quiet and somewhere to relax. There are many dive sites that can be reached from the shore, and a whole range of dive shops offers trips to these sites.

From the varied reef top around Dahab, the reef generally slopes gently down to between 80 and 100 ft/ 25 and 30 m. Beautiful dive sites include the Southern Oasis and, in the north, the Canyon, a deep cleft that begins at 50 ft/15 m and has its lowest exit point at a depth of more than 165 ft/50 m. As there are only a few exit points in between, careful planning is necessary.

Just over 1 mile/2 km north lies the legendary and mysterious Blue Hole, a cylindrical hole that drops vertically down to 400 ft/120 m. At 180 ft/56 m there is an exit known as the Arch. The Blue Hole, with a diameter of 80 ft/25 m, is a Mecca for technical divers equipped with special gas mixtures for these depths. Unfortunately, the site has acquired the awful nickname of "Diver's Cemetery."

29 FACTS

- **Depth:** 3–395 ft/1–120 m
- **Visibility:** 50–115 ft/15–35 m
- **Water temperature:** 66–84°F/ 19–29°C
- **Best time of year:** Mar–Nov
- **Level of difficulty:** ■–■■■■■
- **Diversity of coral species:** ■■■■
- **Diversity of fish species:** ■■■■
- **Big fish:** ■■
- **Wrecks:** ■■
- **Caves:** ■■■■
- **Walls:** ■■■■■
- **Snorkeling:** ■■■■

Below left: The devil scorpionfish is one of the most dangerous creatures in this region.

Below right: This flathead is very well camouflaged.

RED SEA: REPUBLIC OF DJIBOUTI

Djibouti

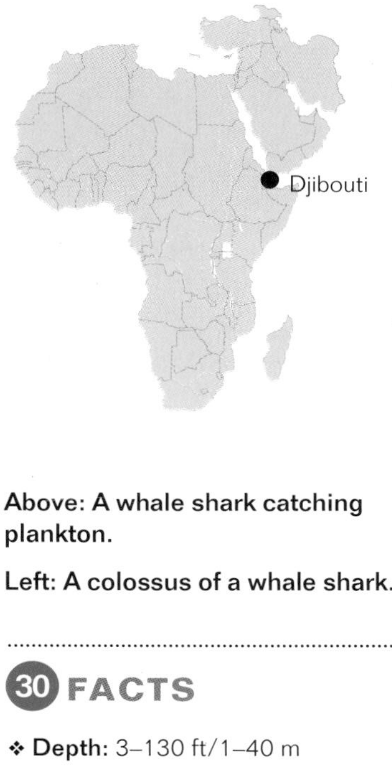

THIS COASTAL STATE BORDERS ON THE RED SEA AND THE GULF OF ADEN. THE SEVEN BROTHERS ISLANDS WERE ONCE FAMOUS FOR THEIR INTACT CORAL GARDENS AND THE MANY SHARKS FOUND THERE. NOWADAYS IT IS THE WHALE SHARKS, WHICH SPEND THE WINTER OFF THE COASTS HERE, THAT ATTRACT THE DIVERS.

In the 1970s, the "Seven Brothers" archipelago between the Red Sea and the Indian Ocean was regarded as a top diving destination because of its magnificent soft corals, its imposing walls, and the numerous sharks found there. However, the sharks were hunted until there were hardly any left. Political unrest was another factor leading to this barren desert land's being avoided by divers for decades.

Meanwhile, however, Djibouti has a new shark highlight to offer, one that is attracting increasing numbers of divers: dozens of whale sharks congregate in the Gulf of Tadjourah in the winter months to gorge themselves and to give birth to their young. They plough through the deep waters along a short section of coast near a French Foreign Legion training camp in search of rising plankton. Unfortunately, the plankton makes the water here very murky, but an encounter with the spectacular whale sharks more than compensates for this.

You have to visit the whale shark sites and the Seven Brothers islands on live-aboards, as there are no dive shops in Djibouti.

Above: A whale shark catching plankton.

Left: A colossus of a whale shark.

30 FACTS

- **Depth:** 3–130 ft/1–40 m
- **Visibility:** 15–65 ft/5–20 m
- **Water temperature:** 77–90°F/25–32°C
- **Best time of year:** Nov–Feb
- **Level of difficulty:** ■
- **Diversity of coral species:** ■■
- **Diversity of fish species:** ■■■
- **Big fish:** ■■■■■
- **Wrecks:** ■■
- **Caves:** ■■
- **Walls:** ■■
- **Snorkeling:** ■■■

The smallest of the world's oceans, lying between Africa, Asia, Australia, and the Antarctic, offers fabulous diving. The waters off East Africa and the wonderfully beautiful island worlds of the Maldives and Thailand, in particular, have everything needed for a successful diving holiday: They are warm, rich in fish, exotic, and have superb coral formations.

INDIAN OCEAN

INDIAN OCEAN: MALDIVES

North Male Atoll

THE MALDIVES ARE A DREAM DESTINATION. THE FIRST HOTELS WERE BUILT ON NORTH MALE ATOLL IN 1972. WITH ITS WHITE SAND BEACHES AND CRYSTAL-CLEAR WATER, THIS IS A PERFECT PLACE TO GET AWAY FROM IT ALL, RELAX, AND DIVE.

The Maldives officially consist of 1,190 islands, spread across 26 atolls. Only 202 islands in the archipelago are inhabited by indigenous people. About 100 others are accessible to tourists, and this number is rising. The ocean makes up 99 percent of this country, which is 510 miles/820 km long and 80 miles/130 km wide.

One of the largest atolls in the Maldives is North Male Atoll. It is home to the capital Malé and boasts an international airport on the island of Hulule. The resorts on the islands are reached by boat or seaplane. During the spectacular approach by plane, you cannot fail to be impressed by this "necklace of pearls" surrounded by blue, blue water. However, if you have been here before, you will notice differences: Some resort islands have changed—they have been enlarged and made the "right" shape to form the "necklace".

The atoll's dive spots are still top-class, and many are not even very far from the capital. The soft corals and fish population are surviving very well, although there are fewer and fewer sharks around the legendary Shark Point. Officially, hunting them within the atolls is banned, but unfortunately the practice continues.

The best dive sites include Rainbow Reef off the island of Soneva Gili in the Himmafushi Kandu channel, which has a strong current flowing through it. The schooling fish and sharks, as well as the magnificent soft and fan corals of extraordinary variety and color, are

31 FACTS

- **Depth:** 5–100 ft/2–30 m
- **Visibility:** 50–165 ft/15–50 m
- **Water temperature:** 81–86°F/27–30°C
- **Best time of year:** Feb–Apr
- **Level of difficulty:** ■–■■■
- **Diversity of coral species:** ■■■■■
- **Diversity of fish species:** ■■■■■
- **Big fish:** ■■■■
- **Wrecks:** ■■■■
- **Caves:** ■■■■
- **Walls:** ■■■■■
- **Snorkeling:** ■■■■■

truly captivating. Banana Reef is a classic and, like Rainbow Reef, is located in a nature reserve. It features hundreds of bannerfish and table coral. On the long outer reef of Paradise Island lies the legendary Manta Point, where these "high-flyers" enjoy being cleaned from time to time by cleaner fish; divers can watch the spectacle live.

When the current in Makunudu Channel is flowing strongly, you'll have a real surprise in store in Blue Canyon. There are fluorescent soft corals living on the walls and overhangs. You are likely to encounter big fish at Woshi Mas Thila, and diving at Barracuda Giri is like swimming in fish soup. Due to its coral formations, the Arena at Madigas is very sheltered.

Wrecks are also an option in the underwater world around North Male Atoll: the *Hembadhoo* wreck, at a depth of between 50 and 80 ft/15 and 25 m, and the wreck of the famous *Maldive Victory*, a 360-ft-long/ 110-m-long freighter, which ran aground on a reef near the airport in 1981. It sits upright at a depth of 115 ft/ 35 m, making it ideal for divers.

Opposite page: Glassfish on the bridge of the *Hembadhoo* wreck.

Above: Enormous soft corals on Rainbow Reef.

Left: At Manta Point off Paradise Island.

INDIAN OCEAN: MALDIVES

South Male Atoll

THE VADOO CHANNEL SEPARATES THE SOUTH AND NORTH MALE ATOLLS. THE CIRCULAR SOUTHERN REEF IS SMALLER THAN NORTH MALE ATOLL, BUT IT TOO HAS DIVE SITES THAT ARE EXTREMELY REWARDING.

South Male Atoll is 13 miles/21 km long and 22 miles/35 km wide. It consists of thirty-two islands. Seventeen of these are open to tourists, and only three are inhabited by local people. The other islands are less suitable for resorts, so it is likely that no further hotels will be built. Some islands have been artificially enlarged by means of dredging and landscaping. Unfortunately, the sand pumps used to do this have already caused major damage to the reef.

The southern islands of the Male Atoll were the second area of the Maldives to be identified for tourism. Many islands now have luxury resorts built on them. The two inhabited islands of Maafushi and Gulhi, where the traditional crafts of mat-weaving and dhoni-building are still practiced, can be visited as part of a day trip.

Like every atoll, South Male Atoll was originally constructed by the most successful master builders of all time—small coral polyps. Atolls are circular limestone formations that may lie above or beneath the water surface. They always have lovely lagoons that generally have a shimmering turquoise color, as well as sand banks and islands.

At the northern end of the Vadoo Reef, you will find the Vadoo Cave dive spot. Under a huge overhang with soft corals, a large school of snappers is usually to be found, and in the current you can observe whitetip sharks, trevally, and tuna. On the Vadoo Island house reef you can see lots of small

32 FACTS

- Depth: 5–100 ft/2–30 m
- Visibility: 50–165 ft/15–50 m
- Water temperature: 81–86°F/ 27–30°C
- Best time of year: Feb–Apr
- Level of difficulty: ■–■■■
- Diversity of coral species: ■■■■■
- Diversity of fish species: ■■■■■
- Big fish: ■■■■
- Wrecks: ■■■■
- Caves: ■■■■
- Walls: ■■■■■
- Snorkeling: ■■■■■

creatures such as gobies, blennies, nudibranchs, scorpionfish, and sand eels. When the current is right, you can enjoy spectacular encounters with fish at Embudu Express. In this protected area, as well as in the southern Guraidhoo Channel, experienced divers can enjoy some real action with gray sharks and eagle rays.

In 1991, off Dhinganfinolhu, a 230-ft-long/70-m-long freighter was sunk on the Kuda Giri as a tourist attraction for divers: today it rests in 110 ft/34 m of water. The superstructure is encrusted with bright red sponges, shrimps dance in the ventilation shafts, and the scene around the rusting giant is one to make any diver's heart beat faster.

Three more sites not to be missed are the large cave called the Cathedral, the caves and wrecks on Potato Reef, and Broken Rock with its gullies, canyons, and photogenic sweetlips.

Opposite page: Oriental sweetlips at the canyon dive spot at Embudu.

Top: Sponges growing on the wreck at the Kuda Giri dive site off Dhinganfinolhu.

Above: A group of sharks, a sight to make a diver's heart pump faster.

Left: Corals in the current at Embudu Thila.

North Ari Atoll

THE ARI ATOLL, WITH 105 ISLANDS, IS THE SECOND-LARGEST ATOLL IN THE MALDIVES. LIKE THE MALE ATOLL, IT IS DIVIDED FOR ADMINISTRATIVE PURPOSES INTO A NORTHERN AND A SOUTHERN HALF. MANY DIVERS WERE ONCE DRAWN THERE BY LEGENDARY SITES SUCH AS THE FISHHEAD.

For years, the entire Ari Atoll was world famous for its excellent shark sites. A glance in the logbook, the diver's diary, reveals the differences between then and now: "July 22, 1989, Place: *Fishhead*, 24 m, 91 min, Notes: lots of gray sharks, rays, must do this dive again." "August 31, 2006, Place: *Fishhead*, 25 m, 42 min. Notes: humphead wrasses and a whitetip shark, not much else around."

For how many thousand years must this underwater cliff have been a meeting point for sharks before it and the sharks here were discovered by divers? There were only nineteen years between those two dives, yet now everything has suddenly changed. This is because in 1994, within the space of one week, the entire shark stocks at many sites of this atoll were caught by local fishermen simply for their fins. This "shark finning" caused worldwide consternation. Quite apart from that, a single live shark brings in significantly more money from the tourism it attracts than the value of the fins, for which the fishermen were earning just ten dollars.

In 1995, the area was finally made a protected zone, but unfortunately far too late. The area and its shark population have still not properly recovered. Nonetheless, there are still plenty of diving highlights in North Ari Atoll, which can be reached from Hulule in about 30 minutes by plane. The traditional diving islands here are putting increasing emphasis on luxury, so divers who are more interested in the beautiful things below the water than in luxury above often rent cruisers.

The most popular sites are Ukulhas Thila, Nika Point, and Angehi Kandu with its many manta rays. You should not miss the beautifully overgrown *Fesdu* wreck, which lies at a depth of between about 80 and 90 ft/24 and 28 m, nor the devil rays at Dhonkalo Thila, Bathala Thila, the *Halaveli* wreck, or the Elaidhoo house reef, which is renowned for its large schools of snapper.

The richly encrusted Maaya Thila is particularly suitable for night dives. One extraordinary top spot is Hafza Thila, with batfish, trevally, gray reef sharks, and turtles.

An experience that has become legendary is the early morning dive at the hammerhead site Big Blue off Kuramathi, the largest hotel island in the Maldives, which is part of the Rasdu Atoll, north of the Ari Atoll.

Opposite page, top: A portrait of a gray reef shark.

Opposite page, bottom: A shoal of bluestripe snappers.

Right: A turtle in the northeast of the Ari Atoll.

33 FACTS

- **Depth:** 5–100 ft/2–30 m
- **Visibility:** 50–165 ft/15–50 m
- **Water temperature:** 81–86°F/ 27–30°C
- **Best time of year:** Feb–Apr
- **Level of difficulty:** ■–■■■
- **Diversity of coral species:** ■■■■■
- **Diversity of fish species:** ■■■■■
- **Big fish:** ■■■■
- **Wrecks:** ■■■
- **Caves:** ■■■
- **Walls:** ■■■■■
- **Snorkeling:** ■■■■■

INDIAN OCEAN: MALDIVES

South Ari Atoll

SINCE THE MID-1980s, THE ENTIRE ARI ATOLL HAS FIRMLY ESTABLISHED ITSELF AS PART OF THE INTERNATIONAL DIVING SCENE. THE SOUTHERN SECTION, WITH ITS WORLD-FAMOUS MANTA POINTS AND WHALE SHARKS, IS A MAJOR ATTRACTION IN THE SPRING.

As far as climate is concerned, the Maldives are definitely a year-round destination—both air and water temperatures are constantly subtropical. As the southwest monsoon, in particular, often brings rain and wind to the southwesterly islands of all the Maldives atolls from May to October, the best time to travel to the South Ari Atoll is between November and April, when the northeast monsoon prevails and it is calmer.

Besides the weather, the presence of a good house reef should also be one of the points to note. You can then dive without the constraint of having to stick to set times, as for example at the Vilamendhoo Island house reef, which has more than ten entry and exit points with a tank service. The MV *Kudhi Maa* sank directly off Machchafushi, and the wreck can safely be dived at any time of day. The house reef wall at Ranveli drops off from 10 to 120 ft/3 to 36 m and is inhabited by many moray eels, snappers, and trevally, lying as it does in the middle of a nutrient-rich channel.

Even though many dive spots in South Ari Atoll are relatively well protected during the northeast monsoon, the channels still sometimes experience strong currents caused by the ebb and flow of the tides and by the phases of the moon, which bring nutrient-rich water to the calmer outer reef. For this reason, whale sharks often visit the southern corner of the atoll at this time of year. The best way to spot these

34 FACTS

- **Depth:** 5–100 ft/2–30 m
- **Visibility:** 50–165 ft/15–50 m
- **Water temperature:** 81–86°F/27–30°C
- **Best time of year:** Nov–Apr
- **Level of difficulty:** ■–■■■■■
- **Diversity of coral species:** ■■■■■
- **Diversity of fish species:** ■■■■■
- **Big fish:** ■■■■■
- **Wrecks:** ■■■■
- **Caves:** ■■■
- **Walls:** ■■■■■
- **Snorkeling:** ■■■■■

creatures is from a boat when the swell is light. Their dorsal and tail fins give them away. When someone suddenly shouts "Whale shark!" there is a flurry of activity on board. Equipped with just mask, snorkel, and fins, everyone then tries to get right up close to these leviathans and swim with them.

Manta rays, too, can often be spotted in the spring. All the islands have their established places, those off Rangali and at Mirihi being particularly recommended. Top spots for fishes and corals of all kinds include the dive sites Thinfushi-Thila, Kudarah-Thila, and Mamigili Faru. On the outer reef of Dhidhoofinolhu, better known as Diva Resort or formerly White Sands, the chances of an encounter with whale sharks are particularly good. You can see bumphead parrotfish and sharks at Dhangethi Corner.

The diving at Panettone, north of the island of Thundufushi, where the underwater world of the Maldives can be seen at its most beautiful, is in a class of its own.

Opposite page: A manta ray at a cleaning station.

Top: A whale shark on the southern outer reef of South Male Atoll.

Above: A sweetlips with cleaner wrasses.

Left: Humpback snappers on the outer reef at Diva Resort island.

Southern Atolls

MOST OF THE MALDIVE RESORT ISLANDS LIE AROUND MALE ATOLL IN THE CENTER OF THE COUNTRY. THE NEARER YOU GET TO THE EQUATOR, THE FEWER DIVERS YOU MEET. HOWEVER, THE SOUTHERN ATOLLS HAVE SOME FANTASTIC DIVE SPOTS.

The Nilandhe, Felidhu, Mulaku, and Addu Atolls in the south of the Maldives have dive sites that are just as diverse as those to be found on Male and Ari Atolls. There are several kinds of reefs, including *giris* (reefs that rise to the surface or just below it), *thilas* (reefs that terminate about 26–33 ft/8–10 m below the water surface, often with strong currents), *farus* (elongated reefs), and *kandus* (channels with powerful inflows and outflows of water that depend on the tides).

The dive sites in north Nilandhe Atoll have for many years enjoyed international status. It is only possible to visit them from a single dive shop on the island of Filitheyo. In addition to a varied house reef up to 300 ft/90 m deep, with eight entry and exit points, there are a further thirty sites within a small radius. The shoals of fish here are reminiscent even today of the Maldives in the 1970s.

The reefs in Felidhu Atoll around the resort islands of Dhiggiri and Alimatha are seldom visited by divers. However, the Golden Wall is extraordinarily colorful, and marvelous pink, red, and yellow soft corals adorn entire blocks on the corner of the channel. With a bit of luck you will see hammerhead sharks in the early morning at Hammerhead Point off the island of Fottheyo. In Rakeedhoo Kandu you will come across lots of schooling fish and fat groupers. Vattaru Channel is a little-known gem.

The southernmost atoll is Addu Atoll, which even has its own airport on the island of Gan. This atoll also has a couple of dozen dive spots where almost untouched hard coral gardens flourish, and where even technical diving is possible. At Muda Kan, you can see manta rays being cleaned by small wrasses, and at Bushy East Channel there are eagle rays, humphead wrasses, and snappers. At Ismahelia, you can observe nurse sharks dozing, turtles grazing, and barracuda hunting.

The largest wreck in the Maldives, the *British Loyalty*, is a 440-ft-long/134-m-long oil tanker, most of which is overgrown with all sorts of coral. Here, too, the coral life has recovered well since the warm El Niño currents, with water temperatures reaching up to 95°F/35°C, damaged almost 70 percent of the coral in 1998. Worst hit by "coral bleaching" were the hard coral gardens just below the surface and in places where no exchange of water could take place with water from cooler, deeper layers.

Opposite page, top: The huge propeller on the wreck of the *British Loyalty* off the island of Gan.

Opposite page, bottom: A school of fusiliers—a common sight in the Maldives.

Above right: Small soft corals on the Golden Wall in Felidhu Atoll.

Below right: A grouper eating a smaller relative.

35 FACTS

- **Depth:** 5–100 ft/2–30 m
- **Visibility:** 50–165 ft/15–50 m
- **Water temperature:** 81–86°F/27–30°C
- **Best time of year:** Dec–Apr; Addu Atoll: Feb–June
- **Level of difficulty:** ■–■■■■■
- **Diversity of coral species:** ■■■■■
- **Diversity of fish species:** ■■■■■
- **Big fish:** ■■■■
- **Wrecks:** ■■■
- **Caves:** ■■■
- **Walls:** ■■■■■
- **Snorkeling:** ■■■■■

Al Mukallah

YEMEN IS RELATIVELY UNDEVELOPED IN TERMS OF DIVING. HOWEVER, THE COUNTRY BORDERS ON THE RED SEA IN THE WEST AND THE INDIAN OCEAN IN THE SOUTH. DIVERS WILL DISCOVER A FAIRYTALE LAND STRAIGHT OUT OF THE *ARABIAN NIGHTS*, BELOW AS WELL AS ABOVE THE WATER.

Most people associate Yemen with mystical tales about the Kingdom of the Queen of Sheba, the Incense Route, and the spice trade, but hardly anyone associates it with diving. Nonetheless, it is well worth making the journey to this country right in the south of the Arabian peninsula—but you should expect a bit of an adventure.

The first permit for a dive center in Yemen was issued in 1995, in the city of Al Mukallah, today a booming port. On no account should you miss the house reef, around which there are what is probably a record number of species of moray eel: ten different species seen in one dive justify its title of the "moray capital." You can also dive the wreck of the freighter *Maldive Image*, which ran aground on the reef near the port.

A little more than 1 mile/2 km from the center are the Rocky Banks, shallows that lie 40–50 ft/12–15 m below the sea surface. The whole gamut of Arabian Sea fishes congregates here: you will be greeted by hundreds of blue triggerfish; you can often see impressive laced morays in front of their holes, and occasionally you even come across sharks, marlins, and tuna.

36 FACTS

- **Depth:** 10–130 ft/3–40 m
- **Visibility:** 30–65 ft/10–20 m
- **Water temperature:** 79–88°F/26–31°C
- **Best time of year:** Nov–Mar
- **Level of difficulty:** ■–■■■■■
- **Diversity of coral species:** ■■■
- **Diversity of fish species:** ■■■■
- **Big fish:** ■■■
- **Wrecks:** ■■
- **Caves:** ■■
- **Walls:** ■■■
- **Snorkeling:** ■■■

Below left: Cuttlefish nuptials.

Below right: A laced moray under observation.

INDIAN OCEAN: TANZANIA

Pemba

THIS "GREEN ISLAND" OFF THE EAST COAST OF SOUTHERN AFRICA GEOGRAPHICALLY FORMS PART OF THE ZANZIBAR ARCHIPELAGO AND POLITICALLY PART OF TANZANIA. THE DIVING GROUNDS AROUND THE ISLAND AND IN THE PEMBA CHANNEL ARE FULL OF PROMISE AND EASY TO REACH, AND YET THEY ARE NOT OFTEN DIVED.

In 1967, this lush, hilly island was made famous by champion diver Jacques Cousteau. Today, it remains a favorite among divers, as Zanzibar's "little sister," like Sleeping Beauty, seems to have fallen into a hundred-year slumber.

At first, the only diving possible on the island was off cruisers based in Kenya. Nowadays, though it is still a far cry from mass tourism, there are some lodges and dive shops on the island, and it is also visited by live-aboards.

The deep Pemba Channel, through which manta rays, whale sharks, and other big fish pass, runs between the mainland of Tanzania and the island. Around the main island there are countless small islands, some of them uninhabited, with luxuriant tropical vegetation.

Around the island of Misali there is a protected marine reserve with many channels that are good for diving. Off Pemba, divers can take their pick of sites, from steep drop-offs to soft coral gardens. The ocean colors range from the blue of deep waters to the turquoise of the shallows, the fish and coral life from huge to minuscule.

Above left: Barracudas shimmering like silver.

Above right: Koran angelfish with electric blue stripes.

Left: A giant barrel sponge.

37 FACTS

- **Depth:** 15–130 ft/5–40 m
- **Visibility:** 30–115 ft/10–35 m
- **Water temperature:** 81–88°F/ 27–31°C
- **Best time of year:** Oct–Mar
- **Level of difficulty:** ■–■■■■■
- **Diversity of coral species:** ■■■
- **Diversity of fish species:** ■■■■
- **Big fish:** ■■■
- **Wrecks:** ■
- **Caves:** ■■
- **Walls:** ■■■■
- **Snorkeling:** ■■■

INDIAN OCEAN: SEYCHELLES

Seychelles

THERE CAN HARDLY BE A MORE PERFECT BACKDROP THAN THE SEYCHELLES. UNDERWATER, THESE GRANITE ISLANDS HAVE A RATHER BLEAKER CHARM, BUT DESPITE THE ABSENCE OF CORALS, THE SPLENDOR OF THE FISHES AND CRUSTACEANS IS CAPTIVATING.

The Seychelles "paradise" consists of 115 islands. It lies east of Africa (northeast of Madagascar) and is divided into an inner and an outer region. The Inner Islands are located on the "Seychelles Bank" around the main islands of Praslin, La Digue, and Mahé, and are the center of tourist and indigenous life on the Seychelles. The Outer Islands are tiny atolls and sandbanks, some of which are more than 600 miles/1,000 km from the main islands. Thanks to their proximity to the equator, they enjoy a constant tropical climate.

There are many dive shops integrated into the hotels on some of the islands. However, a cruise around the archipelago offers far greater variety. The Seychelles have more than a hundred listed dive sites, and the underwater scenery at these is often very similar. Unfortunately, visibility is not always good, and divers should not expect to see colorful soft corals and reef-building hard coral gardens. Sadly, the few corals that do exist were badly damaged in 1998 when El Niño raised the water temperature by 12.6°F (7°C). The tsunami in 2004 also had a negative impact on some islands, both below and above the water.

The underwater scenery in the Seychelles is characterized by large, picturesque blocks of rock, similar to those that can be seen on land. These form canyons and gullies that are reminiscent of diving in the Atlantic. Around the two islands of Les Soeurs, these underwater rocks look, with a bit of imagination, like high-rise buildings, which is why the area has been

38 FACTS

- **Depth:** 15–130 ft/5–40 m
- **Visibility:** 15–80 ft/5–25 m
- **Water temperature:** 73–86°F/23–30°C
- **Best time of year:** Apr/May and Oct/Nov (monsoon transition)
- **Level of difficulty:** ■–■■■
- **Diversity of coral species:** ■■
- **Diversity of fish species:** ■■■■
- **Big fish:** ■■■■
- **Wrecks:** ■■■
- **Caves:** ■■
- **Walls:** ■■■
- **Snorkeling:** ■■■

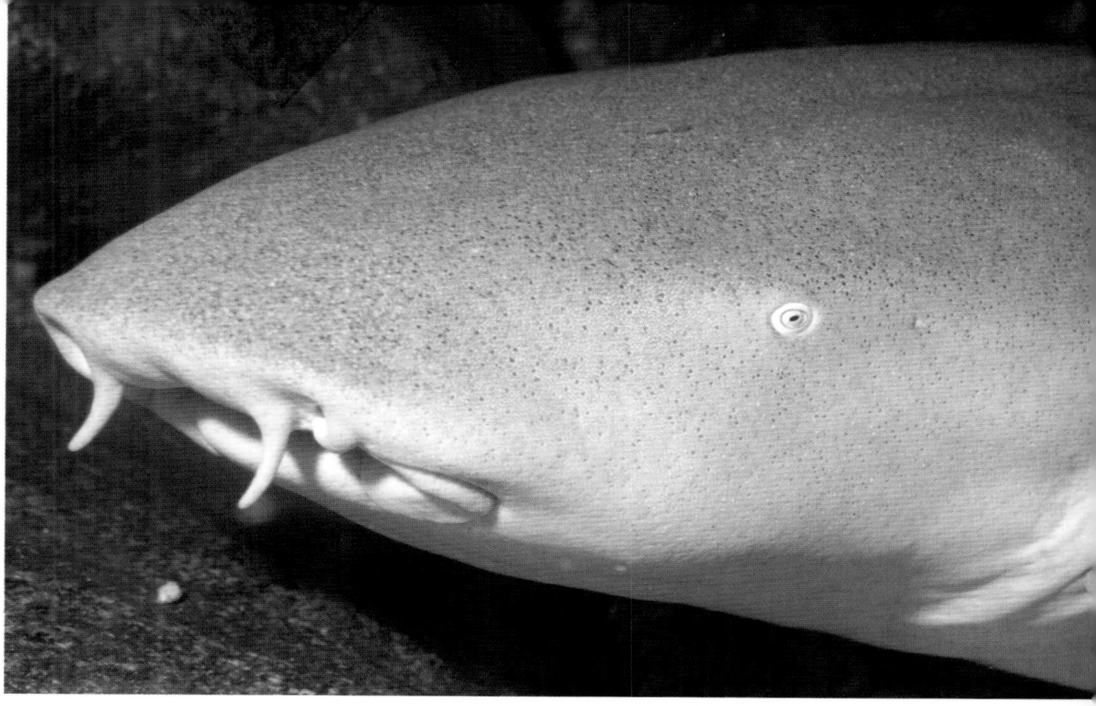

christened "Manhattan." The gullies between them form alleyways in which predators like trevally hunt yellowback fusiliers, and barracuda stand guard as reef police. Some "skyscrapers" reach almost to the surface and are decorated with colorful sponges—like art on a building.

At the site of the small wall off the island of Marianne, there are often gray and whitetip sharks circling; divers just need to be patient. From time to time you will even see whale sharks cruise past with golden trevally and remoras, and sometimes eagle rays also fly past through the water.

Biter Rock between Praslin and La Digue is an uncharted top diving spot. There are outstanding sites with all sorts of rays off the world-famous Anse Lazio beach on Praslin and off Booby Island. In addition, the Aldabra group, which forms part of the Outer Islands, is renowned throughout the world for its giant tortoises.

Opposite page: Remora and golden trevally accompanying a whale shark.

Top: An impressive specimen of a basking shark.

Above: Guitarfish making its way along the sea bed.

Left: A grouper being cleaned by shrimps.

INDIAN OCEAN: THAILAND

Phuket

THIS SOUGHT-AFTER TROPICAL ISLAND IN THE ANDAMAN SEA IS A REAL DIVING STRONGHOLD. IT OFFERS LOTS OF GOOD SITES FOR SNORKELERS, NOVICES, AND EXPERIENCED DIVERS, AND HAS BEEN ABLE TO RECOVER QUICKLY FROM THE DEVASTATION CAUSED BY THE 2004 TSUNAMI.

Phuket lies approximately 550 miles/900 km south of Bangkok and, with an area of 210 square miles/543 square km, is the largest island in Thailand. Picturesque sandy beaches, lovely hotels, reasonable prices, night life, and excellent flight connections make the island a tourist magnet. Diving, in particular, is booming: Its 80+ dive shops bear witness to the popularity of Phuket and the surrounding dive areas, which offer a glimpse into a fantastic underwater world, rich in color and marine life.

Trips in the indigenous longtail boats have long been a thing of the past. Nowadays, the divers who travel here from all over the world have a whole fleet of state-of-the-art dive boats available to them for day trips or longer tours. In Chalong harbor there is a "dive terminal," where every morning special vehicles ferry batches of divers to the various boats, which wait at the end of a long pier for their passengers.

Beginners generally dive around the reefs just offshore, while more experienced divers are drawn to the dive sites one or two hours' journey away. In the protected area around Shark Point, which lies a ninety-minute boat ride to the east, you can often see sea snakes and territorial leopard sharks. The area's soft and fan corals are an additional attraction. Close by, the wreck of the *King Cruiser* slumbers in an upright position: this former ferry sank in May 1997. The three levels of the ship are at depths of

39 FACTS

- ❖ **Depth:** 15–130 ft/5–40 m
- ❖ **Visibility:** 30–80 ft/10–25 m
- ❖ **Water temperature:** 81–88°F/27–30°C
- ❖ **Best time of year:** Nov–Apr
- ❖ **Level of difficulty:** ■–■■■■■
- ❖ **Diversity of coral species:** ■■■■
- ❖ **Diversity of fish species:** ■■■■
- ❖ **Big fish:** ■■■
- ❖ **Wrecks:** ■■
- ❖ **Caves:** ■■■
- ❖ **Walls:** ■■■■
- ❖ **Snorkeling:** ■■■

40–100 ft/12–30 m, and they are guarded by lionfish, moray eels, and crustaceans. The nutrient-rich open water also attracts a variety of schools of fish. At the nearby Anemone Reef, there are striking large fields of anemones living in symbiosis with clown fish.

There is a good chance of seeing manta rays and leopard sharks at the uninhabited Racha Noi island south of Phuket. The neighboring island, Racha Yai, is relatively undisturbed and also good for snorkeling, with a wide range of tropical fish and colorful soft and hard corals. This site is usually done as a drift dive: You let yourself drift along in the current and are picked up by the boat again at the end of the dive.

The sites around the Phi-Phi islands east of Phuket, which can be reached in three hours, are a real delight. Here, you can dive in limestone caves where thousands of glassfish flit to and fro.

Opposite page: A leopard shark at Ko Bid Noc.

Above: Perfect camouflage—a ghost pipefish on a harp coral.

Left: A sea star doing the splits.

Ko Lanta

THE TWO LANTA ISLANDS LIE IN PHANG-NGA BAY IN SOUTHWEST THAILAND. FROM LANTA YAI, THERE ARE TRIPS TO DIVE SITES WHERE SPECTACULAR SOFT CORALS ARE GUARANTEED AND ENCOUNTERS WITH BIG FISH ARE A REAL POSSIBILITY.

Opposite page: Hin Daeng dive spot—how many thousands of fish must be in that shoal?

Top: A devil scorpionfish opening its jaws wide.

Center: Well-camouflaged poisonous stonefish.

Bottom: A colorful anemone.

Southeast of Phuket and about 40 miles/70 km south of the town of Krabi, in Mu Ko Lanta National Park, lie the two islands of Lanta Noi and Lanta Yai. The first is virtually uninhabited, while Lanta Yai is—compared to hectic Phuket—a fairly tranquil tourist island with pretty beaches. There are also some dive centers based here.

The surrounding dive spots to the west and south of the islands are accessed on day trips or on two-day tours. These destinations are also served by a number of cruise boats coming from Phuket. During the rainy season in the summer months, the often murky water makes diving at all the sites unattractive.

The most beautiful sites, which are in the area around Ko Lanta, include the small rock Hin Bida, which projects above the water at low tide. There are often leopard sharks dozing on the sandy bed, and on the east side there are thriving beautiful soft coral formations. Thrilling drop-offs with fan corals are waiting to be explored at the two rocks of Koh Bida Nai, where spiny lobsters and other crustaceans hide in the many crevices.

Ko Ha, which means "five islands," lies about an hour's boat ride away from Saladan pier on Lanta Yai. Around this island group there are a number of good spots from which you can take your pick: At Ko Ha Yai there is an enticing cathedral-like cave with white whip coral, around which lurk scorpionfish, stonefish, and lionfish. Off the neighboring island, Ko Ha Nua, a wonderfully encrusted chimney rises from 55 to 15 ft/17 to 5 m deep and is wide enough that you can dive through it without feeling claustrophobic. There are generally hundreds of small barracuda swimming around it.

About 12 miles/20 km southwest of the Ko Rok Nok nature reserve lie the area's two top dive spots: Hin Muang and Hin Daeng. The "purple rocks" of Hin Muang rise to about 40 ft/12 m below the surface and are almost entirely covered with purple soft corals; farther down there are often leopard sharks dozing. This is the deepest wall in Thailand, going down to about 230 ft/70 m and offering visibility of 30–130 ft/10–40 m. Not 400 yd/400 m away, three small rocks protrude above the water: the "red rocks" of Hin Daeng are also named after the soft coral found there. Hundreds of thousands of tiny schooling fish live here, and from January to April divers may experience a real thrill, as whale sharks and manta rays like to visit the site in these months.

40 FACTS

- **Depth:** 15–130 ft/5–40 m
- **Visibility:** 30–130 ft/10–40 m
- **Water temperature:** 79–86°F/26–30°C
- **Best time of year:** Nov–Apr
- **Level of difficulty:** ■–■■■■■
- **Diversity of coral species:** ■■■■■
- **Diversity of fish species:** ■■■■
- **Big fish:** ■■■■
- **Wrecks:** ■
- **Caves:** ■■■
- **Walls:** ■■■■
- **Snorkeling:** ■■■■

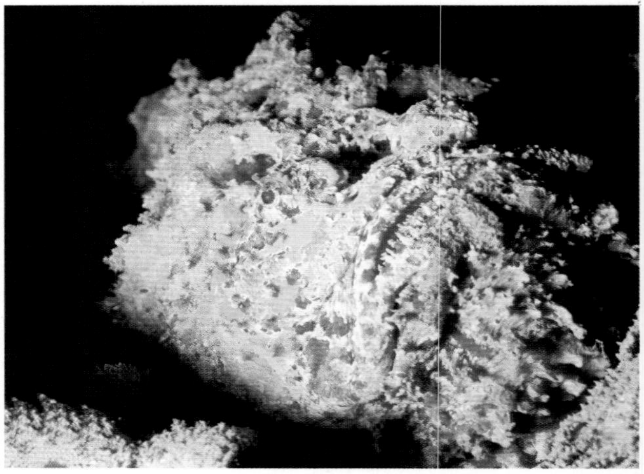

INDIAN OCEAN: THAILAND

Similan Islands

WHEN THESE NINE GRANITE ISLANDS WERE FIRST PROTECTED IN 1982, THEIR CORAL REEFS, RICH IN FISH LIFE, WERE DEEMED AN INSIDER TIP. NOW THEY ARE WORLD FAMOUS AND A FAVORITE DESTINATION FOR SAFARI BOATS IN PARTICULAR.

The Similan Islands lie 60 miles/100 km to the northwest of Phuket in the Andaman Sea and are part of the 49-square-mile/128-square-km uninhabited Mu Ko Similan National Park. Dive tourism on the islands has increased markedly, with ever-increasing numbers of live-aboards coming from Phuket. Added to these are the many high-speed day boats coming from Khao Lak, about 35 miles/60 km away.

This 15-mile-long/25-km-long chain of islands comprises a total of nine islands, hence the name "Similan," which is Malaysian for "nine." For the sake of simplicity, the islands have been numbered from south to north, but they do also have their own Thai names. The two dozen or so dive sites in the national park are some of the best in southeast Asia. Fishing is banned, and if you want to dive here you have to pay a daily entry fee.

In these islands, a distinction is made between the western side, polished by the wind and waves and exposed to the southwest monsoon, with impressive granite blocks forming underwater canyons, overhangs, and caves, and the gently sloping reefs on the eastern side, where the diving is more relaxed. More than 200 species of stone coral and 350 different soft corals have been recorded around the islands. Unfortunately, the encounters with whale sharks which you could previously count on here, are now a thing of the past.

41 FACTS

- **Depth:** 15–130 ft/5–40 m
- **Visibility:** 65–150 ft/20–45 m
- **Water temperature:** 79–86°F/26–30°C
- **Best time of year:** Oct–May
- **Level of difficulty:** ■–■■■■■
- **Diversity of coral species:** ■■■■■
- **Diversity of fish species:** ■■■■■
- **Big fish:** ■■■■
- **Wrecks:** ■■
- **Caves:** ■■
- **Walls:** ■■■■
- **Snorkeling:** ■■■■■

A popular dive is the openwater descent to Sharkfin Reef on island no. 3, where reef fish abound. Off island no. 4, large stone blocks are adorned with sea fans at Stonehenge, and colorful parrotfish populate the Chinese Wall. Ko Payu, island no. 7, is outstanding, with three top spots for novices and experienced divers alike: Canyons and barrel sponges await the diver at Deep Six; East of Eden, with magnificent coral, turtles, moray eels, and sea snakes, is one of the most beautiful reefs on the archipelago; and at Sea Fan City there are fan corals, sponges, soft corals, and shoals of fish in the current.

Ko Similan is island no. 8 and the largest in the whole archipelago. To the southwest of it lies Elephant Rock. The idyllic Donald Duck Bay with its picture-postcard scenery offers an anchorage and good night dives. On the western side there is a great spot with lots of soft corals called Fantasea Reef. The former cruiser *Atlantis* now rests on Beacon Reef at a depth of 40 ft/12 m and is swarming with rays, moray eels, and batfish.

In the north, the popular island no. 9, Ko Bangu, has seven dive sites to its name, the best being Snapper Alley, North Point, and Christmas Point.

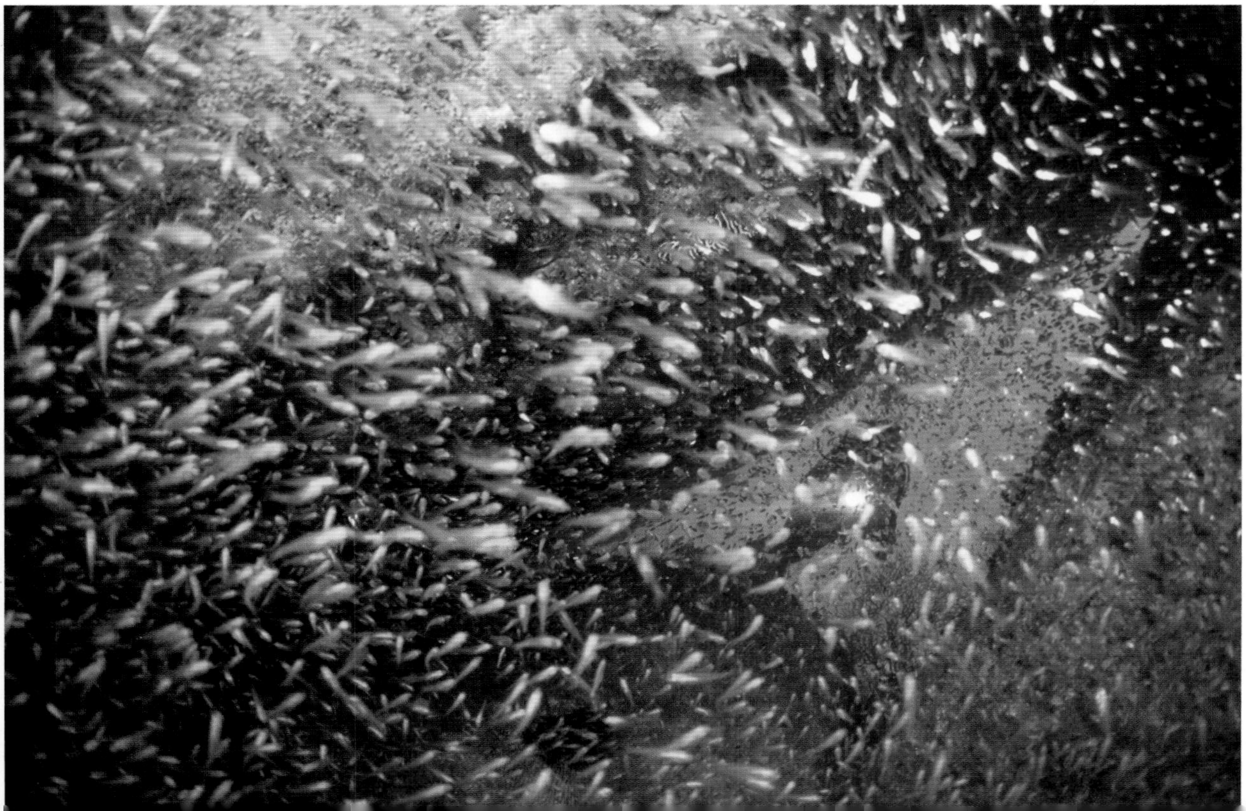

Opposite page: Coral block at the East of Eden dive site on the Similan Islands.

Above: Filigree tubeworms.

Left: Glassfish at the Elephant Rock site, all but obscuring the view.

Surin Islands

THE SURIN ISLANDS LIE CLOSE TO THE BORDER WITH MYANMAR. LIKE RICHELIEU ROCK, KO TACHAI, AND KO BON, THEY FALL WITHIN THE MU KO SURIN NATIONAL PARK. PEOPLE TRAVEL HERE TO SEE ONE THING IN PARTICULAR: BIG FISH.

Opposite page, top: Feather star catching plankton.

Opposite page, bottom: Soft corals on Pastel Ridge.

Above right: Living up to its name, the copperband butterflyfish.

Below right: A true leviathan—the whale shark.

42 FACTS

- **Depth:** 15–130 ft/5–40 m
- **Visibility:** 15–80 ft/5–25 m
- **Water temperature:** 79–86°F/26–30°C
- **Best time of year:** Oct–May
- **Level of difficulty:** ■–■■■
- **Diversity of coral species:** ■■■■
- **Diversity of fish species:** ■■■■
- **Big fish:** ■■■■
- **Wrecks:** ■
- **Caves:** ■
- **Walls:** ■■■■
- **Snorkeling:** ■■■■

A little farther to the north of the Similan Islands in the Andaman Sea, you will come across the Surin Islands. In 1981, this archipelago, which includes five islands and some rock formations, was also declared a national park. The islands are for the most part uninhabited, the only people living there being the park rangers together with the inhabitants of a single village of Moken (a southeast Asian tribe of sea nomads).

As this region lies about 125 miles/200 km from Phuket and is thus too far away to be included in the popular four-day tours, you will see fewer cruise boats than on the Similan Islands. However, those who undertake the journey will be rewarded with top-class dive sites: Richelieu Rock, Ko Tachai, and Ko Bon also lie within the national park.

The hard coral gardens of the Surin Islands are regarded by dive experts as the most beautiful in the whole of Thailand, but the soft corals and the diversity of fish species are not quite as good as those in the south of the Andaman Sea. A hard coral plateau with large staghorn corals, which is good for snorkeling, extends along the east coast of Ko Torinla. At Staghorn Point on Ko Surin Tai island, there are two parallel rock faces with reef sharks patrolling in the current, and in places there are fan corals for divers to admire. Among the interesting things to explore are ribbon eels and shellfish. Watch out for titan triggerfish, which defend their territory assiduously against intruders and have a powerful bite, as more than one diver has discovered.

Probably the most popular dive spot in Thailand is Richelieu Rock. It was incorporated into the park in 2005 in order to protect its underwater flora and fauna from Burmese fishermen. At low water the rocks just graze the surface of the water. Divers were once guaranteed to see big fish here, but even today the chances of seeing whale sharks and manta and eagle rays are still good. There are always plenty of barracuda, trevally, camouflaged anglerfish, and ghost pipefish. Richelieu Rock is definitely a site where you should plan on making several descents.

The islands of Ko Bon and Ko Tachai are famous for their marvelous soft coral gardens, and here, too, with a bit of luck, you may encounter whale sharks. Around the seamounts off Ko Tachai, at depths of 45–115 ft/14–35 m, there are often strong currents. The crest of Pastel Ridge at Ko Bon, which is clothed in colorful soft corals, lies a little deeper, and leopard sharks and manta rays are frequently seen there.

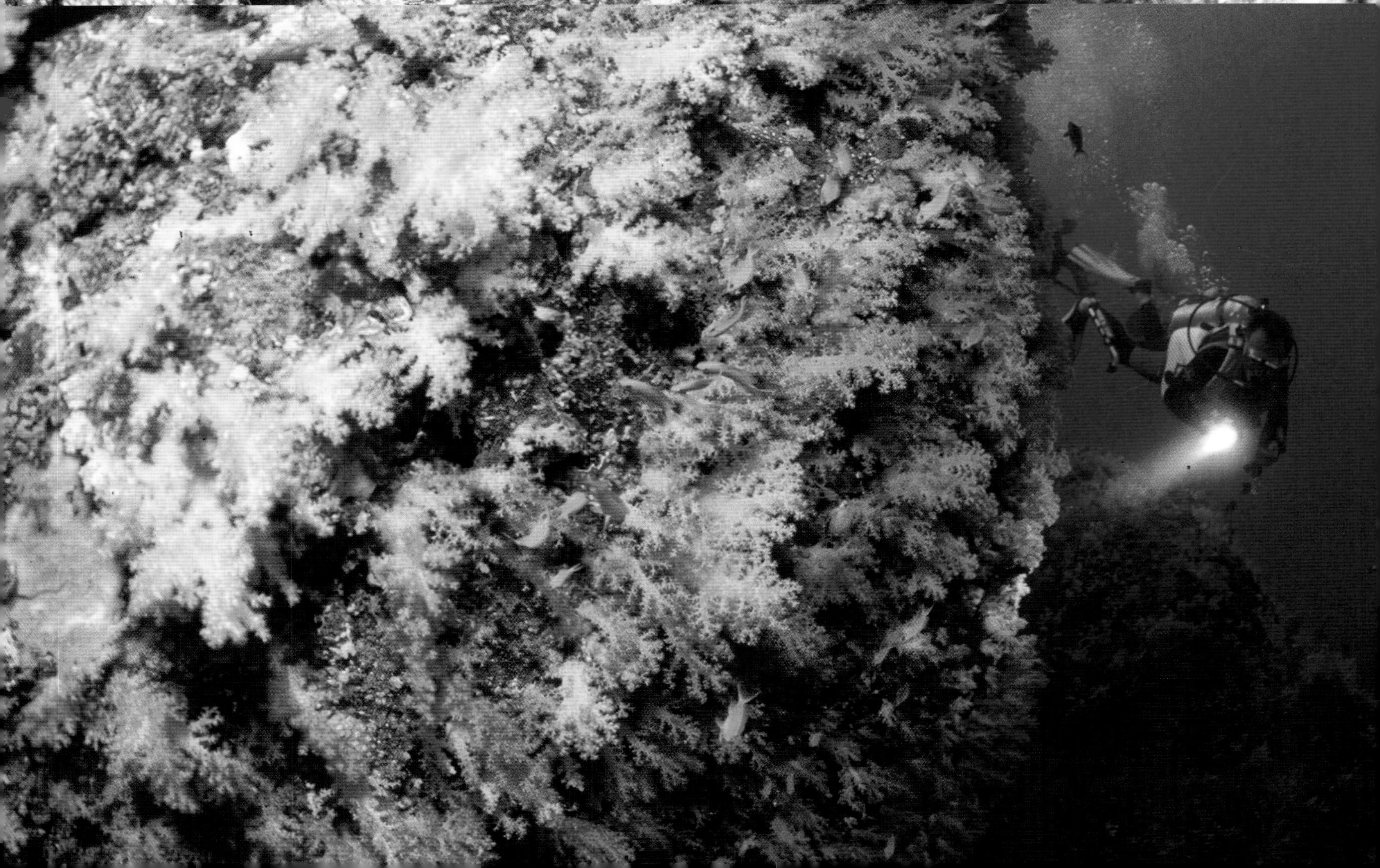

INDIAN OCEAN: MYANMAR

Myanmar

THE UNDERWATER WORLD AROUND THE MERGUI ARCHIPELAGO AND THE BURMA BANKS IS A PRISTINE ENVIRONMENT AND AN ADVENTUROUS DIVE DESTINATION: ONLY A FRACTION OF THIS VAST EXPANSE HAS PREVIOUSLY BEEN DIVED.

Diving holidays to Myanmar (formerly known as Burma) are something of a voyage of discovery. There are two diving areas, both lying in the south of the country and in the north of the Andaman Sea: the Mergui archipelago and the Burma Banks.

The Mergui archipelago consists of more than 800 densely wooded islands, of which only a few have been inhabited for centuries by small numbers of sea nomads. The Moken live a secluded life, spend much of their time on boats, and subsist by catching fish. Myanmar was ruled by Britain until 1948, and today it is a socialist republic ruled by military dictatorship. The latter first opened the Mergui archipelago as a diving area in 1997.

Macleod Island houses the one and only dive resort in the entire archipelago. For this reason, most divers take dive cruises to the islands. These depart either from Kawthaung, a town near the border, or else from Phuket or from Tablamu pier in Phang Nga, in Thailand. However, boats from Thailand also have to pass through Kawthaung to deal with the necessary border formalities.

At Haa Mile Hin, as at many dive sites in the Mergui archipelago, there are beautiful walls, fantastic coral growth, and deep canyons. Other well-known sites include Shark Cave, where gray reef sharks swim through shoals of anchovies in a ravine, and Three Islets, where these elegant hunters also make their rounds.

43 FACTS

- **Depth:** 15–130 ft/5–40 m
- **Visibility:** 30–100 ft/10–30 m
- **Water temperature:** 77–84°F/25–29°C
- **Best time of year:** Nov–Apr
- **Level of difficulty:** ■■■–■■■■■
- **Diversity of coral species:** ■■■■
- **Diversity of fish species:** ■■■■
- **Big fish:** ■■■■
- **Wrecks:** ■
- **Caves:** ■■■
- **Walls:** ■■■■
- **Snorkeling:** ■■

About 125 miles/200 km northwest of Kawthaung, Black Rock is a magnet for a variety of sharks and manta rays. However, it should be made clear that sharks are hunted in this area, and the archipelago was first declared a "shark protection zone" in 2004. The government is now aiming to create a national marine park.

Farther west, the Burma Banks, a colorful underwater plateau in the middle of nowhere, are totally unprotected. It is really well worth making a detour to visit them, and it has been possible to do so from bases in Thailand since 1990. The region used to be a real favorite, but unfortunately the silvertip and nurse sharks on Silver Tip Bank have been decimated, though there are still plenty of huge potato cod there. Other sites on Burma Banks include Big Bank, Rainbow Bank, Roe Bank, and Heckford Bank.

Opposite page: Potato cod on Silver Tip Bank.

Top: A silvertip shark gliding through the Indian Ocean.

Above: A nurse shark at Silver Tip Bank.

Left: A large stingray at Black Rock.

North of Australia, the Indo-Pacific forms the transition zone between the Indian Ocean and the western Pacific. Together with its marginal seas, it contains the widest variety of coral and fish species in the world. Island states such as the Philippines, Indonesia, and Malaysia have thousands of dive sites, whose magnificent underwater flora and fauna no diver should miss.

NDO-PACIFIC

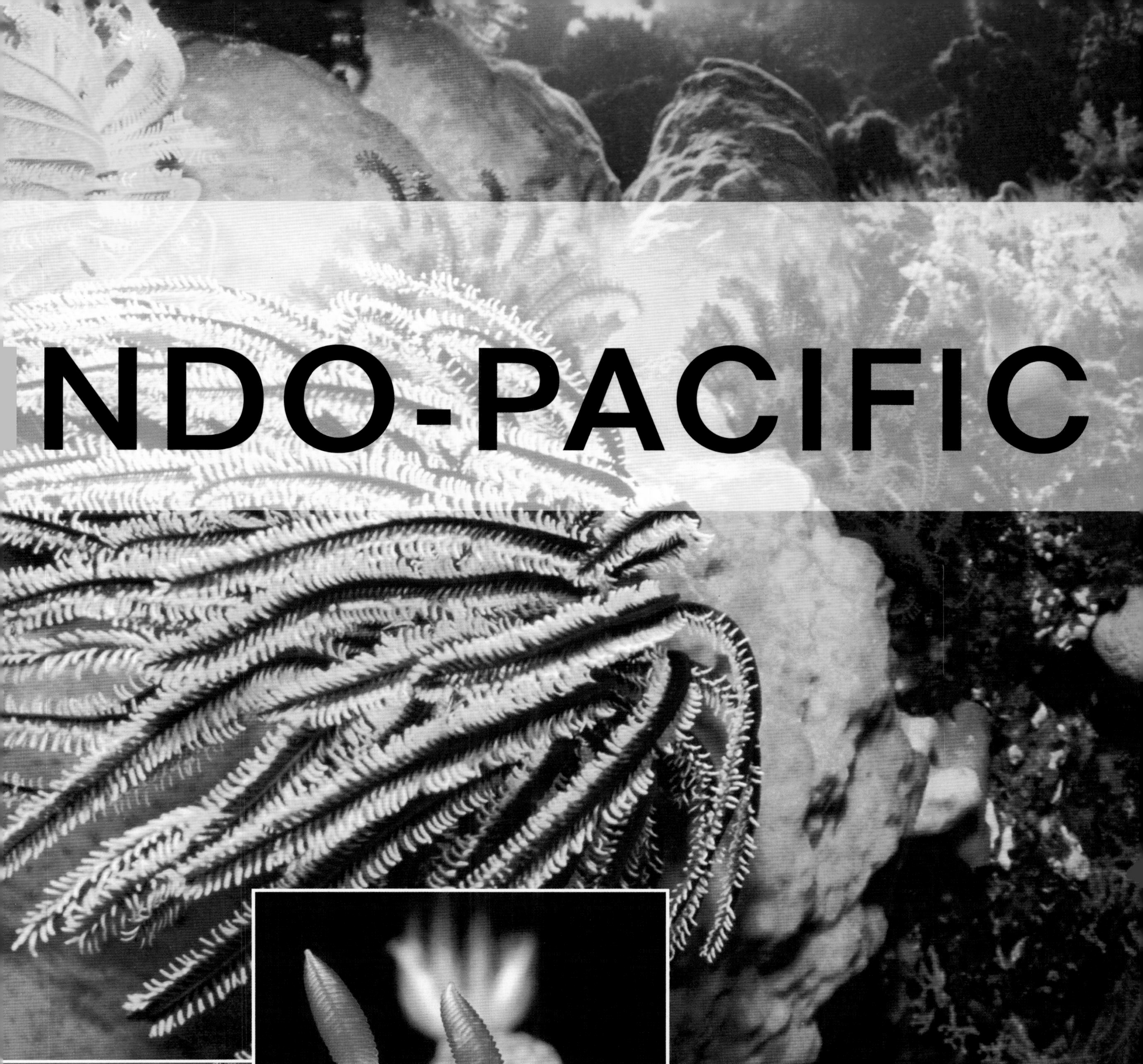

INDO-PACIFIC: INDONESIA

Raja Ampat

THE RAJA AMPAT ARCHIPELAGO LIES OFF THE COAST OF INDONESIA, FAR REMOVED FROM CIVILIZATION. THE AREA IS A REAL DIVERS' PARADISE AND IS HOME TO THE ISLAND OF KRI, WHICH CURRENTLY HOLDS THE WORLD RECORD FOR THE NUMBER OF FISH SPECIES.

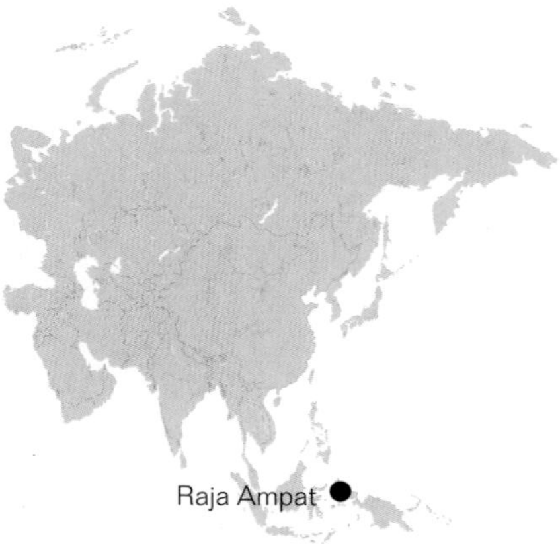

Opposite page: A brightly colored bouquet of soft corals.

Top: A pygmy sea horse.

Center: A manta ray gliding through a shoal of fusiliers.

Bottom: Mantis shrimp off the island of Wai.

The journey to these islands off the coast of the Indonesian province of West Papua is long but it is definitely well worth the effort. In the Raja Ampat archipelago itself there are only three dive centers, but for some time now a number of dive boats have included in their itineraries the sites around the larger islands of Waigeo, Batanta, Salawati, and Misool (*see spot no.* 45), together with some more small islands west of Sorong.

Dutchman Max Ammer has been exploring this region ever since 1990. He has found large Japanese ship and aircraft wrecks dating from World War II, but more importantly, an environment unmatched for the variety of its fishes and corals. The year 2001 was a lucky one for Raja Ampat, as it was then that the scientist Dr. Gerald Allen counted the fish on the house reef off the island of Kri. When he emerged, his slate showed the number 283—a new world record for the number of species seen in a single dive, which had previously been held by the renowned Milne Bay in the east of Papua New Guinea, with about 200 species. The current total of different fish species found in Raja Ampat stands at 970, while the number of hard coral species stands at 565, representing half the world's known hard coral species.

The manta ray sites off the island of Mansuar in the north of the archipelago, near the dive center on Kri, are sensational. Here, huge devil rays come to be cleaned in the mornings, and in the afternoons they mill around at the surface in a feeding frenzy. Rare bamboo sharks spend the days here resting in small caves. Beneath an unprepossessing pier on the island of Arborek, millions of glittering silversides dart around. At Mike's Point, three different species of pygmy sea horse have been discovered, and there are various species of sweetlips hovering under table corals. Snorkelers can marvel at the gorgonian sea fans which grow here at depths as shallow as 10 ft/3 m.

A really extraordinary place here is the Passage between the islands of Gam and Waigeo. You boat in at high tide through the green labyrinth of Blue Water Mangroves, a nursery for many fish species. The current in the Passage, which is a kind of channel only 65 ft/20 m wide, can be very strong. However, this provides plenty of food for soft corals, sponges, nudibranchs, and fish. The wobbegong, or carpet shark, is found here, and various species of goby live on the sandy bed.

Many dives in this region are drift dives and thus more suitable for experienced divers. However, there are also some calmer spots for novices.

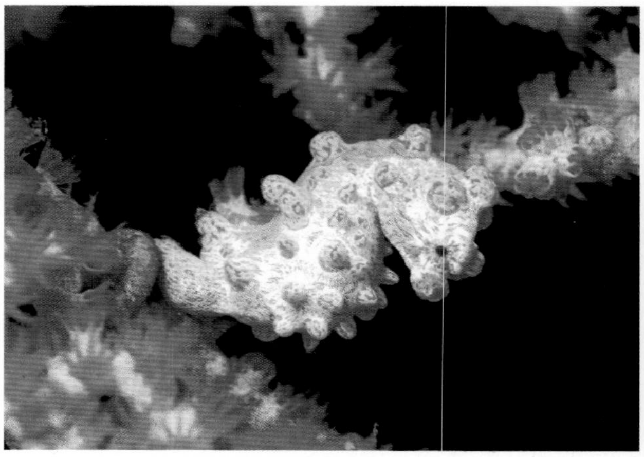

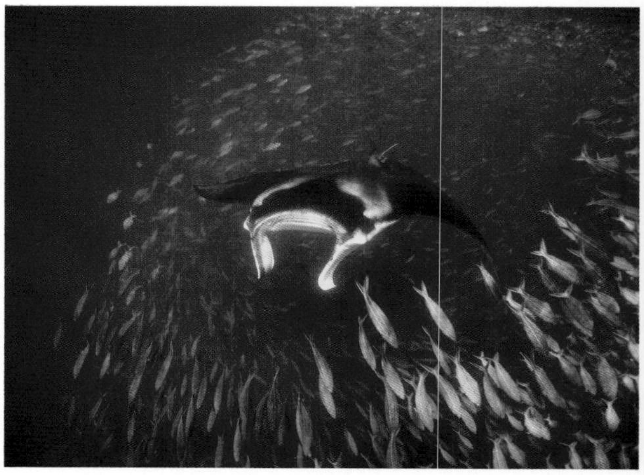

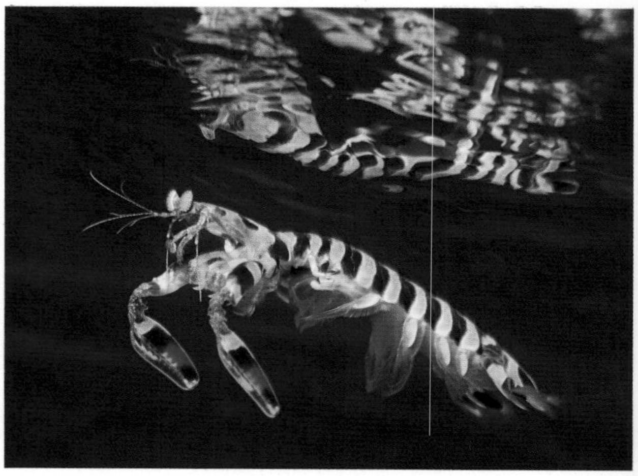

44 FACTS

- **Depth:** 5–130 ft/2–40 m
- **Visibility:** 30–100 ft/10–30 m
- **Water temperature:** 81–86°F/27–30°C
- **Best time of year:** Sept–Feb and Apr–July
- **Level of difficulty:** ■–■■■■■
- **Diversity of coral species:** ■■■■■
- **Diversity of fish species:** ■■■■■
- **Big fish:** ■■■■
- **Wrecks:** ■■■■
- **Caves:** ■■■
- **Walls:** ■■■■
- **Snorkeling:** ■■■■

INDO-PACIFIC: INDONESIA

Misool

TO THE SOUTH OF RAJA AMPAT, THE WORLD LEADER IN TERMS OF CORAL BIODIVERSITY, LIES THE ISLAND OF MISOOL. IT IS SURROUNDED BY A VERITABLE LABYRINTH OF ISLANDS, WHICH IN 2007 WAS DECLARED A MARINE PROTECTED AREA.

In the huge area surrounding Misool, southwest of the so-called bird's head of Papua, formerly known as Irian Jaya, there are hundreds of tiny islands. Some of these are unnamed and are not even marked on the most recently updated charts. This labyrinth of limestone and basalt lies just below the equator and provides every diver with the chance to be the first to discover a dive site. Marine biologists are constantly discovering new coral species on their expeditions.

The only tourists in the area around Misool are in a small diving resort on the private island of Batbitim or on cruise boats. Most diving safaris start in Sorong, on the west coast of New Guinea. In the language of the Biak, the first people to settle in this area, Sorong means "deep sea," but in fact the waters around the many small islands off the coasts of Misool are not that deep. Here, you can dive in channels and on walls off mushroom-headed lush green islands with palm trees and orchids.

At Killer Cave every square inch is covered with life, there is an abundance of shapes and colors, and even at the 10-ft/3-m decompression stop there are 3-ft-tall/1-m-tall gorgonian sea fans competing for the best places. Fan, cauliflower and whip corals also abound at Papua Phanta Sea. At Gamfi island you will find tiny pygmy sea horses. The decorative reefs around the Damfu site drop away steeply to a depth of 230 ft/70 m, and the seamount peak attracts many fish.

45 FACTS

- **Depth:** 5–130 ft/2–40 m
- **Visibility:** 30–100 ft/10–30 m
- **Water temperature:** 79–86°F/ 26–30°C
- **Best time of year:** Oct–May
- **Level of difficulty:** ■–■■■■■
- **Diversity of coral species:** ■■■■■
- **Diversity of fish species:** ■■■■■
- **Big fish:** ■■■
- **Wrecks:** ■
- **Caves:** ■■■
- **Walls:** ■■■■■
- **Snorkeling:** ■■■■■

The Swiss diver Edi Frommenwiler has been exploring this area since 1992 in his boat *Pindito* and knows the underwater world around Misool better than anyone else. He has discovered more than a hundred dive sites here, and his favorites are Fiabajet, an interesting area of shallows in the midst of currents, and Vrenelis Gärtli, where there are all sorts of marine creatures living in caves.

During the day, the spots around Misool sparkle with a variety of fan corals, colorful nudibranchs, fusiliers, and humphead wrasses. Night dives are particularly worth doing here, when you can see crabs camouflaged with anemones and corals.

Opposite page: Various feather stars putting on a fireworks display.

Above: Fabulous corals outdoing one another in a magnificent display of colors.

Left: Clownfish live in symbiosis with anemones.

INDO-PACIFIC: INDONESIA

Banda Sea

PART OF THE AUSTRALASIAN MEDITERRANEAN, THE BANDA SEA LIES BETWEEN SULAWESI, THE SMALL SUNDA ISLANDS AND THE MOLUCCAS. THIS CURRENT-PRONE REGION OFFERS EXPERIENCED DIVERS IN PARTICULAR ALL THEY COULD WISH FOR.

The Banda Sea measures approximately 750 by 375 miles/1,200 by 600 km. In the middle of this sea, popular with diving connoisseurs because of its magnificent coral and rich fish life, lies the Banda archipelago. It forms part of the Moluccas, and until the middle of the nineteenth century it was famous for its trade in spices, particularly nutmeg. The Banda region also includes the following islands: Ambon, Seram, Saparua, Molana, Nusa Laut, Manuk, and the Lucipara islands.

As well as the permanent dive centers on some of the islands, there is also a good selection of cruise boats. Anyone wanting a broader overview of the region should book a place on a cruise. Most dive cruises start out from the town of Ambon on the island of the same name.

Underwater photographers and filmmakers will be particularly enthralled by the macro flora and fauna of the area around Ambon and Saparua. Here they will be able to point their lenses at hungry-looking ribbon eels, multicolored leaf scorpionfish, and mantis shrimps. At Nusa Laut they will have to switch to a wide-angle lens to capture the walls of gorgonian sea fans, massive shoals of tuna, and occasional large hammerhead sharks found at Batu Karang.

At Karam Peketo, a completely intact reef off Haya on the southern side of Seram, there are giant fans, fields of whip coral, and tall barrel sponges. Black corals, hundreds of batfish, turtles, and really fat

46 FACTS

- **Depth:** 5–130 ft/2–40 m
- **Visibility:** 50–130 ft/15–40 m
- **Water temperature:** 81–86°F/27–30°C
- **Best time of year:** Oct–Dec, Mar–Apr
- **Level of difficulty:** ■■■–■■■■■
- **Diversity of coral species:** ■■■■■
- **Diversity of fish species:** ■■■■■
- **Big fish:** ■■■■
- **Wrecks:** ■■
- **Caves:** ■■■
- **Walls:** ■■■■■
- **Snorkeling:** ■■■■■

groupers inhabit the premium dive site at Tempat Susa at the eastern tip of the island. With a bit of luck, you will even see groups of rays on the sands.

The island of Manuk, which towers up from the deep sea like a pin head, is visited only when the weather conditions are good. This volcanic island is still active beneath the waves. It is not charted on any map but forms part of the "Ring of Fire." Manuk has become famous for its large number of sea snakes, and unfortunately also because of the shark finning that is often practiced there.

The volcano on the Banda island of Api last erupted in 1988. At the place where the lava flow entered the water, table corals grew to a diameter of 8 ft/2.5 m within ten years, and a new species has even been discovered in the very clear water. Other famous sites include the Cathedral, with its fan coral measuring up to 65 square ft/6 square m, and the two seamount peaks of Batu Kapa, between which the sea teems with fish.

Opposite page: A hammerhead rising from the blue depths.

Top: A poisonous sea snake in its lair.

Above: Love among the nudibranchs.

Left: A cone shell—warning, danger!

INDO-PACIFIC: INDONESIA

Komodo

THIS ISLAND BELONGS TO THE LESSER SUNDA ISLANDS AND LIES IN A NATIONAL PARK THAT HAS BEEN RECOGNIZED BY UNESCO AS A WORLD HERITAGE SITE. THE UNDERWATER ENVIRONMENT HERE PROVIDES AN EXTRAORDINARY BUT CHALLENGING DIVE LOCATION.

Komodo Island is nicknamed "Dragon Island" because of the famous Komodo dragons that live here. The Komodo National Park, which was founded in 1980, originally as a protected area for the monitor lizards, lies about 300 miles/ 500 km east of Bali, between Sumbawa and Flores. It includes the three larger islands of Komodo, Rinca, and Padar, together with several smaller islands. The park, which was declared a UNESCO World Heritage Site in 1991, now covers an area of 702 square miles/1,817 square km, of which approximately two-thirds is made up by the protected marine reserve.

There are about 4,000 people living within the national park. Nowadays, most dive tourists arrive by cruise boat from Bali. There is also a dive center on the large neighboring island of Flores, to the west, which has been organizing trips to the Komodo area since 1991. Right from the outset, divers have been amazed by the flora and fauna around Komodo and Rinca.

The absolutely incredible diversity of species and interesting reef structures here make the underwater scenery first class. Besides bizarre crabs and fascinating smaller coral fish such as the cunningly disguised frogfish, scorpionfish, poisonous stonefish, and quaint squid, you can also count on seeing larger fishes.

The strong currents that prevail year-round where the warmer Sea of Flores meets the

rather colder Indian Ocean provide a plentiful supply of food, especially to the south of Komodo. This means that you will sometimes see sharks, manta rays, large schools of bumphead parrotfish, eagle rays, tuna, and even dugongs, sunfish and whale sharks. The "washing-machine effect" at some dive sites makes the area somewhat difficult for diving so it may not be ideal for novices. Divers are expected to take responsibility for themselves, all the more so as the nearest decompression chamber is on Bali.

Besides the dragon island, "must-see" sites for any diving schedule include GPS Point, an area of shallows where lots of big fish congregate, and Highway to Hell, where action-packed diving is guaranteed. In Horseshoe Bay off Rinca, there are several top spots, for example the world-famous Cannibal Rock and Yellow Wall with its impressive colors. If night dives are on offer, you should not pass up this opportunity.

Above left: Exquisite reefs off the island of Rinca.

Above right: An impressive coral landscape.

Left: The eyes of a mantis shrimp.

47 FACTS

- **Depth:** 15–130 ft/5–40 m
- **Visibility:** 15–100 ft/5–30 m
- **Water temperature:** 68–82°F/20–28°C
- **Best time of year:** North: Apr–Oct; South: Oct–Mar
- **Level of difficulty:** ■■■–■■■■■
- **Diversity of coral species:** ■■■■■
- **Diversity of fish species:** ■■■■■
- **Big fish:** ■■■■
- **Wrecks:** ■
- **Caves:** ■■■■
- **Walls:** ■■■■■
- **Snorkeling:** ■■■

INDO-PACIFIC: INDONESIA

Bali

BALI IS THE MOST POPULAR OF ALL THE INDONESIAN ISLANDS AMONG DIVERS. WITH A HUGE VARIETY OF DIVE SPOTS, THE "ISLAND OF GODS AND DEMONS" BEWITCHES NOVICES AND EXPERTS ALIKE.

The most westerly of the Lesser Sunda Islands is probably the most famous island in Indonesia. In its capital, Denpasar, in the south, there is a large international airport, so the tourist centers in the south like Kuta, Legian, and Sanur are constantly growing and becoming more crowded and more luxurious. There are almost a hundred dive shops on Bali, but many of the places where you can dive are a bit off the beaten track and have been able to retain a cozy charm.

It would be impossible to dive all the spots around the island during one holiday. You need two weeks just to get a rough overview of the diving here, taking into account long journey times or moving between hotels. Everywhere you go on the island you will be accompanied by an intoxicating scent—a mixture of flowers, incense sticks, and clove cigarettes—apart from when you are underwater, breathing filtered air through your regulator.

In the northwest of Bali, directly opposite Java, lies the natural harbor and dive site Secret Bay. If demons do live in the water, as the Balinese believe, then it is here. Through your mask, frogfishes, ghost pipefishes, stonefishes, scorpionfishes, and many others seem to take on a really spooky appearance. Even farther north, in the middle of a nature reserve, lies the island of Menjangan: almost all its reefs have walls and an immense diversity of fish life, and are densely overgrown with corals, sponges, and gorgonian sea fans.

48 FACTS

- **Depth:** 15–130 ft/5–40 m
- **Visibility:** 30–130 ft/10–40 m
- **Water temperature:** 73–86°F/ 23–30°C
- **Best time of year:** Apr–Nov
- **Level of difficulty:** ■–■■■■■
- **Diversity of coral species:** ■■■■
- **Diversity of fish species:** ■■■■
- **Big fish:** ■■■■
- **Wrecks:** ■■■
- **Caves:** ■■■
- **Walls:** ■■■■■
- **Snorkeling:** ■■■■

These are regarded as the best in the whole of Bali and also have the best visibility.

At Lovina on the north coast, there are several dive shops, but as you go farther east it gets quieter again. The diving resort of Alam Anda, with its beautiful and easy-to-dive house reef, is still a little-known favorite today. Every dive guide is familiar with the nearby wreck of the *Liberty* in Tulamben, which displays much of the wealth of marine species found in the Indo-Pacific along its 400-ft/120-m length.

The reefs around Amed, in the east of Bali, are frequently visited. Off Candidasa lie the islands of Tepekong and Gili Mimpang, where the currents are often strong and there is the prospect of seeing sharks and sunfish. These can also be seen around the island of Nusa Lembongan and Nusa Penida. Depending on the season, you can even see manta rays, the gentle giants of the oceans, gliding by. They are enticed here by the plentiful food brought by the tidal currents in the deep trench of the Lombok Strait, which separates Bali from the Asiatic continental shelf.

Opposite page: The view through a porthole on the *Liberty*.

Top: A well-disguised dragonet.

Above: Inquisitive catfish.

Left: Tiny bobtail squid in iridescent colors.

Maratua Atoll

MARATUA ATOLL LIES OFF THE EAST COAST OF KALIMANTAN, THE INDONESIAN PART OF BORNEO. THERE HAS BEEN A SUSTAINABLE DIVE RESORT ON THE ISLAND OF NABUCCO HERE SINCE 2001, AND THERE ARE FABULOUS DIVE SITES OFF THE SURROUNDING ISLANDS.

After landing at Balikpapan in the south of Borneo, you take another flight to Berau, followed by a three-hour boat ride—that's all it takes to reach the diving paradise of Maratua Atoll! Around Maratua, the largest island in the atoll, with its huge lagoon, the Celebes Sea plunges in places to depths of up to 6,500 ft/2,000 m. To the east of the lagoon there are a few small islands, of which Nabucco is one. Its Indonesian name, Pulau Papahanan, means "coral island."

The Nabucco Island Resort shows that environmental awareness and luxury can go hand in hand: you live in comfortable water bungalows built in the native style, which have been built with nature in mind without felling a single palm tree. There is an environmentally friendly sewage system and an in-house fresh water treatment plant, and water is heated using solar energy.

Between Nabucco and Maratua there are some interesting channels in which extreme drift diving is often possible. In the nutrient-rich channel called Big Fish Country, you can see huge shoals of hundreds of barracuda and other big fish.

The many dive spots around the atoll are easily reached. You can almost always see large nurse sharks and whitetip sharks in caves, and with a bit of luck even gray reef sharks, leopard sharks, or thresher sharks. There are always trevally and tuna hunting off the coral-encrusted walls, and you can see big, trusting turtles almost everywhere. The area around the atoll also has a lot to offer: frogfish, scorpionfish, and dragonets are to be found here, as well as nudibranchs.

Sangalaki Island, about an hour's boat ride away, is a great place for an excursion. This island has achieved worldwide renown for its manta population, the coral life, and the turtles, which come here to lay their eggs. Manta rays can be seen almost all the year round. Their presence is betrayed by their wingtips at the surface, and some divers report seeing more than eighty specimens in a single dive. It is also possible here to snorkel with these "eagles of the sea," which is a real treat.

In 2008, another eco-friendly resort was opened on the island of Nunukan on the southern tip of Maratua Atoll, where you can dive straight off the house reef, a wall more than 150 ft/45 m deep. It is also possible to dive the spots around Nabucco from here, or you can head off to the as yet unexplored areas of the region farther afield.

Opposite page, top: A manta ray off Sangalaki.

Opposite page, bottom: Within touching distance of a turtle.

Below: Myriads of barracuda swimming in formation.

49 FACTS

- **Depth:** 15–150 ft/5–45 m
- **Visibility:** 15–100 ft/5–30 m
- **Water temperature:** 81–86°F/27–30°C
- **Best time of year:** Apr–Oct
- **Level of difficulty:** ■–■■■■■
- **Diversity of coral species:** ■■■■
- **Diversity of fish species:** ■■■■
- **Big fish:** ■■■■
- **Wrecks:** –
- **Caves:** ■■■
- **Walls:** ■■■■■
- **Snorkeling:** ■■■

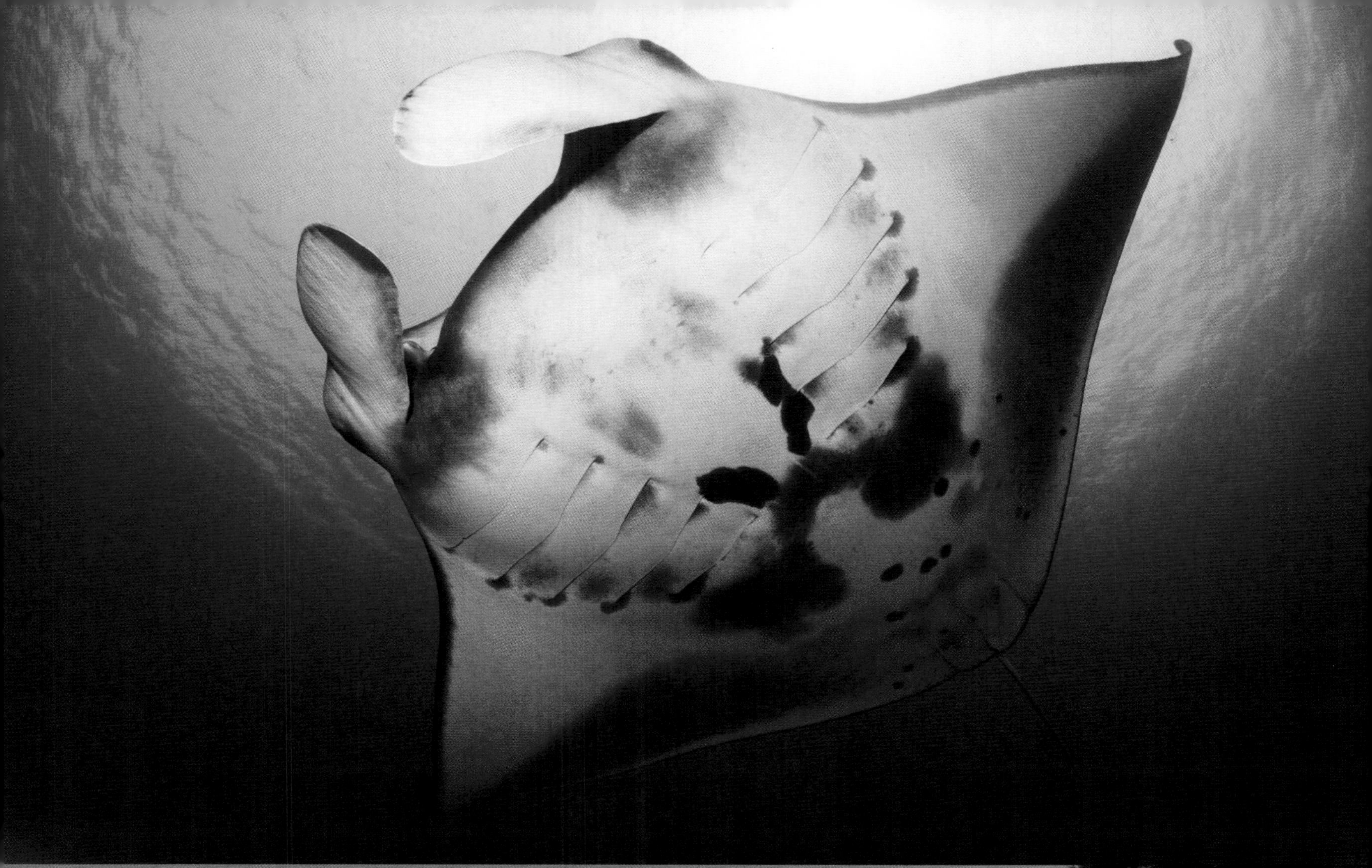

Cressi

Kakaban

THIS ISLAND CONTAINS A GEOLOGICAL AND BIOLOGICAL GEM: A 2-SQUARE-MILE/5-SQUARE-KM JELLYFISH LAKE, WHICH IS SLIGHTLY SALINE BUT HAS NO DIRECT CONNECTION TO THE SEA. DIVING HERE IS A UNIQUE EXPERIENCE.

Opposite page, top: A variety of sponges on a mangrove root.

Opposite page, bottom: Non-stinging jellyfish.

Below left: A poisonous sea snake with snorkeler in Jellyfish Lake.

Below right: If you are very lucky you may see monitor lizards. This one is getting its breath back after diving.

In the Celebes Sea, off the east coast of Borneo between the islands of Maratura and Sangalaki, lies the uninhabited island of Kakaban. Unfortunately, some of the reefs around it have been damaged, but at Barracuda Point off its southwest tip, where the currents are strong, it is possible to encounter big fish, for example the magnificent leopard shark.

However, most divers come to Kakaban in search of quite a different diving experience. In the middle of the island there is a lake about 10,000 years old, which is full of jellyfish.

Jellyfish Lake was formed in the Holocene, the most recent geological age in the earth's history, when the island rose from the depths. This brackish lake, separated from the sea, today occupies 70 percent of the island. As the water level of the lake is subject to the tides, scientists believe that there is an exchange of water with the sea above the lake bed. However, the low salinity is not sufficient to support many marine species. It is therefore assumed that vital nutrients are formed in the lake and recycled.

The lake can be reached from the coast in about ten minutes on foot. Wooden steps and boardwalks lead across the spine of the island, a bizarre reef edge about 1,000 ft/300 m wide and 165 ft/50 m high, and through the jungle. If you want to, you can even dive in the lake with your scuba gear, but just a mask, fins, and snorkel are quite adequate, as the best scenes take place directly below the surface.

Over the millennia, a unique ecosystem has developed here, and you can see plants and animals that normally occur only in estuaries. The main attraction is thousands of non-stinging jellyfish. Four different species of jellyfish live on Kakaban: Some swim near the surface and follow the sun, while others lie on the algae-covered lake bed with their tentacles facing upward. They have no large natural enemies here, but they constitute a new food source for small anemones: these prey on the considerably larger jellyfish. Snorkelers and divers must move extremely carefully around Jellyfish Lake in order to avoid injuring these gelatinous creatures.

Yet another sensational experience is provided by the enchanting atmosphere of the underwater landscape near the shores of the lake. Under the mangroves, a variety of different sponges has evolved, providing a splash of color in the greenish lake. Besides eight different species of fish, sea cucumbers and nudibranchs also live in the lake. With a bit of luck you will even come across diving monitor lizards in what is truly a wonder of nature.

50 FACTS

- **Depth:** 0–55 ft/0–17 m
- **Visibility:** 25–50 ft/8–15 m
- **Water temperature:** 81–86°F/27–30°C
- **Best time of year:** Apr–Oct
- **Level of difficulty:** ■
- **Diversity of coral species:** –
- **Diversity of fish species:** ■■
- **Big fish:** –
- **Wrecks:** –
- **Caves:** –
- **Walls:** –
- **Snorkeling:** ■■■■■

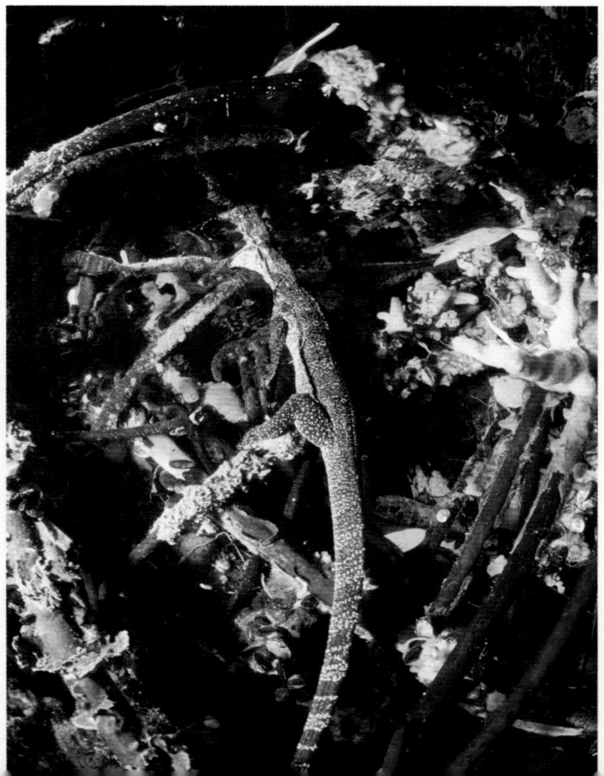

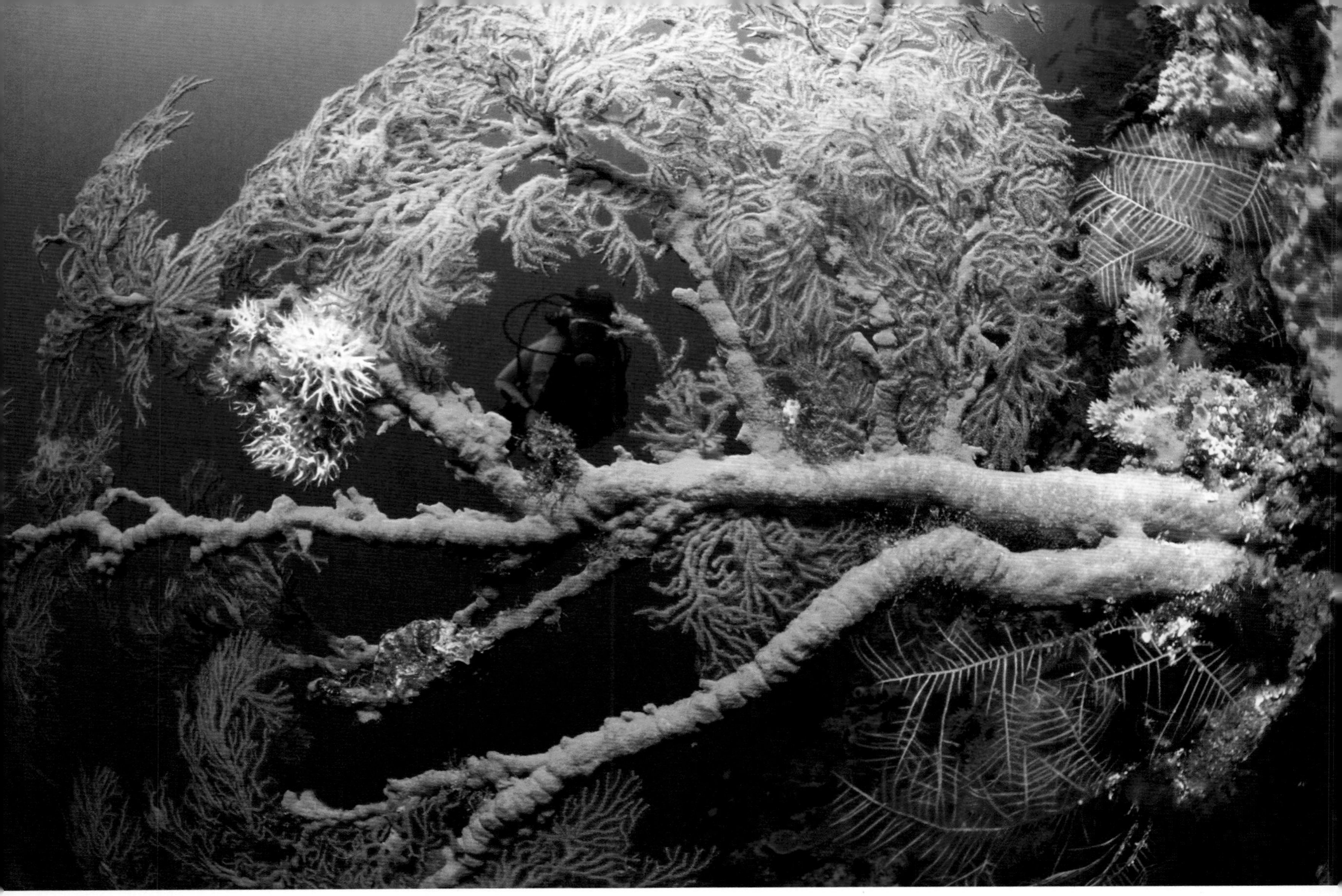

INDO-PACIFIC: INDONESIA

South Sulawesi

AROUND THE ISLAND OF SULAWESI THERE ARE MANY EXCEPTIONAL DIVE SPOTS. IN THE SOUTH, THE HIGHLIGHTS ARE LOCATED OFF THE ISLANDS OF SELAYAR IN THE CELEBES SEA AND TOMIA IN THE BANDA SEA. BOTH THESE ISLANDS ARE HOME TO ECO-FRIENDLY DIVE RESORTS.

The Indonesian island of Sulawesi, formerly known as Celebes, lies between Borneo and New Guinea. South of it is the island of Selayar, where the Selayar Dive Resort has been built on a wonderful secluded beach on the east coast. The operator is committed to eco-tourism and campaigned to get the underwater world around his resort protected. Since the marine reserve was established in 2000, there has been a noticeable increase in the fish population. Even though the island is already well known among divers, it is still possible to dive in seclusion here, away from the masses. The reason for this is probably the lengthy journey necessary to get here from the airport in Makassar on Sulawesi.

The resort has a long, intact house reef, on which you can dive independently at any time. You reach the edge of the fringing reef either via a long jetty or by swimming about 110 yd/100 m through varied coral gardens, which are also enthralling for snorkelers. In the waters off the resort, one dive site leads to another—it is hard to say where one ends and the next begins. The showpiece dive site is called Shark Point and takes about ten minutes to get to by boat. Here, you can observe large predators in the current on a fascinating reef.

About 250 miles/400 km away, in the southeast of Sulawesi, lies the Tukang Besi archipelago. On the small island of Onemobaa, off Tomia, is the world-famous Wakatobi Dive Resort, which has taken up the

51 FACTS

- **Depth:** 5–165 ft/2–50 m
- **Visibility:** 50–130 ft/15–40 m
- **Water temperature:** 77–84°F/25–29°C
- **Best time of year:** Apr–June, Sept–Nov
  Selayar: closed May–Oct
- **Level of difficulty:** ■–■■■■■
- **Diversity of coral species:** ■■■■■
- **Diversity of fish species:** ■■■■■
- **Big fish:** ■■■■
- **Wrecks:** ■
- **Caves:** ■■■■
- **Walls:** ■■■■■
- **Snorkeling:** ■■■■■

cause of involving the local population in protecting the environment. It can be reached from Bali in two and one-half hours by plane—the resort has its own airfield. Thanks to the strenuous efforts of the resort management, the entire region has been declared a marine protected area, which is managed sustainably. Wakatobi therefore offers an extremely high level of biodiversity within an intact ecosystem, providing an unforgettable diving experience.

The dive sites and the virtually pristine reefs around them are absolutely world-class. The house reef, with its magnificent fish and coral life, is bewitching, and has several times been voted one of the best in the world. In the immediate vicinity of this well-appointed dive resort there are forty-three more amazing spots. Particularly recommended are Roma, Magnifica, Teluk, Maya, Blade, Fan 38, and Pinki's Wall, all of which will captivate you with their gorgeous corals. A luxurious live-aboard is available for trips farther afield.

Opposite page: Marvelous walls with impressive gorgonian sea fans.

Above: The famous "Window" on the Wakatobi house reef.

Left: A large frogfish lying in ambush.

INDO-PACIFIC: INDONESIA

North Sulawesi

THE BEST DIVE SPOTS IN NORTH SULAWESI ARE TO BE FOUND AROUND THE TOWN OF MANADO, IN THE BUNAKEN NATIONAL PARK, AND IN THE BANGKA ARCHIPELAGO. THE LEMBEH STRAIT IS WORLD-FAMOUS FOR THE MUCK DIVING PRACTICED HERE.

The capital of the province of North Sulawesi is Manado. To the north and south there are lots of smart dive resorts, almost all of which have thrilling house reefs to offer. The macro life here is particularly fascinating for divers.

In Manado Bay lie the islands of Nain, Montehage, Manado Tua, Siladen, and Bunaken, which all form part of the Bunaken National Park. This was created in 1989, and 97 percent of it is covered in water. The region contains areas for fishing and diving and also rest zones where the flora and fauna can recover. Entrance fees are used to finance ongoing maintenance, monitoring, and compensation payments to the inhabitants, whose fishing has been restricted. There are more than a dozen designated dive sites around Bunaken, many of which have beautifully encrusted walls where you can do drift dives.

Around Siladen and the dormant volcano Manado Tua, an area known for its shoals of fish, the coast drops away steeply. Montehage is surrounded by a large area of shallows. Due to a number of accidents that have occurred at depth, the island of Nain is only accessible to experienced divers.

All the dive centers in the north region offer trips to the northern tip of Sulawesi. Around the islands of Bangka and Gangga, where there are also well-known dive resorts, are the islands of Talisei, Kinobohutan, Tindila, and Tamperong, which still

52 FACTS

- **Depth:** 3–130 ft/1–40 m
- **Visibility:** 50–150 ft/15–45 m; Lembeh: 25–80 ft/8–25 m
- **Water temperature:** 79–86°F/26–30°C; Lembeh: 72–84°F/22–29°C
- **Best time of year:** Manado & Bunaken: Mar–Nov; Bangka: Mar–June; Lembeh: Aug–Oct
- **Level of difficulty:** ■–■■■■■
- **Diversity of coral species:** ■■■■■
- **Diversity of fish species:** ■■■■■
- **Big fish:** ■■■
- **Wrecks:** ■■■
- **Caves:** ■■■
- **Walls:** ■■■■■
- **Snorkeling:** ■■■■■

have small fishing villages on them today. The fish life in this area is attracted by the currents, which are often strong. The unique soft coral gardens in all the colors of the rainbow and the many varieties of nudibranch are particularly impressive.

The Lembeh Strait, between the town of Bitung and the offshore island of Lembeh, is a macro paradise known for muck diving, which is also possible around Manado. Increasing numbers of divers from all over the world are traveling here to search for minute creatures hidden in the dark sand—comical and bizarre figures that are so well camouflaged you only notice them on the second glance. There are also coral gardens, but large fish are seldom encountered.

Opposite page: Zebra lionfish, one of the poisonous scorpionfishes.

Above: Bizarre ghost pipefish.

Left: A well-camouflaged coral crab.

INDO-PACIFIC: INDONESIA

Sangihe Islands

BETWEEN NORTH SULAWESI AND THE PHILIPPINES, ABOUT 50 TROPICAL VOLCANIC ISLANDS RISE UP OUT OF THE DEEP SEA. THESE ARE THE SANGIHE ISLANDS. UNDERWATER THERE ARE MARVELOUS HARD CORALS, GIANT SPONGES, AND EVEN AN ACTIVE VOLCANO.

The landscape above the water is impressive: small, lush islands with tall tropical rain forests, among which there are volcanoes that are still active today. The Sangihe Islands form part of the Pacific Ring of Fire and can only be dived on cruises.

The first to explore this area, in 1992, was the Indonesian diving pioneer Dr. Han Batuna. He gave an account of the underwater volcano off the island of Nahangetan, which rises from a depth of 2,600 ft/800 m to just below the surface. This dive spot is easy to find thanks to the stream of bubbles rising from it, which smell of sulfur. The scenery underwater is eerie, rather like a moon landscape. The rays of the sun struggle to penetrate the yellowish, murky water, and the dark-brown sand around the millions of rising bubbles is hot.

To find life—giant sponges, black gorgonian sea fans, and the first fish—you have to move farther away. At other sites in the archipelago, large hard corals and colorful soft corals thrive on slopes and walls. Many places are still unknown and are just waiting to be discovered.

Top: There is a constant stream of bubbles from the underwater volcano.

Below left: Square spot anthias.

Below right: Colorful sponges.

53 FACTS

- **Depth:** 15–130 ft/5–40 m
- **Visibility:** 30–115 ft/10–35 m
- **Water temperature:** 79–86°F/ 26–30°C
- **Best time of year:** Mar–June
- **Level of difficulty:** ■■■
- **Diversity of coral species:** ■■■■
- **Diversity of fish species:** ■■■■
- **Big fish:** ■■■
- **Wrecks:** ■■
- **Caves:** ■■■
- **Walls:** ■■■
- **Snorkeling:** ■■■■

INDO-PACIFIC: MALAYSIA

Sipadan

THIS SMALL ISLAND TO THE EAST OF BORNEO IS THE MOST POPULAR DIVE DESTINATION IN MALAYSIA AND ONE OF THE BEST DIVE SPOTS IN THE WORLD. IT HAS BEEN PROTECTED SINCE 2004 BECAUSE OF ITS TURTLES AND ITS EXCEPTIONAL SPECIES DIVERSITY.

Until the end of 2004 there were several dive resorts on the island, but nature conservationists had justifiably been complaining for a long time that there were too many divers. Diving around the island, which has beautifully overgrown walls with strong currents, is still permitted, but numbers are restricted. Now you have to stay on the neighboring islands of Mabul or Kapalai, which are highly regarded for their excellent macro life.

Sipadan rises vertically from a depth of 2,600 ft/800 m in the Sulu Sea in the shape of a giant mushroom, with the island forming the cap and the surrounding fringing reef the rim.

There are dozens of dive spots around the island, and the list of attractions is impressive: schools of wheeling barracuda, trevally, and stately bumphead parrotfish, whitetip sharks lying on the sea bed, reef sharks circumnavigating the island, and hundreds of turtles. These are Sipadan's trademark features, which have made it famous worldwide.

Above left: A turtle diving.

Above right: A shoal of trevally against the light.

Left: Feather stars in the Sulu Sea.

54 FACTS

- **Depth:** 15–130 ft/5–40 m
- **Visibility:** 30–115 ft/10–35 m
- **Water temperature:** 81–86°F/27–30°C
- **Best time of year:** Mar–Oct
- **Level of difficulty:** ■■■–■■■■■
- **Diversity of coral species:** ■■■■
- **Diversity of fish species:** ■■■■■
- **Big fish:** ■■■■
- **Wrecks:** –
- **Caves:** ■■■
- **Walls:** ■■■■■
- **Snorkeling:** ■

INDO-PACIFIC: PHILIPPINES

Tubbataha Reefs

THE LARGEST CORAL REEF IN THE PHILIPPINES CONSISTS OF TWO ATOLLS WITH A TOTAL OF MORE THAN 40 MILES/70 KM OF UNDERWATER WALL. IT LIES IN THE "CORAL TRIANGLE" AND IS A UNESCO WORLD HERITAGE SITE.

The Philippines encompasses 7,107 islands and possesses a diving gem: the Tubbataha Reefs in the semi-enclosed Sulu Sea. The north island of Tubbataha lies 113 miles/182 km southeast of Puerto Princesa, the capital of the province of Palawan and the departure point for cruises to the reefs. Due to the otherwise difficult weather conditions, these take place only between the months of March and June, when the Sulu Sea is relatively calm.

In 1988, the two atolls became the Tubbataha Reefs National Park, and in 1993 it was declared a UNESCO World Heritage Site. This means that commercial fishing is banned, and a ranger station monitors this as well as diving from live-aboards. The reef system forms the apex of the "Coral Triangle," the area with the largest coral species diversity in the world. This extends as far as Borneo in the west and New Guinea in the east.

The north and south atolls are separated by a 4-mile-wide/7-km-wide channel. Tubbataha means something like "long reef that appears at low tide," and it is certainly the case that many of the sandbanks and reefs are not visible at high tide. Underwater there are myriad fishes, and the vast numbers of corals and sponges create a fascinating variety of color. And all this despite the fact that illegal fishing methods using dynamite and cyanide as well as drag nets were still causing considerable damage as recently as the early 1990s. The gently sloping reefs, which in parts consist

merely of coral debris, are now in the recovery stage. The gigantic walls deeper down have not suffered any damage.

The exposed parts of the reef, with overhangs, gullies, caverns, and caves, are a real thrill. You can see many species of shark, guitarfish, barracuda, trevally, tuna, turtles, and sometimes even manta rays and dolphins. In addition to this, there are innumerable smaller reef fish in a superb coral landscape.

The atolls are recommended only for experienced divers, not merely because of their isolated location, but also because of the currents that suddenly arise and the deep walls, which call for absolutely perfect buoyancy control.

Above: A perfect "house" for the longnose hawkfish.

Left: Huge fan corals growing on the walls at Tubbataha Reef.

55 FACTS

- **Depth:** 5–200 ft/2–60 m
- **Visibility:** 50–150 ft/15–45 m
- **Water temperature:** 79–84°F/ 26–29°C
- **Best time of year:** Mar–June
- **Level of difficulty:** ■■■–■■■■■
- **Diversity of coral species:** ■■■■
- **Diversity of fish species:** ■■■■
- **Big fish:** ■■■■
- **Wrecks:** ■
- **Caves:** ■■■■
- **Walls:** ■■■■■
- **Snorkeling:** ■■■

INDO-PACIFIC: PHILIPPINES

Dauin

THIS SMALL VILLAGE ON THE ISLAND OF NEGROS IS BECOMING INCREASINGLY POPULAR THANKS TO ITS MARINE RESERVES. A SPECIALITY HERE IS MUCK DIVING, SEARCHING FOR MARINE MASTERS OF DISGUISE IN THE BLACK VOLCANIC SAND.

Negros is the fourth-largest island in the Philippines and, like the famous dive locations of Cebu, Bohol, Leyte, Palawan, Panay, and Samar, belongs to the Visayas, one of the three island groups that make up the country. Dauin lies in the south of the island, below the regional capital Dumaguete.

The resorts all have house reefs, and in addition, with the permission of the authorities, artificial reefs including scrapped cars, boats, tires, and barrels, have been set up. Here, you can dive independently and marvel at the interesting underwater life that has rapidly made these new objects home.

At many sites, divers can go muck diving and discover various well-camouflaged scorpionfish, ghost pipefish, and frogfish, as well as rare octopuses, sea horses, eels, unusual nudibranchs, and many more bizarre creatures.

The dive resorts around Dauin are becoming increasingly popular—partly because of the good value they offer—and more and more hotels are springing up along the black-sand coast. This is not least due to the marine reserves, the so-called sanctuaries, set up by the local authorities. Fishing is forbidden in these zones, so the sandy beaches, which were formerly lacking in fish and unpopular, now attract all kinds of fishes and form a thriving nursery for the underwater life here.

56 FACTS

- **Depth:** 3–100 ft/1–30 m
- **Visibility:** 30–100 ft/10–30 m
- **Water temperature:** 79–88°F/26–31°C
- **Best time of year:** Nov–June
- **Level of difficulty:** ■–■■■
- **Diversity of coral species:** ■■■–■■■■■■
- **Diversity of fish species:** ■■■■
- **Big fish:** ■■
- **Wrecks:** ■■
- **Caves:** –
- **Walls:** – (Siquior/Apo Island: ■■■■)
- **Snorkeling:** ■■■–■■■■

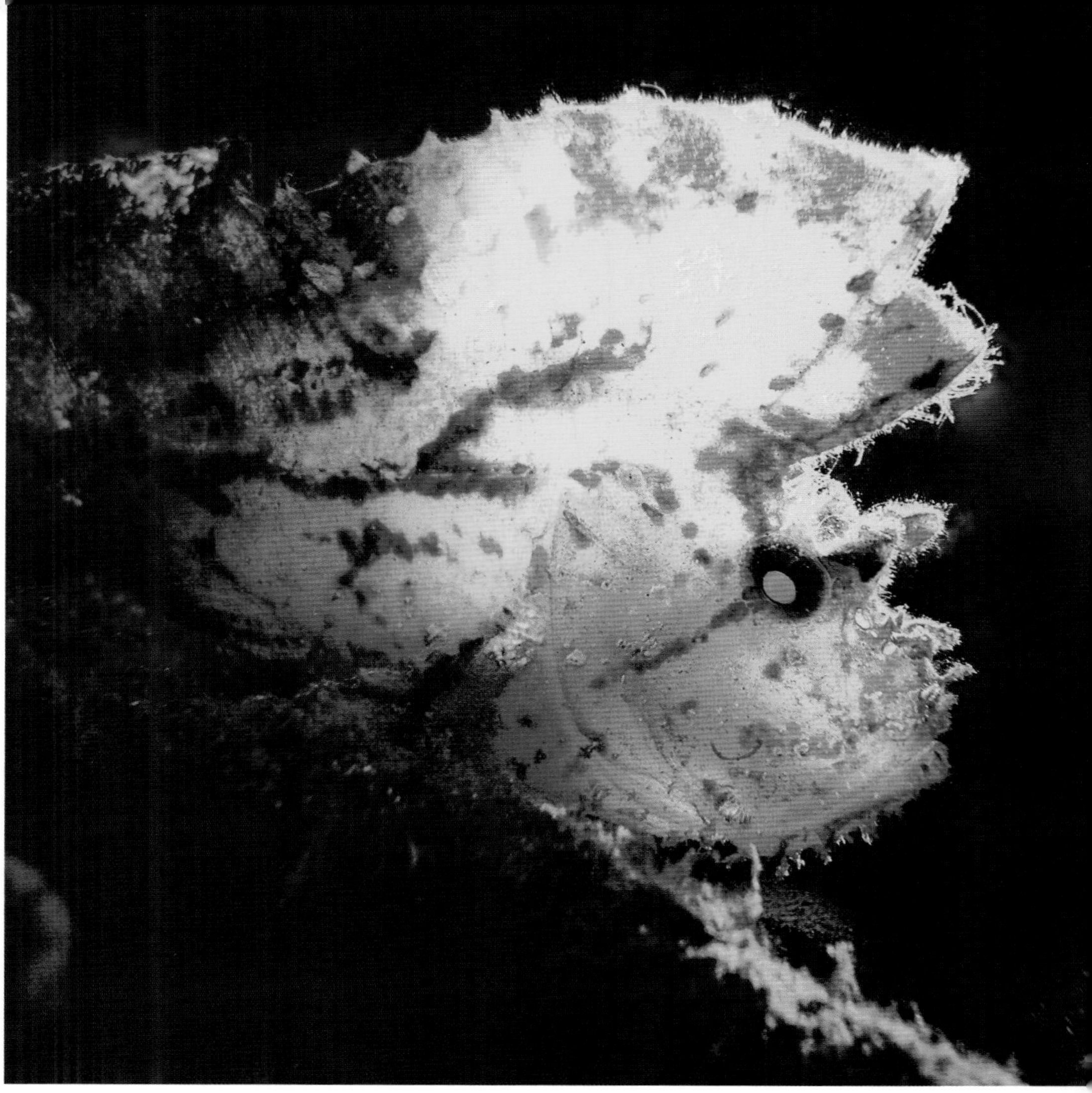

The marine reserves nearby, Dauin Sanctuaries and Masaplod Sanctuaries, can be quickly reached by boat. They are full of life and make a perfect studio for underwater photographers. You will seldom see such a quantity and variety of marine inhabitants in a single dive. One extraordinary dive is Ducomi Pier in Bacong: You can find rare fish and tiny crabs on the pillars of the pier, which are encrusted with beautiful sponges and corals, as well as in the muck on the sea bed.

If you love colorful coral reefs, you should take a day trip to the island of Siquior or to Apo Island marine reserve. Both islands have dive centers and many good dive spots, which are famed far beyond the country's borders.

Due to its central location in the archipelago, Dauin is also the departure point for the "island-hopping" dive safaris to other islands, lasting several days, which are organized by the dive operator "Sea Explorers." Bangkas, the local outrigger boats, are used to reach the best sites at other locations. This is an experience where everything is provided for, both above and below the water; your diving equipment stays on board all the time, and hotels are available for overnight stays and meals.

Opposite page: A pair of Coleman's shrimps living between the spines of a fire urchin.

Above: The lighting shows off this almost transparent leaf scorpionfish to perfection.

Left: The poisonous devilfish likes to bury itself in the sand.

Moalboal

THE ISLAND OF CEBU HAS LONG HAD AN ESTABLISHED REPUTATION AMONG DIVERS. THE FOCAL POINT OF RECREATIONAL DIVING HERE IS MOALBOAL ON THE WEST COAST AND, IN PARTICULAR, THE WATERS OFF THE COAST OF THE SUBLIME CORAL ISLAND OF PESCADOR.

East of the Philippine island of Negros lies the island of Cebu, which also belongs to the Visayas group. In the island's capital, also called Cebu, there is an international airport, and you should allow about three hours for the 55-mile/90-km journey to Moalboal. On a peninsula a short distance away from the town center lies Panagsama Beach, with bars, restaurants, and a few small mid-price dive resorts. Guests from all over the world have a number of different dive locations available to them: the resorts' own house reefs, various spots on the peninsula's long wall, the marine park around the offshore island of Pescador, or Sunken Island farther to the south.

The house reefs are coral-covered walls that drop from their tops to depths of about 130 ft/40 m. The dive shops here allow you to dive independently with a buddy. In order to get to the ten dive spots along the peninsula, you need a boat. Bangkas, the boats typical to this area, bring divers the short distance to spots like Marine Sanctuary in the north or to White Beach, Talisay, Tongo Point, Sampaguita, or Airport, where there is a small plane. Most of the sites also offer dives on coral-covered drop-offs with overhangs down to about 130 ft/40 m, with small to medium-sized fish. In shallower areas you will find all kinds of nudibranchs and worms, and lots of crustaceans and photogenic shrimps. These dive spots are also suitable for novices.

The area's most popular dive destination is without doubt the island of Pescador to the west of Moalboal, which can be reached by outrigger in about 15 minutes. From a depth of 1,000 ft/300 m, the small protected island rises to 20 ft/6 m above sea level. It is encircled at a depth of 10–30 ft/3–9 m by a completely intact, brightly colored coral fringe. Even deeper, there are walls which are covered in sponges, gorgonian sea fans, and soft corals, and which extend right around the island, dropping away steeply. One of the prime sites is the Cathedral: You dive into this tunnel at a depth of 115 ft/35 m and emerge again at 50 ft/15 m, and inside you are greeted by a beautiful display of sunlight playing on the scene around you. Right around the island, the many small shoals of sea bass provide a kaleidoscope of magnificent colors.

Sunken Island, a spot located in the open sea, is best dived in the early morning. However, the 80-ft/24-m freefall descent through open water down to the reef amidst exuberant shoals of fish and numerous lionfish and frogfish is only for experienced divers.

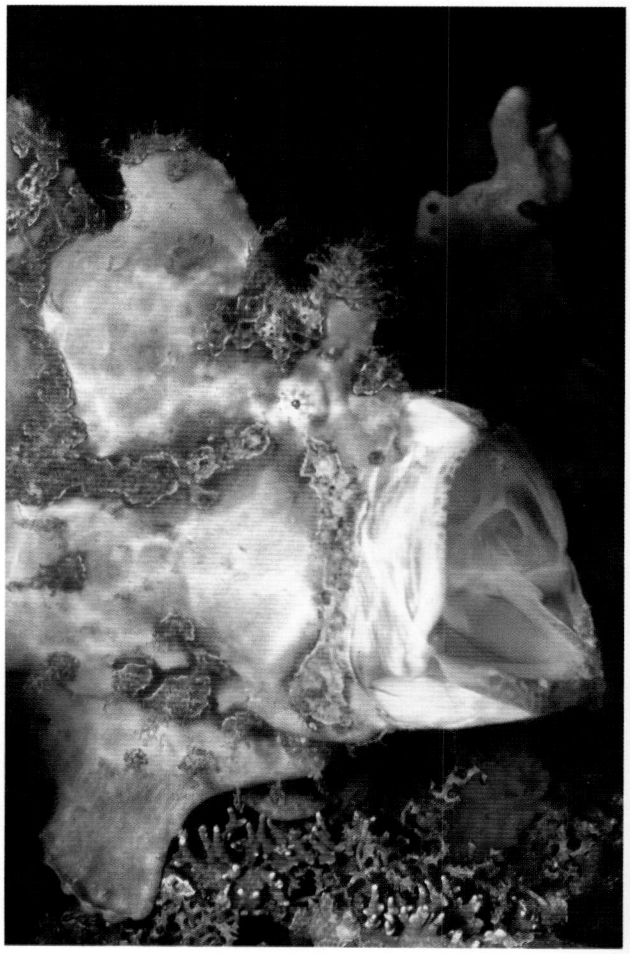

Opposite page: Luxuriantly overgrown walls around Pescador.

Above right: Porcupinefish "parking" in a barrel sponge.

Below right: Giant frogfish searching for food.

57 FACTS

- **Depth:** 10–130 ft/3–40 m
- **Visibility:** 30–100 ft/10–30 m
- **Water temperature:** 79–88°F/26–31°C
- **Best time of year:** Nov–June
- **Level of difficulty:** ■–■■■■■
- **Diversity of coral species:** ■■■■
- **Diversity of fish species:** ■■■■
- **Big fish:** ■■■
- **Wrecks:** ■
- **Caves:** ■■
- **Walls:** ■■■■■
- **Snorkeling:** ■■■■

INDO-PACIFIC: PHILIPPINES

Cabilao

THIS SMALL ISLAND IN THE VISAYAS GROUP LIES EAST OF CEBU AND WEST OF BOHOL. IT IS STILL SEEN AS A HOT DIVING TIP TODAY AND IS A BYWORD FOR RELAXATION, FIRST-CLASS REEF DIVING, AND SITES OF RARE QUALITY.

On Cabilao, about 25 miles/40 km north of the divers' stronghold of Alona Beach on the island of Panglao, there is not a trace of the latter's hustle and bustle and large numbers of dive boats. If you are looking for bars and nightlife, you will be disappointed, as the resorts maintain a family atmosphere and, next to diving, peace and relaxation are given absolute priority.

The island can be reached from Cebu by high-speed ferry to Tagbilaran on Bohol, then transfer by car, followed by an additional short boat ride. It lies in the popular diving triangle of Cebu-Bohol-Negros and is featured on the itineraries of many island-hopping tours. The underwater flora and fauna around the island are completely intact, thanks to traditional fishing methods and a protected nature reserve. This, coupled with good visibility beneath the waves at almost all times, means that Cabilao is on its way to becoming a real divers' paradise. The fact that some people make up to five dives a day speaks for itself.

The Lighthouse, to the northeast of the island, is a top-quality dive site. There is a slope that falls away from 15 to about 70 ft/5 to about 22 m, and an expert local dive guide will help you find the spots where there are devilfishes, stargazers, leaf scorpionfishes, mantis shrimps, ghost pipefishes, or even sea moths. Night dives are highly recommended in order to see the reefs in their full glory.

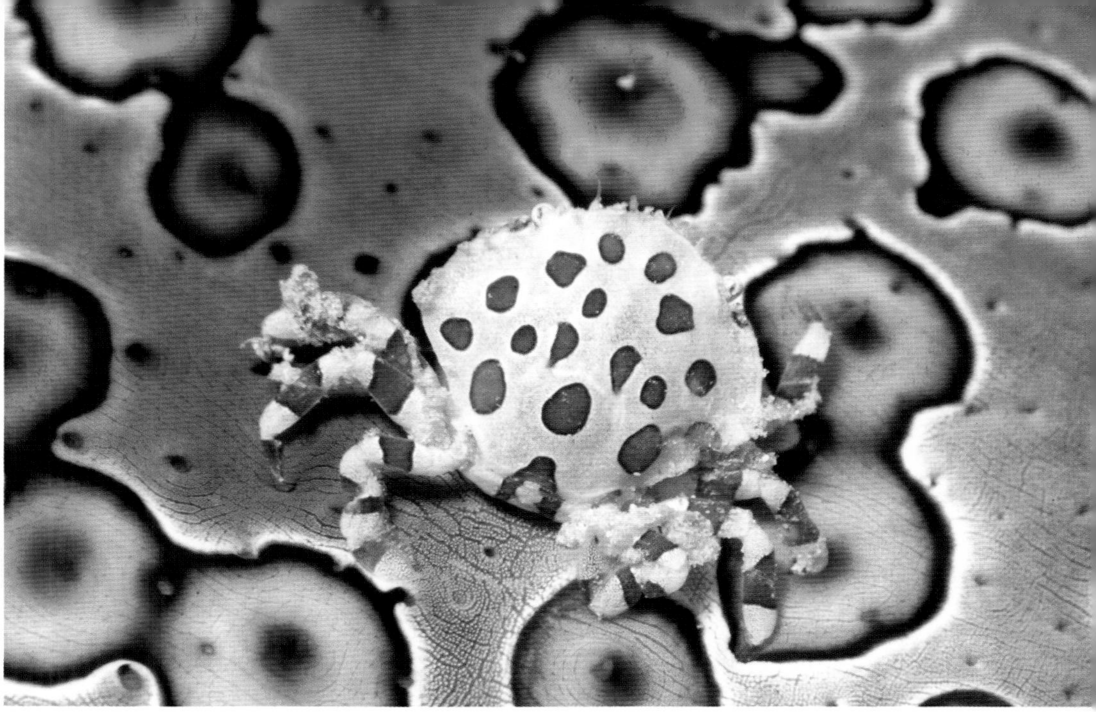

58 FACTS

- **Depth:** 10–200 ft/3–60 m
- **Visibility:** 30–100 ft/10–30 m
- **Water temperature:** 79–88°F/ 26–31°C
- **Best time of year:** Nov–June
- **Level of difficulty:** ■–■■■■■
- **Diversity of coral species:** ■■■■
- **Diversity of fish species:** ■■■■
- **Big fish:** ■■■
- **Wrecks:** –
- **Caves:** ■■
- **Walls:** ■■■■■
- **Snorkeling:** ■■■■

Not far away, on the wall at Shark View Point there are gorgonian sea fans inhabited by a number of pygmy sea horses. At one time, whole schools of hammerheads could be seen from the wall, but unfortunately that time belongs to the past. Today, you may with luck encounter lone specimens.

At South Point, there is a really steep drop-off. The coral slope extends along the coast at a depth of 10–40 ft/3–12 m and includes the island's most beautiful hard corals. The wall then plunges more than 130 ft/40 m vertically down into the depths. In the wall are various caves in which young whitetip sharks conceal themselves during the day. The reef is fantastically illuminated, particularly in the afternoons.

Cambaquiz lies at the northeast tip of Cabilao and is popular for its immense wealth of fish species. Though there is less coral here, turtles and baby sharks can occasionally be seen. The dive spot Fallen Tree is suitable for drift dives. Here, fusiliers swim around between large barrel sponges, leather corals, and gorgonian sea fans.

Opposite page: In the coral forest of Cabilao.

Top: A small crab on a sea cucumber.

Above: An orangutan crab in a bubble coral.

Left: Master of camouflage: A stargazer lies hidden in the sand.

INDO-PACIFIC: PHILIPPINES

Malapascua

SHARKS, SNAKES, AND WRECKS DRAW DIVERS FROM ALL OVER THE WORLD TO MALAPASCUA, A SMALL CORAL ISLAND 5 MILES/8 KM NORTHEAST OF CEBU. HOWEVER, THE MACRO WORLD OF UNDERWATER FLORA AND FAUNA ALSO HAS MUCH TO OFFER.

Malapascua is only 1¼ miles/2 km long by just more than ½ mile/1 km wide. There are no cars here, just one mini-truck and a few mopeds which serve as taxis. Instead of roads, there are paths on which you can easily lose your way, especially at night. Approximately 4,000 people live on the island. They used to subsist primarily from fishing but now rely increasingly on tourism. More and more small beach resorts and dive shops have appeared, but the island has nonetheless remained fairly tranquil and, with its idyllic palm-fringed beaches, is reminiscent of the Maldives.

The elegant thresher sharks are the main attraction. In order to get a sight of them, you will have to get up very early. At the crack of dawn, you ride out in a boat for about half an hour to the underwater plateau Monad, which begins at a depth of 40 ft/12 m and is about 1 mile/1.5 km in diameter. There is a particular point about 75 ft/23 m down called Shark Point, where these predators, which can be up to 13 ft/4 m in length, come to be cleaned by small fish in the mornings. However, divers must be calm and patient if they are to have a chance of observing these shy creatures.

There are several wrecks around the island that can be visited by divers. The *Dona Marilyn*, a 300-ft-long/90-m-long freighter, sank during a typhoon in 1982 and lies on her starboard side at a depth of 105 ft/32 m to the north of Malapascua.

59 FACTS

- ❖ **Depth:** 15–130 ft/5–40 m
- ❖ **Visibility:** 30–100 ft/10–30 m
- ❖ **Water temperature:** 79–88°F/26–31°C
- ❖ **Best time of year:** Nov–June
- ❖ **Level of difficulty:** ■–■■■■■
- ❖ **Diversity of coral species:** ■■■
- ❖ **Diversity of fish species:** ■■■■
- ❖ **Big fish:** ■■■■
- ❖ **Wrecks:** ■■■■
- ❖ **Caves:** ■■■
- ❖ **Walls:** ■■■
- ❖ **Snorkeling:** ■■

In 1944, a Japanese transport ship was hit and sunk by US aircraft. The artificial reef created as a result is an oasis in the sea and has been colonized by a large number of fish. This colorful wreck, which is easy to dive, rests at a depth of 60–90 ft/18–27 m. Nearby lies another wreck suitable for novice divers, that of the *Don Macario*, at a depth of 62 ft/19 m. Three more Japanese ships are located at depths of 100–130 ft/30–40 m and can be visited only by experienced divers.

One of the first highlights off the coast of Malapascua to become famous were the "sleeping sharks of Gato" in Gato Cave. You can dive through this cave and observe whitetip sharks sleeping during the day. There are also black-and-white banded sea snakes, many nudibranchs and photogenic sea horses at the dive sites around the island of Gato, which fall within the marine park and can be reached by boat in approximately forty minutes from Malapascua.

Opposite page: A black-and-white banded sea snake.

Top: Pacific cleaner shrimp cleaning a small sea bass.

Above: A sea horse between soft corals and a prickly sea urchin.

Left: A sleeping shark with a remora in Gato Cave.

This, the world's largest ocean, covers more than one-third of the earth's surface. The range of opportunities for divers is correspondingly varied. Dream destinations like the Galapagos Islands and Cocos Island, the innumerable islands of Micronesia, South Sea paradises like Papua New Guinea and Polynesia, and, to the east of Australia, the world's largest barrier reef, await the diver here.

PACIFIC OCEAN

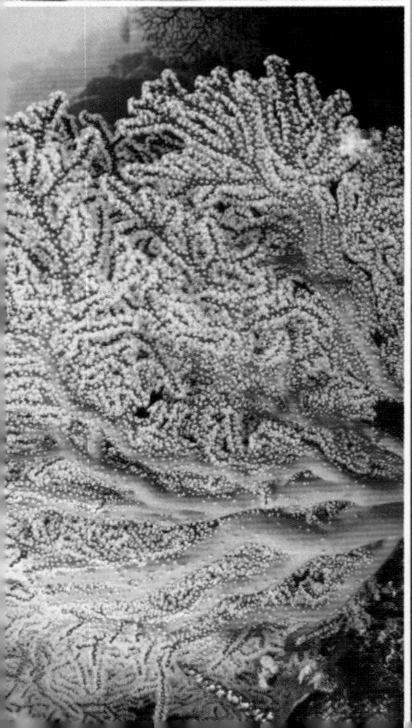

Palau

THE UNDERWATER WORLD OF PALAU IS CONSIDERED BY MANY TO BE THE ULTIMATE DIVE DESTINATION, AS THERE IS A HUGE VARIETY OF THINGS TO SEE: DROP-OFFS, BIG FISH, VAST CAVES, WRECKS, JELLYFISH LAKES, GREAT MACRO LIFE, AND EVEN CROCODILES.

Opposite page: An enormous giant clam in Clam City.

Below left: Remnants of breathing masks on the *Helmet* wreck.

Below right: Jellyfish in Jellyfish Lake.

The Palau Islands slumber in the western Pacific east of the Philippines and north of New Guinea. The islands, which are the westernmost island group of the Carolines as well as part of Micronesia, are an independent state. Palau did not attain official independence until 1994, after it had been administered for nearly fifty years by the US as a district of the UN Trust Territory. Until 2006, it was ruled from Koror, the former capital, but the seat of government today is Melekeok, on the largest island, Babeldaob.

Koror is also where most of the dive shops are located. Tours to many spots around the eight inhabited main islands and the many smaller lush tropical coral islands are on offer. In this dream setting, the daily trips out and back have their own quite special allure—the route to the southern dive sites takes you past the world-famous Rock Islands.

There is also the possibility of heading out to Palau's diving spots on a live-aboard. That way, you can usually anchor close to the dive site and have the opportunity to be the first to dive in the early morning hours, which always holds out the promise of excitement and a chance of seeing big fish. Furthermore, the schedule on board allows you to enter the water up to five times a day.

Palau's most famous and fascinating dive sites are the Blue Hole caves, Blue Corner, and the walls off the islands of Ngemelis and Peleliu. Apart from these quite exceptional locations, to which spots nos. 61 and 62 are devoted, there are many other impressive dive sites.

The caverns and caves of Palau are numerous and varied. Besides the Blue Hole, other sites that should not be missed include Siaes Tunnel, Virgin Blue Hole, and the Chandelier Cave, which lies in a natural harbor close to Koror. This cave system is made up of five enormous chambers that are reached through an entrance at a depth of 13 ft/4 m. The water will be crystal clear provided no one has stirred up the fine sediment on the bottom just before you. Long

60 FACTS

- **Depth:** 3–130 ft/1–40 m
- **Visibility:** 23–100 ft/7–30 m on wrecks, caves up to 150 ft/45 m
- **Water temperature:** 79–88°F/26–31°C
- **Best time of year:** Dec–Apr
- **Level of difficulty:** ■–■■■■■
- **Diversity of coral species:** ■■
- **Diversity of fish species:** ■■■■
- **Big fish:** ■■■■
- **Wrecks:** ■■■■■
- **Caves:** ■■■■■
- **Walls:** ■■■■■
- **Snorkeling:** ■■■■■ (Jellyfish Lake, Mandarinfish Lake, Clam City, mangroves)

Above: A humphead wrasse at Blue Corner.

Opposite page, top: An aerial photo of Seventy Islands.

Opposite page, bottom left: A red gorgonian sea fan at Big Drop-Off—wall-diving at its finest.

Opposite page, bottom right: Diving on the wreck of a Japanese seaplane.

stalactites that hang down from the ceiling of the cave break through the surface of the water, creating fantastic scenery. In the first cave, it is even possible to surface, but the other chambers should only be dived with a guide who is familiar with the site.

The many wrecks originating from World War II provide a further highlight. On account of its strategically useful position, the Japanese requisitioned the archipelago for use as a naval base during the Pacific War. At the end of March 1944, the US launched an aerial assault, during which sixty ships and aircraft were sunk in the surrounding bays. Francis Toribiong, one of the first divers on Palau, together with German diver Klaus Lindemann, discovered the lost fleet.

The *Helmet* wreck now lies at a depth of 30–90 ft/10–28 m. The supply vessel was laden with grenades, munitions, and spare parts for Zero Fighter planes, as well as carrying many helmets, which are still visible today and gave the wreck its name. The freighter *Chuyo Maru* is 270 ft/83 m long, and both the bridge and the engine room, as well as the deck gun, are well preserved and worth exploring. Measuring 500 ft/153 m in length, the *Amatsu Maru* is the largest wreck around Palau. It lies at a maximum depth of 120 ft/37 m and has been colonized by black corals. The wreck of the *Iro* and the *Jake* and Zero fighter aircraft wrecks are also well worth diving.

Another attraction is to be found on the island of Eil Malk, which is one of the world-renowned Rock Islands, a protected site. There is a jellyfish lake here that has become world-famous. You can snorkel in the lake in the midst of millions of non-stinging jellyfish which have been living here for millennia. Mangroves, whose roots have been colonized by sponges and anemones, grow along the shore. Just a few minutes' boat ride away at Clam City, there are giant clams measuring almost 6 ft/2 m across and weighing up to 1,100 lb/500 kg, some of which are a century old.

To the south and not far from Koror lies one of the Rock Islands' numerous saltwater lakes, Mandarinfish Lake, where tiny colorful and photogenic mandarinfish live. For the very bold, there are even organized dives with crocodiles in the mangrove swamps of Kuror—it's not exactly cheap, but it promises a thrilling adventure.

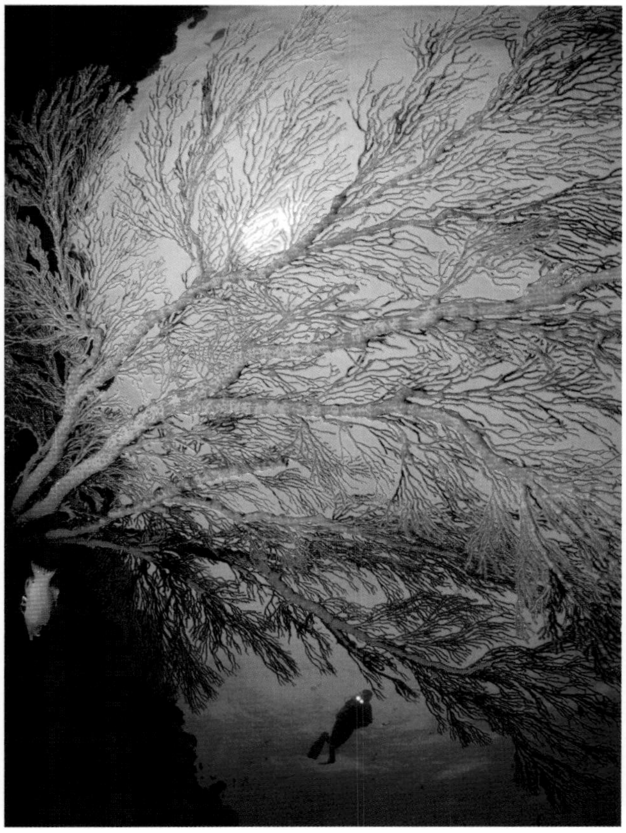

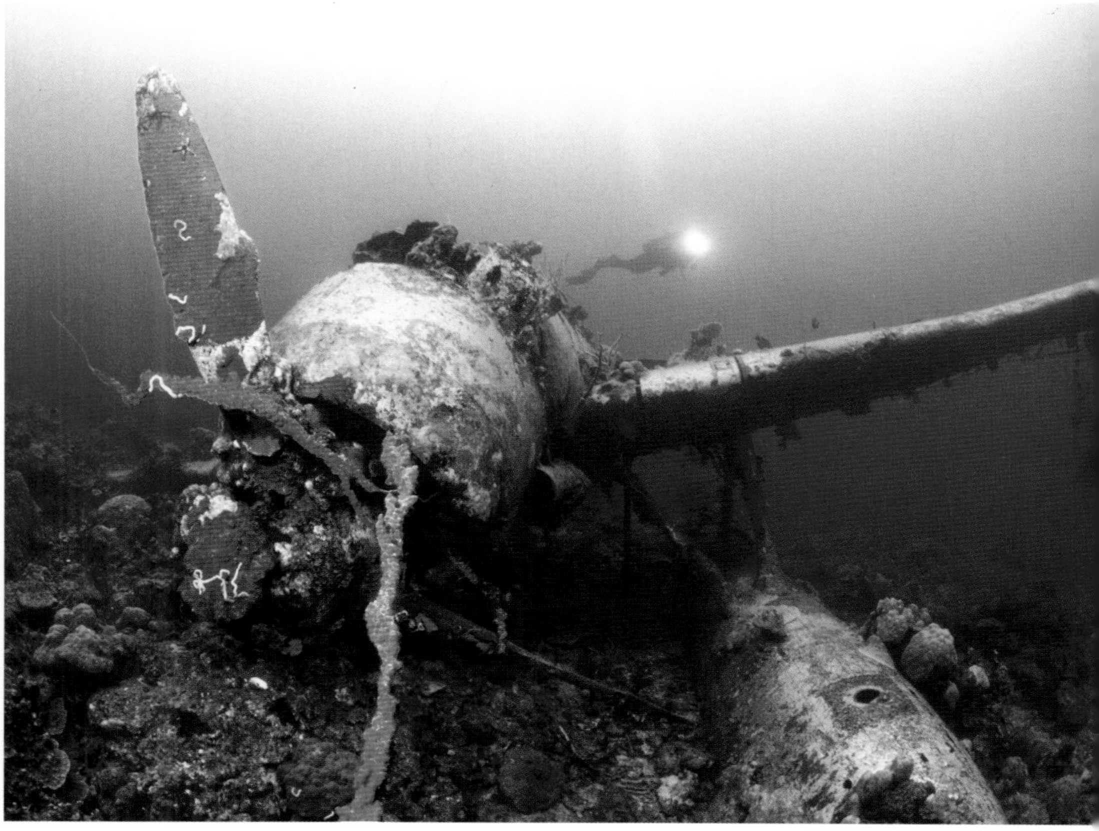

NORTH PACIFIC: PALAU

Blue Corner & Blue Holes

TWO DIVE SPOTS IN THE SOUTHWEST OF PALAU ARE REAL SITES OF PILGRIMAGE FOR THE INTERNATIONAL DIVING COMMUNITY. THEY ARE THE REASON THIS ISLAND GROUP IS ALWAYS RIGHT AT THE TOP OF THE CHARTS OF THE WORLD'S BEST DIVE SITES.

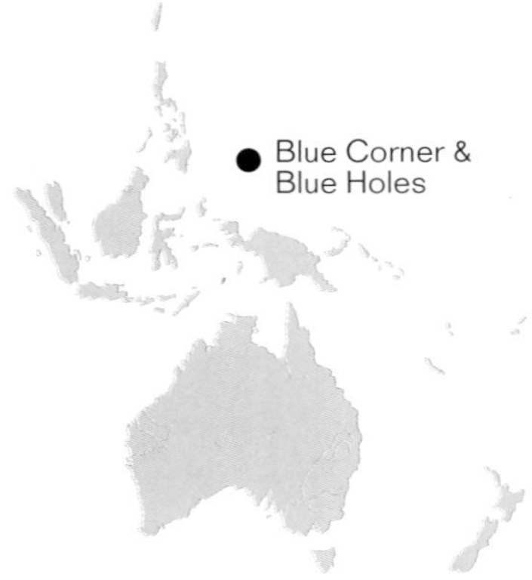

The Blue Holes hold out the promise of excellent cave diving. Erosion over the millennia has created four holes in the roof of the reef through which, when the sea is calm, you can dive vertically down into a vast cavern. A mystical blue light falls through the approximately 65-ft-long/20-m-long chimneys into the cave, the bottom of which is in places as deep as 130 ft/40 m. A small exit at 50 ft/15 m and a larger one below 90 ft/27 m lead divers conveniently back into open water. Inside the cave, divers can descend even deeper into the Temple of Doom, in which even turtles have lost their way—their skeletons are evidence of this.

Francis Toribiong, the famous diving pioneer from Palau, was the first to discover this spot. In 1978, drifting in the strong current on his way back from Blue Holes, he arrived by chance at Blue Corner. Suddenly he found himself facing a plateau surrounded by an armada of curious sharks, snappers, trevally, and barracuda. Today, even though the shark population is declining somewhat, Blue Corner remains a magnet for divers. At high tide, the powerful and nutrient-rich current at this exposed corner of the reef provides sufficient food for both large and small fish. Giant humphead wrasse, sea bass, rays, sleeping whitetip sharks and turtles are always present, and even dolphins pass by the reef from time to time.

Right: A gray reef shark.

Below: Blue Holes, one of Palau's highlights.

61 FACTS

- **Depth:** 10–130 ft/3–40 m
- **Visibility:** 50–165 ft/15–50 m
- **Water temperature:** 81–88°F/27–31°C
- **Best time of year:** Dec–Apr
- **Level of difficulty:** ■■■–■■■■■
- **Diversity of coral species:** ■■■
- **Diversity of fish species:** ■■■■
- **Big fish:** ■■■■■
- **Wrecks:** –
- **Caves:** ■■■■■
- **Walls:** ■■■■■
- **Snorkeling:** ■■■

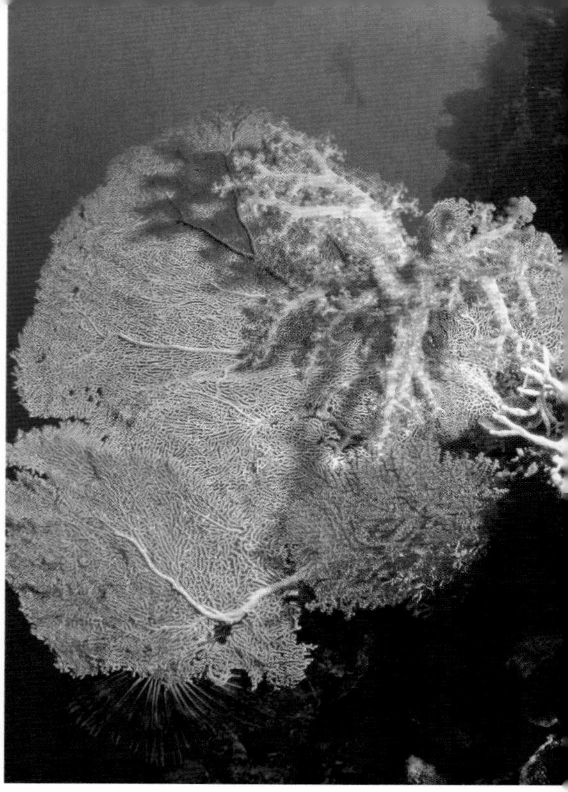

NORTH PACIFIC: PALAU

Ngemelis & Peleliu

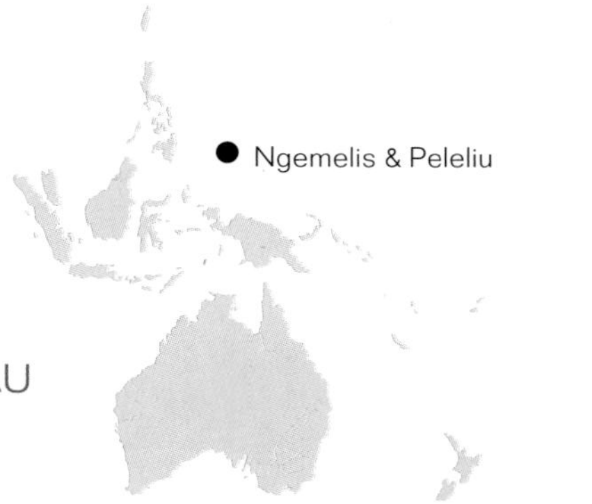

WALLS ARE ALWAYS FASCINATING FOR DIVERS, AND THOSE OFF THE SOUTHERN PALAU ISLANDS ARE BREATHTAKING. ALL KINDS OF CORALS GROW ON THEM, AND THERE IS ALWAYS THE POSSIBILITY OF ENCOUNTERING SOMETHING EXTRAORDINARY.

On the southwestern side of the uninhabited island of Ngemelis, the wall at Big Drop-Off falls away to a depth of more than 900 ft/ 280 m. Here, it is essential to have perfect buoyancy control, maintain continuous contact with the wall, and constantly check the dive computer. The wall teems with thousands of tropical fish, and with luck you may even spot a nautilus, a primeval deep-sea-dwelling cephalopod, as it occasionally climbs up this vertical garden of coral.

The more westerly New Drop-Off also falls away steeply. Here, however, the current can pull very strongly, so a reef hook is an essential part of your diving equipment. If you want to observe the patrolling sharks and other hunters at a particular place quietly, you can place the large hook, which is connected by a line to the buoyancy control device, around a rock—making sure you don't damage anything. The wall is extremely beautifully overgrown with soft corals, fan corals, and rod corals. Other walls to the south of the island include Turtle Wall, Ngemelis Coral Garden, and Ngemelis Wall.

There are also perfect dives near the island of Peleliu. Highlights are the Yellow Wall, named after its covering of yellow soft corals, the Peleliu Cut dive site, the Wall, where there are giant fans, and the Peleliu Express with its schools of sweetlips and snapper.

Above left: Rod corals at New Drop-Off.

Above right: Soft corals at Big Drop-Off.

Left: A nautilus, a creature from primeval times.

62 FACTS

- **Depth:** 5–130 ft/2–40 m
- **Visibility:** 65–130 ft/20–40 m
- **Water temperature:** 79–88°F/ 26–31°C
- **Best time of year:** Dec–Apr
- **Level of difficulty:** ■–■■■■■
- **Diversity of coral species:** ■■■■■
- **Diversity of fish species:** ■■■■
- **Big fish:** ■■■■
- **Wrecks:** –
- **Caves:** ■■
- **Walls:** ■■■■■
- **Snorkeling:** ■■■■

NORTH PACIFIC: FEDERATED STATES OF MICRONESIA

Chuuk (Truk Lagoon) I

CHUUK ATOLL IS CONSIDERED THE BEST WRECK-DIVING AREA IN THE WORLD. BESIDES WRECKS WHERE CONDITIONS ARE IDEAL FOR ALL DIVERS, THERE ARE ALSO SOME FOR WHICH SPECIAL TRAINING IS NEEDED. CHUUK ALSO OFFERS EXCELLENT SHARK SITES.

The volcanic islands of Chuuk, which are still known today under their former name of Truk, are part of the eastern Caroline Islands and form one of the Federated States of Micronesia. Eleven larger and forty-six smaller emerald-green islands are encircled by a 140-mile-long/224-km-long barrier reef that has formed around the edge of a sunken crater. There are no beaches to speak of, nor comfortable hotels. Divers are the only people who stray this way, in order to dive the many wrecks dating from World War II. Two hotels currently have dive shops attached to them, and these offer daily tours that include two to three dives.

Because of its isolated location in the middle of the Pacific, this island group was of great importance strategically. It formed a protected military base for the Japanese, who anchored a large part of their Pacific fleet here. In February 1944, the US launched Operation Hailstone, a surprise attack on this fortress, which was thought to be secure, and sank cruisers, destroyers, submarines, and transport ships. It is estimated that about 400 aircraft were destroyed and just under eighty ships sunk.

Today, superb coral gardens grow on this ghost fleet, and sponges and other lower animal forms have colonized the steel giants. Fishes, too, have found a new home, for example on the picture-book wreck of the *Fujikawa Maru*, which is covered with soft corals, to the southwest of the island of Eten. The 433-ft-long/132-m-long transport ship lies upright at a moderate depth, between 40 and 110 ft/12 and 34 m. In the hold you can see aircraft cockpits, wings, torpedoes, chinaware, and bottles. The engine room, the ship's guns, and the deck superstructure are all impressive.

Another great spot is the wreck of the 500-ft-long/152-m-long tanker *Shinkoku Maru*, north of the island of Param. Its masts begin at a depth of just 30 ft/9 m, the wheelhouse lies at 50 ft/15 m, and the deck guns at about 100 ft/31 m. Other wrecks that are very easy to dive include the *Sankisan Maru*, the *Hanakwa Maru*, the *Gossei Maru*, and the *Yamagiri Maru*. The wrecked aircraft *Betty Bomber* to the west of Eten is also a very worthwhile dive.

Sharks circle around some of the wrecks, but if you want to see more, you should not miss Shark Island, where more than a dozen gray reef sharks can be observed at close quarters.

Opposite page: Soft corals on the king posts of the *Fujikawa Maru*.

Top: The wreck of the *Betty Bomber*.

Center: An engine telegraph covered with sponges.

Bottom: A gray reef shark being cleaned.

63 FACTS

- **Depth:** 29–130 ft/9–40 m
- **Visibility:** 30–130 ft/10–40 m
- **Water temperature:** 82–86°F/28–30°C
- **Best time of year:** Dec–Apr
- **Level of difficulty:** ■–■■■
- **Diversity of coral species:** ■■■■
- **Diversity of fish species:** ■■■
- **Big fish:** ■■■–■■■■
- **Wrecks:** ■■■■■
- **Caves:** –
- **Walls:** –
- **Snorkeling:** ■

NORTH PACIFIC: FEDERATED STATES OF MICRONESIA

Chuuk (Truk Lagoon) II

IN TRUK LAGOON, EXPERIENCED DIVERS WITH SPECIAL TRAINING CAN DESCEND TO ENTHRALLING DEEP-LYING WRECKS. MOST OF THESE LIE AROUND THE ISLANDS OF WENO, FEFAN, UMAN, AND TONOWAS, AND ON NO ACCOUNT SHOULD THEY BE UNDERESTIMATED.

In 1964, twenty years after the sinking of Japan's Pacific fleet, a local witness to the event, Kimio Aisek, discovered the first wrecks in Chuuk Lagoon. Under the name Truk Lagoon, it has now become the wreck-diving mecca of the international diving community. This is due first to the fact that, in contrast to the situation in Pearl Harbor, no effort has been made in Chuuk to remove the remnants of war—quite the opposite: the entire lagoon has been declared an "underwater historical monument." In order to protect it from souvenir hunters, dive tours, which are not cheap, are permitted only with diving guides. Secondly, compared with other wreck areas, the conditions here are optimal: the protected location inside the lagoon with no currents, the warm clear water, and the shallow depths of many of the wrecks make for pleasant dives.

This said, however, there are some wrecks for which a lot of experience is required, one example being that of the *Nippo Maru*, whose role was to supply the other ships with drinking water. It was lying at anchor east of Tonowas when it was attacked and had extra cargo on board: a tank, trucks, artillery, machine guns, and a lot of munitions in the cargo holds. The wreck appears to be intact and lies, colorfully overgrown, upright in the sand. When you are on the deck, your dive computer will show 100 ft/31 m, and the no-decompression limit, within which you can surface without making additional intermediate stops, is correspondingly short.

The 420-ft-long/128-m-long *San Francisco Maru* is another one of the lagoon's deeper wrecks. The main deck on the foreship lies in about 130 ft/40 m of water, while the keel lies at a depth of 203 ft/62 m. Among the attractions are the three tanks on deck, and in the various cargo holds you can see some trucks, a lot of crockery, mines, depth charges, torpedoes, and cases of ammunition. In order to dive into the wreck precise instructions are needed, as the space is limited and some of the munitions may possibly still be live.

An experienced dive guide is needed to investigate the interior of the *Rio de Janeiro Maru*, even though it is located at an easy-to-dive depth of between 45 and 120 ft/14–37 m. However, the fact that the former passenger ship lies on its starboard side, makes it considerably more difficult to orient yourself. Further highlights for specialists are the *Hoki Maru*, the *Heian Maru*, and the *Unkai Maru*, as well as *Submarine I-169*.

Opposite page: Tanks on the *Nippo Maru*.

Above: In the engine room of the *Rio de Janeiro*.

Left: Skulls can still be found today on some wrecks.

Below left: Military trucks in the hold of the *Hoki Maru*.

64 FACTS

- **Depth:** 50–203 ft/15–62 m
- **Visibility:** 30–130 ft/10–40 m
- **Water temperature:** 82–86°F/28–30°C
- **Best time of year:** Dec–Apr
- **Level of difficulty:** ■■■–■■■■■
- **Diversity of coral species:** ■■■■
- **Diversity of fish species:** ■■■
- **Big fish:** ■■■
- **Wrecks:** ■■■■■
- **Caves:** –
- **Walls:** –
- **Snorkeling:** ■

NORTH PACIFIC: FEDERATED STATES OF MICRONESIA

Yap

THE ISLAND OF YAP IS KNOWN AMONG DIVERS PRINCIPALLY FOR THE MANTA RAYS IN THE CHANNELS (SEE SPOT NO. 66), BUT THERE IS FAR MORE TO SEE UNDERWATER HERE: WALLS, CAVERNS, SHARKS, MACRO SPOTS, AND EVEN MANDARINFISH.

The Yap Islands are part of the archipelago of the western Caroline Islands and lie north of New Guinea and east of the Philippines, far from any tourist routes. Divers frequently visit them on tours that also include a visit to Palau, just 280 miles/450 km away. The four main islands are known as Yap Proper and are enclosed by a coral reef, and together with the more distant Outer Islands they form one of the Federated States of Micronesia.

Only in Colonia, the capital of Yap, are there any hotels or dive shops. An unusual feature of this island is the fact that landowners also own the sea just offshore from their respective pieces of land. It is therefore not at all easy for the dive shop owners to obtain the necessary dive permits for the many spots around the island. These cannot simply be purchased; they have to be acquired through a process of long, ceremonial negotiations. In the meantime, divers have more than thirty diving spots available to them around the 15-mile-long/25-km-long and 5-mile-wide/8-km-wide island.

One of the diving highlights here is Vertigo Wall in the west, where you will be greeted underwater by large numbers of blacktip and gray reef sharks. At a corner of the reef lies Big Bend, where the guides attract curious silvertip, whitetip, and oceanic sharks by making special noises. Sea fans and soft corals grow beneath overhangs here, and black corals thrive at Cherry Blossom Wall.

65 FACTS

- **Depth:** 5–165 ft/2–50 m
- **Visibility:** On reefs 65–200 ft/20–60 m, in the lagoon 15–50 ft/5–15 m
- **Water temperature:** 82–86°F/28–30°C
- **Best time of year:** Dec–Apr
- **Level of difficulty:** ■–■■■
- **Diversity of coral species:** ■■■–■■■■■
- **Diversity of fish species:** ■■■■
- **Big fish:** ■■■■■
- **Wrecks:** ■■
- **Caves:** ■■■ (only in the south)
- **Walls:** ■■■■
- **Snorkeling:** ■■■

At Gilman Wall, to the south of the island, well-camouflaged yellow frogfish lie in wait, and at Yap Caverns, where there are some territorial leaf scorpionfish, divers can experience magnificent light shows in the caverns. In this labyrinth of reefs, trevally hunt and bumphead parrotfish eat coral—something you cannot fail to hear.

The eastern side of the island is close to the Yap Trench, the world's second-largest oceanic trench. It is important to keep an eye on the open water, as big fish encounters are possible at any time. In the east, the reefs fall away gradually into the depths and have fascinating and completely intact hard-coral gardens. The best spots are Sakura Terrace and Gapow Reef, which all have very good visibility.

Close to the capital of Colonia lie two wrecks and a macro site with nudibranchs, symbioses, cardinal fishes, and frogfishes. Brightly patterned mandarinfish live off O'Keefe Island, and these can best be observed after sunset.

Opposite page: A portrait of a gray reef shark.

Top and above: Colorful mandarinfish.

Left: Fighting parrotfish.

NORTH PACIFIC: FEDERATED STATES OF MICRONESIA

Yap: The channels

THE ISLAND OF YAP HAS BECOME KNOWN AMONG DIVERS WORLDWIDE FOR THE MAJESTIC MANTA RAYS IN ITS CHANNELS. THESE ARE BEST DIVED ON A RISING TIDE, WHEN THE WATER IS AT ITS CLEAREST AND THE MOST ACTIVITY IS TAKING PLACE.

Yap is chiefly volcanic in origin and has rolling hills covered in tropical forest. The island is encircled by a ring of coral, and a number of separate channels lead from the sea into the lagoons. The coasts are covered in mangrove jungle, and many inhabitants still live in unspoiled villages with a unique traditional culture based on fishing and agriculture. The legendary stone money that was quarried in Palau and transported to Yap in canoes, and which still plays a genuinely important role today, is put on display in front of their houses and on paths.

In 1984, dive pioneer Bill Acker discovered the manta rays that come to the channels to be cleaned and to filter the water for plankton. Acker, who is known by divers worldwide as the "manta man," has encountered and studied these peaceful giants on thousands of dives. He owns a dive resort on Yap and guarantees his guests manta encounters all year round. He also runs biology courses in which he teaches the correct way of handling manta rays. In front of his dive shop there is a board showing photos of more than 100 different manta rays with their respective names. They can be distinguished by the markings on their undersides, by their color and size, and by the bases of their tails.

The manta rays, whose wingspans can measure up to 16 ft/5 m and make them appear to by flying, search out specific locations at which small fish can free them of parasites. The occurrence of manta rays in the channels, where sharks and other fish also feel at home, is dependent on both the season and the time of day. The rays mate in winter, from December to April. For this, they prefer the Mi'l Channel on the northwestern side of the island, which is calmer at that time of year. In summer, they pass through the Goofnuw Channel in the northeast, usually in the mornings. The best times to dive here are at full moon and new moon, when the current is strongest. An incoming tide means clear water, while an outgoing tide brings murkier conditions.

These "beauty salons" are the favorite dive sites: there are five spots in the Mi'l Channel and three in the Goofnuw Channel where the strikingly elegant "fliers" come to be cleaned. Tzimoulis Ridge, which is named in honor of the famous American diver and underwater photographer, is one of the world's best manta sites.

Opposite page: A manta ray flying over Tzimoulis Ridge.

Below left: A portrait of a manta ray against the light.

Below right: A soft-coral wall in Mi'l Channel.

66 FACTS

- **Depth:** 30–90 ft/10–28 m
- **Visibility:** 15–130 ft/5–40 m
- **Water temperature:** 82–86°F/ 28–30°C
- **Best time of year:** Dec–Apr
- **Level of difficulty:** ■–■■■
- **Diversity of coral species:** ■■■
- **Diversity of fish species:** ■■■
- **Big fish:** ■■■■■
- **Wrecks:** ■■ (only in the main channel)
- **Caves:** –
- **Walls:** ■■■
- **Snorkeling:** ■■■

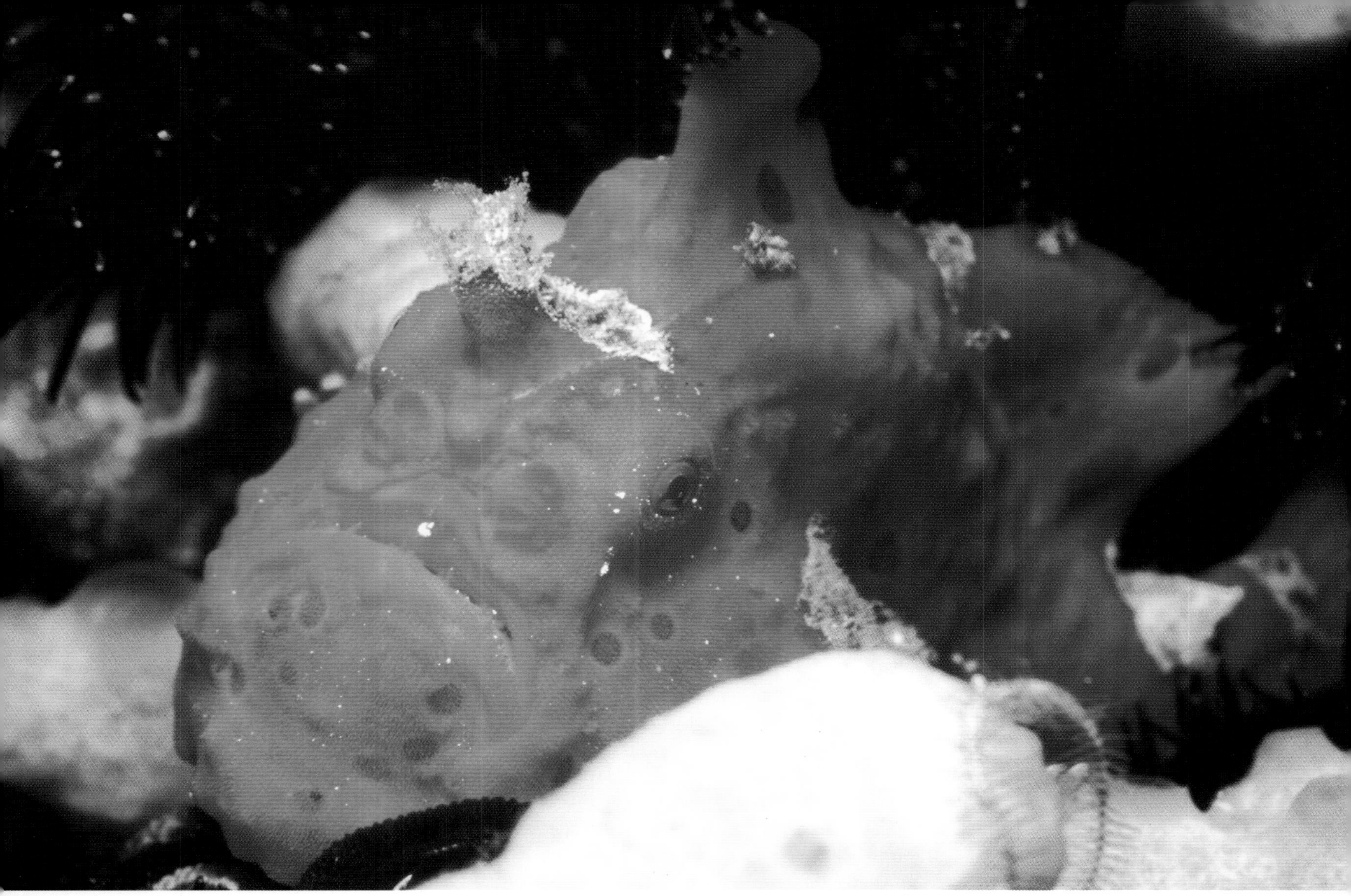

SOUTH PACIFIC: SOLOMON ISLANDS

Solomon Islands

THE SOLOMONS ARCHIPELAGO CONSISTS OF TWO ISLAND CHAINS RUNNING ALMOST PARALLEL FOR A DISTANCE OF NEARLY 600 MILES/1,000 KM. BELOW THE WATER THERE ARE EXCELLENT WALLS, CORAL GARDENS, AND WRECKS FROM THE BATTLE OF GUADALCANAL.

The Solomon islands group stretches from northwest to southeast and is the third-largest archipelago in the South Pacific. The northern islands belong to Papua New Guinea, which lies to the west, and the southern islands form the state of the Solomon Islands. Along with hundreds of small islands, there are a number of larger volcanic islands that are inhabited. The six main islands are Santa Isobel, San Cristobal, Malaita, New Georgia, Choiseul and Guadalcanal, home to the capital Honiara, where most of the dive centers are located as well as the starting points for one- to two-week dive cruises.

In the recent past, the islands have been in the headlines because of political unrest and a tsunami, and before that they were known for their role during the Pacific War. The Japanese occupied the islands in 1942, but very soon afterward the US launched its first offensive, leading to the Battle of Guadalcanal, which did not come to an end until February 1943. The wrecks around Honiara date from this period. Divers find the Bonegi wrecks, which are overgrown with soft corals, and a Japanese submarine particularly fascinating. The region around Munda on the island of New Georgia was also the scene of heavy fighting during the war, so this is a particularly rewarding site for wreck lovers. There are also drop-offs, big fish, and an exciting cave.

While many of the dive sites around Uepi, an island to the northwest on which a dive center also

67 FACTS

- **Depth:** 15–130 ft/5–40 m
- **Visibility:** 50–165 ft/15–50 m
- **Water temperature:** 75–84°F/24–29°C
- **Best time of year:** July–Nov
- **Level of difficulty:** ■–■■■■■
- **Diversity of coral species:** ■■■■
- **Diversity of fish species:** ■■■■
- **Big fish:** ■■■■
- **Wrecks:** ■■■■■
- **Caves:** ■■■
- **Walls:** ■■■■■
- **Snorkeling:** ■■■

operates, may not be quite so well known, they are extremely worthwhile to visit. Here, you will be enthralled by magnificent coral gardens, a variety of sharks, and tiny biological treasures.

Shorter dive safaris head for the reefs around the Russell and Florida islands, while longer tours lead into Western Province to less developed areas around the island of Gizo. Off this island lies the well-preserved wreck of the former Japanese transport ship, the *Tao Maru* (25–130 ft/8–40 m deep). It still contains a large part of its cargo, from bottles of sake to tanks. The long Marovo lagoon in the center of the New Georgia archipelago offers a mix of imposing walls, exciting wrecks, and deep-sea fish.

One really colorful diving wall bears the name of former US president John F. Kennedy, who was able to seek shelter on the small island when the torpedo boat on which he was serving as a soldier during World War II was rammed by a Japanese destroyer.

Opposite page: Hard to miss—frogfish in glowing red.

Above: A blue-ringed octopus—small and pretty, but highly venomous.

Left: A small blenny peeping out of its hiding place.

Papua New Guinea

THIS ISLAND STATE NORTH OF AUSTRALIA AND SOUTH OF THE EQUATOR IS THE DREAM LOCATION FOR MANY DIVERS. THE UNDERWATER WORLD THAT AWAITS THEM BOASTS UNPARALLELED REEFS, NUMEROUS WRECKS, AND AN IMMENSE DIVERSITY OF FISH AND CORAL SPECIES.

New Guinea, the world's second-largest island, is divided politically into two halves: the Indonesian province of West Papua and, in the east, the independent state of Papua New Guinea, to which the offshore islands also belong. The country is part of Melanesia, but geographically forms part of the continent of Australia. It is characterized as much by the fascinating cultures of its more than 700 ethnic groups as by its contrasting landscapes. The main island features high mountains, glaciers, rainforests, rivers, volcanoes, mangrove swamps, and savannas.

Most divers who end up in Papua New Guinea, despite the difficulty of getting there, come because of the species diversity of the underwater flora and fauna, which is highly praised on all sides and makes the region one of the finest diving locations in the world.

Added highlights are the hundreds of wrecks dating from World War II, which are scattered along the country's offshore waters. The capital city, Port Moresby, was the US headquarters at that time, and after the Japanese had conquered the northern part of New Guinea in 1941, three years of bitter fighting between Japan and the Allies followed. The best ship, aircraft, and submarine wrecks dating from this period are today to be found around the towns of Rabaul, Kavieng, Madang, Tufi, and Port Moresby.

In these areas, there are numerous resorts that have already received international awards. Many of the dive sites that can be visited from these resorts have acquired worldwide renown. The dive centers in Kimbe Bay, also known as the Coral Triangle, on the island of New Britain in the Bismarck Sea are famous, and it is said that 800 different corals and 460 fish species have been counted here.

Farther to the north, between the islands of New Ireland and New Hanover, where the Bismarck Sea meets the Pacific Ocean, lie tiny coral islands featuring magnificent wall sites, schools of fish, and sharks. Diving with the rare creatures in Milne Bay, to the east of the main island between the Coral Sea and the Solomon Sea, is unrivalled. The area's world-famous trademark is the weedy scorpionfish (genus *Rhinopias*). The region around Tufi to the east of Port Moresby features high crags and deep fjords, and the macro life is also particularly good.

All the well-known areas are visited by luxurious live-aboards, and you should plan on spending at least ten days on board.

Opposite page: Gazing through a red sea fan.

Below: Weedy scorpionfish with impressive markings.

68 FACTS

- **Depth:** 15–130 ft/5–40 m
- **Visibility:** 30–165 ft/10–50 m
- **Water temperature:** Coral Sea: 73–84°F/23–29°C Bismarck Sea: 84–86°F/29–30°C
- **Best time of year:** Kimbe Bay & Kavieng: Apr–Dec; Tufi: May & Nov–Jan; Milne Bay: Apr–May & Oct–Jan
- **Level of difficulty:** ■–■■■■■
- **Diversity of coral species:** ■■■■■
- **Diversity of fish species:** ■■■■■
- **Big fish:** ■■■■■
- **Wrecks:** ■■■■■
- **Caves:** ■■■
- **Walls:** ■■■■■
- **Snorkeling:** ■■■■■

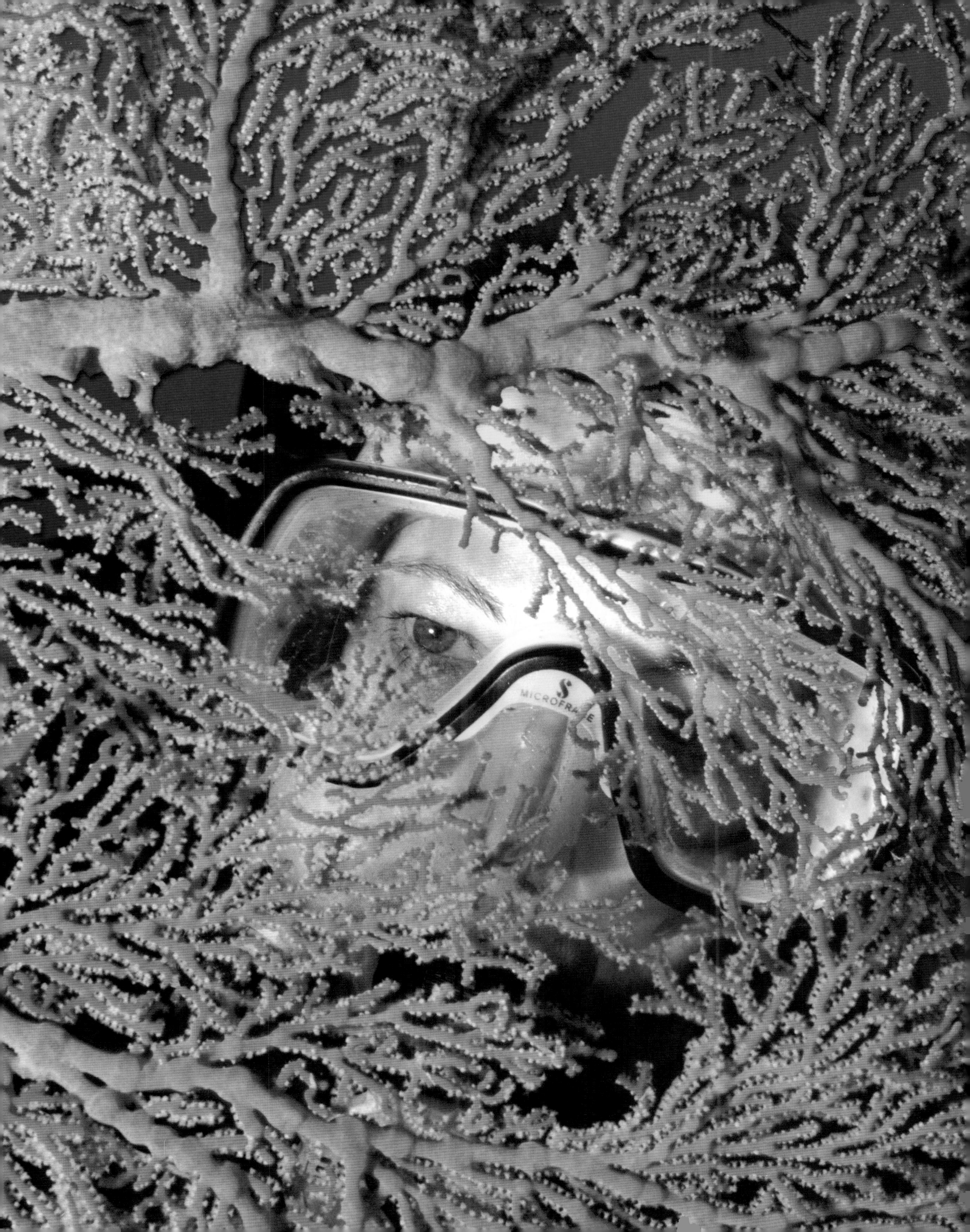

SOUTH PACIFIC: FRENCH POLYNESIA

Moorea

THIS ATOLL IN THE SOUTH PACIFIC FORMS PART OF THE SOCIETY ISLANDS IN FRENCH POLYNESIA. IN THIS SOUTH SEAS IDYLL YOU WILL FIND FIRST-RATE DIVING AMONG SHARKS AND GENTLE RAYS. HUGE HUMPBACK WHALES ARE A FURTHER ATTRACTION.

The French overseas territory of French Polynesia consists of five archipelagos comprising a total of 130 volcanic islands and atolls. Moorea is one of the Windward Islands. It lies to the west and within sight of Tahiti, where Papeete, the capital of French Polynesia, is located. From Papeete, this small diving paradise can be reached in about half an hour by boat or in ten minutes by plane.

You will find that Moorea is everything you would imagine a South Sea island to be: it has mountains, incised valleys, luxuriant vegetation, heavenly sandy beaches, and protected turquoise-colored lagoons enclosed by a reef. Clean, clear water at bathtub temperatures and 3,000 hours of sunshine a year make the island an ideal and safe (yet not overrun) diving destination for both novices and experts.

There are three distinguishable diving zones. The first are the protected lagoons, whose calm waters and flat areas of sand with occasional solitary coral formations are perfect for novices to learn in. There are a lot of interesting things to see here, such as, for example, the many hand-tame rays, which are regularly fed with fish waste and are consequently very attached to people. Anyone under the water during feeding should, however, be mindful of the fact that these are stingrays and not cuddly toys.

The second zone available to divers consists of the slopes outside the lagoon that fall away gradually from the island's outer reef. Typical features here are the many

69 FACTS

- **Depth:** 30–130 ft/10–40 m
- **Visibility:** 30–100 ft/10–30 m
- **Water temperature:** 79–86°F/ 26–30°C
- **Best time of year:** July–Dec
- **Level of difficulty:** ■–■■■■■
- **Diversity of coral species:** ■■■
- **Diversity of fish species:** ■■■■
- **Big fish:** ■■■■■
- **Wrecks:** –
- **Caves:** –
- **Walls:** –
- **Snorkeling:** ■■■

hard corals. Encounters with a number of big fish, as well as with schools of barracuda, humphead wrasses, and turtles, are also a daily occurrence. One dive center even offers guaranteed shark diving. The third zone is formed by the passages through the encircling reef, where there is always action for divers to enjoy when currents are flowing. However, some experience is required for diving in this environment.

One pleasant aspect of Moorea is that all the dive spots are conveniently located not far from the dive shops. One of the top dives starts in the Coral Rose Garden in the north of Moorea, where a wide variety of corals can be admired. You then emerge in Lemon Shark Valley, where the highlight is, as you would expect, a large number of lemon sharks. Some of their relations, such as gray sharks, nurse sharks, and blacktip and whitetip sharks, will invariably be encountered at the dive spots of Tiki and Taotoi at the northwestern tip of the island.

In the summer months, you may even be fortunate enough to be able to snorkel with enormous humpback whales that pass by close to the coast—a high point in any diver's life.

Opposite page: A majestic whale in the waters of Tahiti.

Above: An encounter between a diver on the decompression line and a shark.

Below: A bird's-eye view of Moorea.

SOUTH PACIFIC: FIJI ISLANDS

Fiji Islands

THIS ISLAND STATE ON THE 180TH MERIDIAN, THE INTERNATIONAL DATE LINE, IS AFFECTIONATELY CALLED THE "SOFT CORAL CAPITAL." THE WORLD-RENOWNED GREAT WHITE WALL, IN PARTICULAR, IS A VERITABLE FEAST FOR THE EYES.

The Fiji Islands lie approximately 1,850 miles/3,000 km to the east of Australia. Up until the end of the eighteenth century the islands were considered dangerous, as there really were cannibals living there. Today, a grave is the only reminder of the last cannibal king, and this picturesque country is considered a very hospitable place. The 332 islands of Fiji have been independent since 1970, and a republic since 1987. Several coups d'etat in recent years have meant that the country has experienced some ups and downs, which have also affected tourism. Nonetheless, dive centers have been established on the main islands of Viti Levu and Vanua Levu, as well as on many other islands. These usually offer one- or two-dive trips or day tours.

The topography of the dive sites ranges from walls and gently sloping reefs to small isolated coral pinnacles, called boomies, which project like mushrooms right up to the surface of the water.

The east of Viti Levu, especially the reefs around the offshore islands of Mamanuca and Yasawa, as well as the island of Nananu-i-Ra off the town of Rakiraki, are very popular. In the north, shark encounters are possible at Breath Taker, and Dream Maker is a spectacular spot with beautiful coral growth. Coral towers can be seen at the Pinnacles and at the dive site Golden Dreams, whose name alludes to the color of the soft corals.

Anyone who dives in the Fiji Islands should not miss the Great White Wall, probably the best-known site in the archipelago. The vertical "white" wall forms part of Rainbow Reef off the island of Taveuni, which can be reached by plane from the capital Suva on Viti Levu in an hour. This site, which is often prone to currents and is festooned over a 55-yd/50-m stretch with small white soft corals, is best reached from the top of the reef through a spectacular tunnel.

This spot is just one of the many in the Somosomo Strait, the narrows between Taveuni and Vanua Levu. The surfaces of many of the reefs are adorned with corals in bright red, purple, pink, yellow, and orange tones. These include, among others, the spots Yellow Grotto, Annie's Boomie, Jerry's Jelly, and The Ledge.

The dive sites in the northeastern Bligh Water Channel are best reached by cruise boat. Here, the E-6 Reef, which rises up from a depth of 3,300 ft/1,000 m, and Mount Mutiny, which lies like an oasis in the surrounding ocean, await the diver. At Cat's Miow or at Human Resorce, thousands of anthias flit around against a backdrop of exploding colors, and in Nigali Passage there is plenty of action going on, with sharks, barracudas, trevally, sea bass, moray eels, and sea snakes.

Opposite page: Various soft corals have colonized a dead table coral.

Above: A nudibranch providing a fascinating display of color.

Left: A soft coral beneath an overhang.

70 FACTS

- **Depth:** 15–130 ft/5–40 m
- **Visibility:** 30–130 ft/10–40 m
- **Water temperature:** 81–86°F/ 27–30°C
- **Best time of year:** Apr–Oct
- **Level of difficulty:** ■–■■■■■
- **Diversity of coral species:** ■■■■■
- **Diversity of fish species:** ■■■■
- **Big fish:** ■■■■
- **Wrecks:** ■■■
- **Caves:** ■■■
- **Walls:** ■■■■■
- **Snorkeling:** ■■■■

New Zealand

THE SPECTRUM OF CREATURES LIVING UNDERWATER IS HIGHLY DIVERSE AND INCLUDES REPRESENTATIVES OF COLD-WATER SPECIES AS WELL AS THOSE PREFERRING WARM WATER. THE MOST POPULAR SPOTS ARE LOCATED AROUND THE POOR KNIGHTS ISLANDS.

The mainland comprises the North and South islands separated by the Cook Strait. Added to these are a further 700 islands, which in the north extend halfway toward Fiji and in the south are considered part of the sub-Antarctic island world. Off the coastline, which has a total length of about 9,300 miles/15,000 km, there is plenty for divers to discover.

Around the South Island, which tends to attract fewer dive tourists, there are a number of worthwhile sites: in the southwest, red and black corals grow at a depth of between just 15 and 65 ft/5–20 m in the Fiordland Marine Reserve, which forms part of the fjord landscape of Milford Sound. Directly to the south, Stewart Island is characterized by an enormous diversity of fish species, and on the east coast, close to the town of Kaikoura, whales, dolphins, sea lions, blue sharks and even mako sharks can be observed. In the north of South Island lies what is probably the clearest spring pool in the world at Waikoropupu Springs, and in Marlborough Sound at the northern tip you can dive the wreck of the Russian ship MS *Mikhail Lermentov*.

On North Island, which is washed by warmer subtropical currents, you will find more dive tourists. Most dive locations lie to the north of Auckland. Offshore from the town of Tauranga, there are well-known crawfish sites, while a little farther to the north you will come across spots with caves, walls, and densely populated kelp forests in the Tuhua Marine Reserve. There are a number of sites for the more adventurous diver scattered around the still-active volcano of White Island, which is located about 30 miles/50 km off the coast from the town of Whakatane.

From Tutukaka it is a mere 13 miles/21 km to the Poor Knights Islands, which have several top diving spots. Northern Arch is a breeding site for large numbers of stingrays, and Blue Maomao Arch is a tunnel inhabited by schools of fish. Amidst the sponges you will discover small blennies and nudibranchs, while representatives of tropical species like the red pigfish, damselfish, moray eels, scorpionfish, and wrasses can be seen swimming along walls or among the kelp.

The former Greenpeace flagship *Rainbow Warrior* was scuttled off the coast of the eastern Cavalli Islands in 1987 after it was damaged in an attack by the French secret service in Auckland harbor in 1985. Over the years, the wreck has become a living reef, colonized by jewel anemones and fishes. A little farther to the south, masses of dolphins cruise near Pahaia.

Opposite page: An elegant fly-past—the rays of Poor Knights Islands.

Below left: The kelp forest, the parlor of the fish world.

Below right: A tiny blue-eyed triplefin lying in wait on a colorful terrace in front of its hole.

71 FACTS

(The data relate to the main diving region around the Poor Knights.)

- **Depth:** 30–120 ft/10–36 m
- **Visibility:** 30–100 ft/10–30 m
- **Water temperature:**
  Jan–Apr: 68–73°F/20–23°C
  May–Sept: 59–61°F/15–16°C
  Sept–Dec: 61–68°F/16–20°C
- **Best time of year:** Jan–Apr
- **Level of difficulty:** ■–■■■■■■
- **Diversity of coral species:** ■■■■
- **Diversity of fish species:** ■■■■
- **Big fish:** ■■■■
- **Wrecks:** ■■■
- **Caves:** ■■■■
- **Walls:** ■■■■
- **Snorkeling:** ■■■

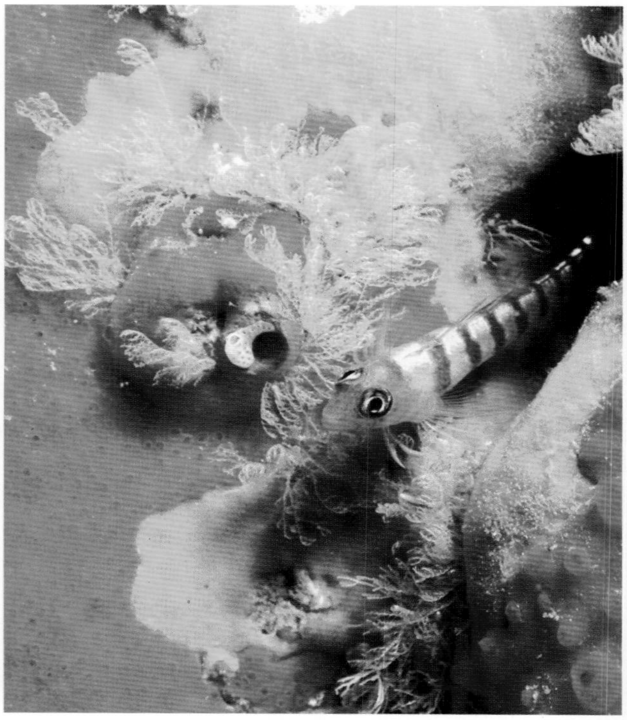

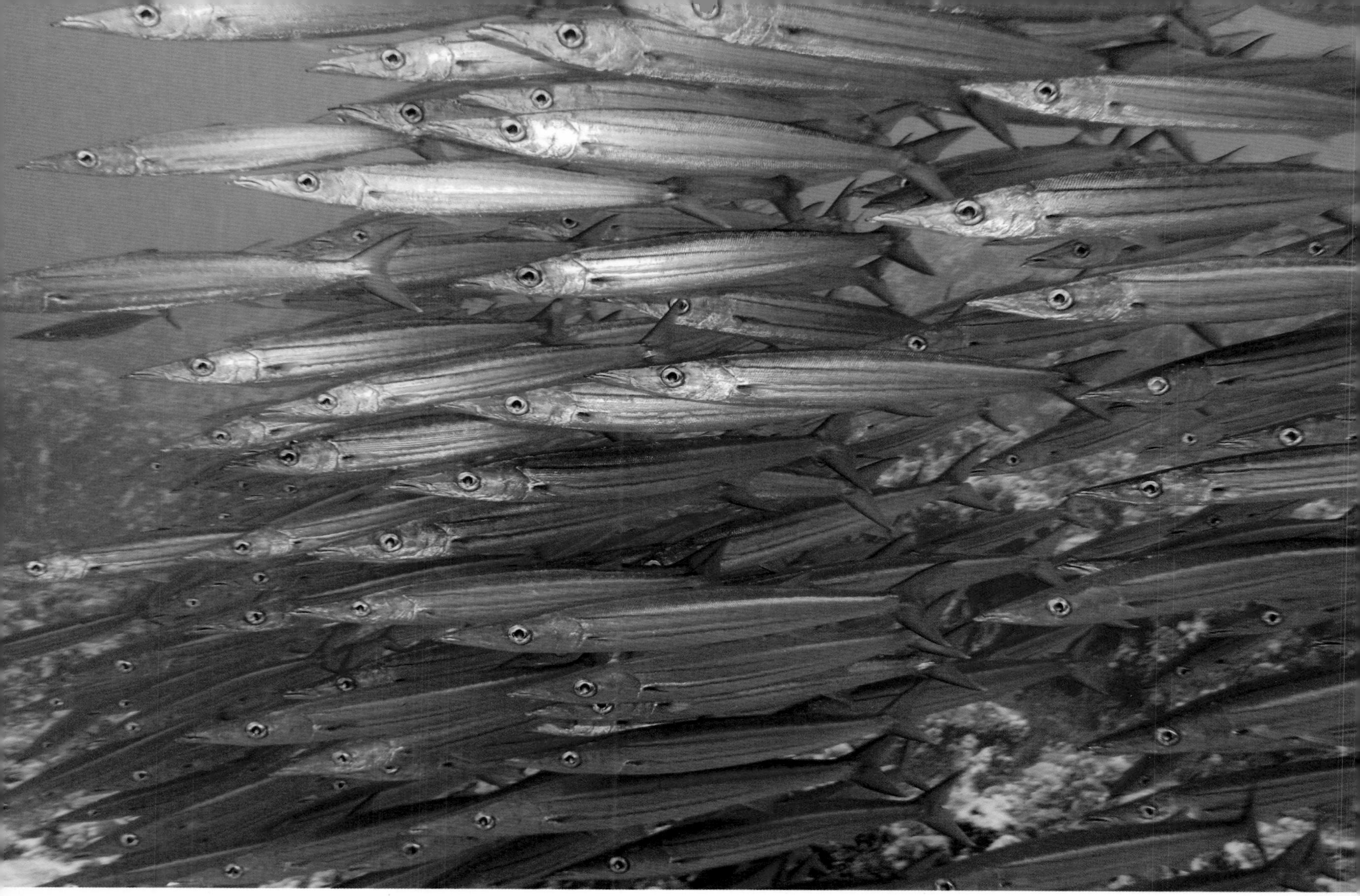

SOUTH PACIFIC: AUSTRALIA

Northern Great Barrier Reef

OFF THE EAST COAST OF AUSTRALIA LIES THE EARTH'S LONGEST REEF SYSTEM, WHICH STANDS UNDER UNESCO PROTECTION AS A WORLD NATURAL HERITAGE SITE. ITS TROPICAL ISLANDS, FISHES, CORALS, AND WHALES ENTHRALL MILLIONS OF TOURISTS EVERY YEAR.

The Great Barrier Reef, measuring about 1,400 miles/2,300 km in length, is the world's largest "structure" created by tiny creatures. Looked at in greater detail, it consists of just under 2,900 individual reefs and almost 1,000 islands surrounded by clear water, with a species-rich underwater flora and fauna. The reef, all of which falls within a protected conservation area, is about 10,000 years old and is often referred to as the eighth wonder of the world.

It runs almost parallel to the coast of the Australian state of Queensland and, on account of its enormous length, is subdivided into various sections. The northern Great Barrier Reef includes the Cairns region, the ribbon reefs, the northern Coral Sea and the Far Northern Reefs east of the Cape York Peninsula.

Diving experts consider the Far Northern Reefs, between Lizard Island and the Torres Strait off the coast of Papua New Guinea, to be the best in the entire region. They are pristine and remote, but the weather conditions there mean that cruises are available only from August to December. Most tours start from Lockhart River, approximately 300 miles/ 500 km north of the town of Cairns. At dive sites on the Far Northern Reefs, visibility is normally extremely good, and a variety of shark species is frequently encountered, as are strong currents.

At many spots on the Great Barrier Reef, a very special event takes place each November: the "coral spawning," when the corals release their eggs and sperm. Many fish are attracted by these tasty morsels, and a fantastically colorful display ensues.

The reefs of the northern Coral Sea rise up almost to the surface of the water from a depth of 3,300 ft/1,000 m. The Osprey Reef, the Holmes Reef, and the Bougainville Reef lie far from Australia and can be accessed only by live-aboards from Cairns or Port Douglas. In return for making the journey of up to 220 miles/350 km out there, you will find breathtaking walls, speedy predators, humphead wrasses, manta rays, and huge corals.

The Cod Hole, with its tame giant groupers, is the most famous dive site on the 60-mile-long/100-km-long ribbon reef off the coast of Cooktown. Your best chance of encountering minke whales here is between May and July.

Off the coast from Cairns and Port Douglas are the most visited dive spots on the Great Barrier Reef, which are cheaper to visit and can be accessed on a day trip. These sites are to be recommended but do not bear comparison with those on the northern reefs.

Opposite page: A school of young barracudas.

Above: An impressive giant clam.

Left: A whale encountering snorkelers.

72 FACTS

- **Depth:** 5–130 ft/2–40 m
- **Visibility:** 50–130 ft/15–40 m
- **Water temperature:** 72–84°F/22–29°C
- **Best time of year:** For northern reefs: Oct–Dec; northern Coral Sea and ribbon reefs: Apr–Jan
- **Level of difficulty:** ■–■■■■■
- **Diversity of coral species:** ■■■■
- **Diversity of fish species:** ■■■■
- **Big fish:** ■■■■■
- **Wrecks:** ■■■
- **Caves:** ■■■
- **Walls:** ■■■■■
- **Snorkeling:** ■■■■■

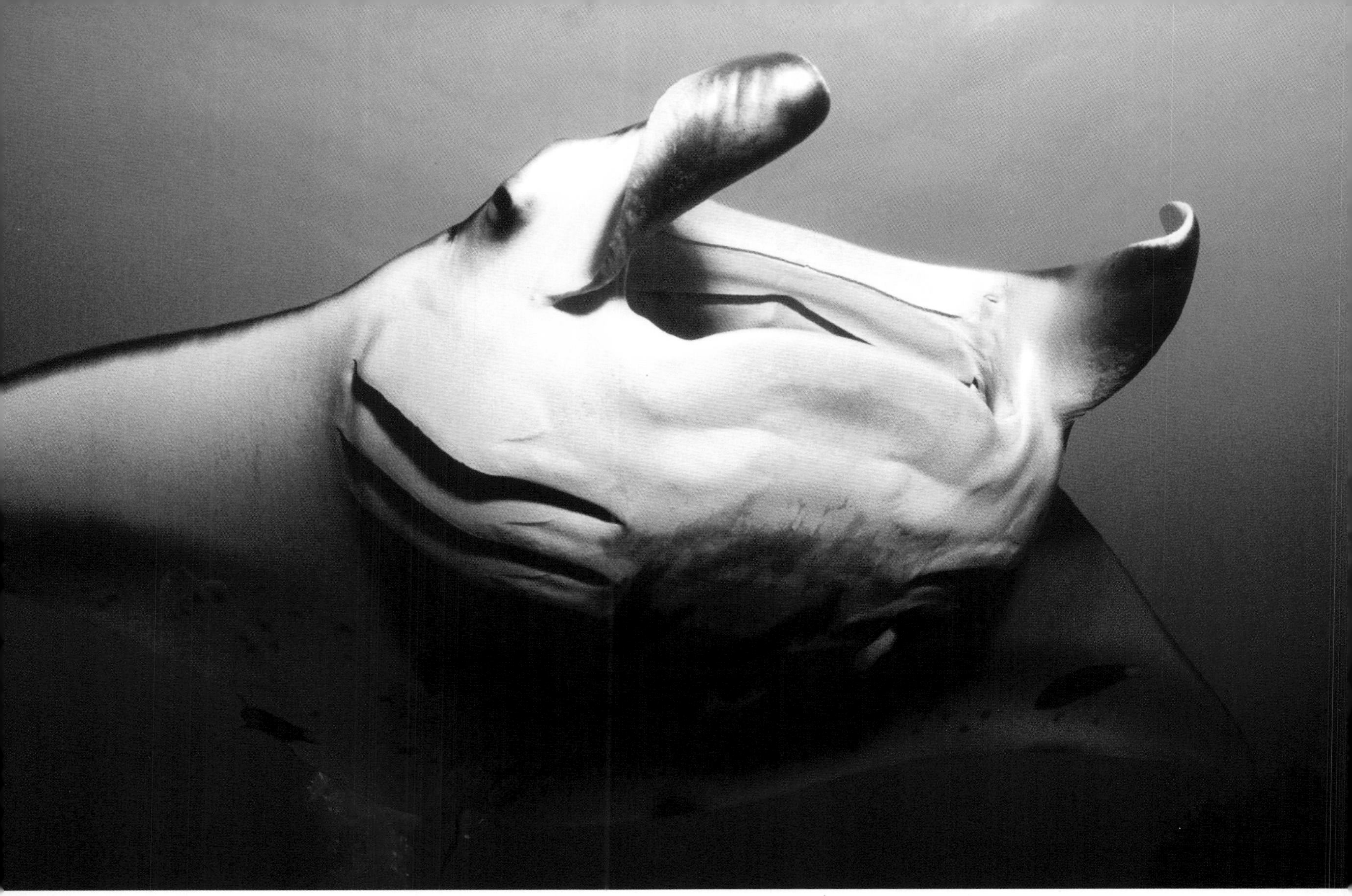

SOUTH PACIFIC: AUSTRALIA

Southern Great Barrier Reef

SOUTH OF CAIRNS LIE THE TWO DIVING REGIONS OF THE SOUTHERN CORAL SEA AND THE SOUTHERN GREAT BARRIER REEF. DEPENDING ON THE SEASON, YOU WILL BE ABLE TO SPOT BABY TURTLES, SHARKS, MANTA RAYS, AND EVEN HUMPBACK WHALES.

As the whole of the Great Barrier Reef lies far from the mainland, you will always need transport to get out to the dive sites. Divers have a whole range of options open to them. If you wish to spare yourself the single-day boat tours, you can fly by helicopter or take a seaplane to the dive sites, or travel around on a live-aboard. Alternatively, you can also choose to be deposited on an island for a certain period of time, or you can opt for a shorter snorkeling tour. The latter are provided not just by the overfilled megaships, but also by specialist tour operators.

In the south, the Great Barrier Reef extends beyond the Tropic of Capricorn to a point level with the town of Bundaberg. In this enormous reef system, the quality of the dive spots varies considerably, as does the level of congestion with dive tourists.

To reach the diving grounds of the southern Coral Sea section of the reef, you will generally start out from Townsville. From here, it is about 140 miles/230 km to most dive sites, which means an approximately 12-hour outward journey. This is frequently a very rough ride, and is only to be recommended to experienced divers and those not prone to seasickness. Once you have reached your destination, you will be richly rewarded: clear visibility conditions, drift dives, deep drop-offs, big-fish encounters with various species of shark, and mantas and other rays are the norm at these sites, together with large fan corals and giant sponges.

73 FACTS

- **Depth:** 5–130 ft/2–40 m
- **Visibility:** 30–130 ft/10–40 m
- **Water temperature:** 70–81°F/21–27°C
- **Best time of year:** Southern Coral Sea: Sept–Jan, Apr–Dec
- **Level of difficulty:** ■–■■■
- **Diversity of coral species:** ■■■■
- **Diversity of fish species:** ■■■■■
- **Big fish:** ■■■■■
- **Wrecks:** ■■■
- **Caves:** ■■■
- **Walls:** ■■■■
- **Snorkeling:** ■■■■■

The thrill of seeing feeding sharks is something you can experience at Flinders Reef, which is also renowned for its turtles. Herald Cay and Dart Reef are visited less often due to their dependence on the weather. The wreck of the 360-ft-long/110-m-long *Yongola* (60–100 ft/18–30 m deep), which sank in a storm in 1911 just 5 miles/8 km off the coast south of Townsville, draws frequent visitors. It is completely cloaked in corals and provides sanctuary for many fish, both large and small.

The largest section of the Great Barrier Reef is the Southern Great Barrier Reef, which can be reached from Gladstone or Bundaberg. It extends from the Whitsunday Islands in the north to "Capricorn & Bunker Marine Park" in the south, where the popular resorts on Heron Island and Lady Elliott Island also lie. The latter are ideal for short trips to their magnificent coral formations, large numbers of tropical fishes, reef sharks, and turtles. There is something on offer here all year round: freshly hatched turtles from January to April, giant humpback whales from June to October, and elegant devil rays from November to February.

Opposite page: A manta ray at a cleaning station.

Above: A lionfish with its venomous spines.

Below: The Great Barrier Reef off Gladstone, Queensland.

Tasmania

NO FEWER THAN FOUR MARINE PARKS LIE OFF THE EAST COAST OF AUSTRALIA'S LARGEST ISLAND. THE DIVERS WHO ARE DRAWN HERE ARE THOSE WHO LOVE KELP FORESTS, CAVES, WRECKS, AND ESPECIALLY SEADRAGONS.

The landscape on this island, which is situated to the southeast of Australia, is so impressive that just under half the island has been designated national park and a quarter has been declared a UNESCO World Heritage Site. There are about a dozen dive centers which cater to guests from all over the world and guide them through the fantastic undersea world off the coast of Tasmania.

Southeast of the capital Hobart lies the popular dive location of Eaglehawk Neck, with its spectacular caves. In places at nearby Waterfall Bay, the high cliffs continue underwater as superbly encrusted rock formations with a colorful, species-rich and extraordinary flora and fauna. Severe erosion has led to the formation of caves and tunnels between different types of rock, one of the most well-known being Cathedral Cave.

Hiding in vast kelp forests are excellently camouflaged common seadragons, better known in Tasmania as weedy seadragons. These unusual relatives of the sea horse are endemic to the south of Australia. The SS *Nord*, which sank in 1915 and now lies at a depth of 140 ft/42 m, is a great wreck with a rich diversity of fishes.

74 FACTS

- **Depth:** 15–130 ft/5–40 m
- **Visibility:** 30–80 ft/10–25 m
- **Water temperature:** 50–63°F/10–17°C
- **Best time of year:** Apr–July
- **Level of difficulty:** ■–■■■■■■
- **Diversity of coral species:** ■■
- **Diversity of fish species:** ■■■■
- **Big fish:** ■■■
- **Wrecks:** ■■■
- **Caves:** ■■■■
- **Walls:** ■■■
- **Snorkeling:** ■■

Below left and right: Weedy seadragons—also known as common seadragons.

PACIFIC: US

California

IN THE WESTERN US, DIVERS CAN EXPERIENCE SOMETHING QUITE SPECIAL IN RATHER COOL PACIFIC WATERS: IN KELP FORESTS UP TO 100 FT/30 M IN HEIGHT, YOU CAN DIVE WITH SEA LIONS, MULTICOLORED FISHES, OR EVEN BLUE SHARKS.

Diving off the coast of the "Golden State" is almost unknown to anyone outside America. A two-hour drive south from San Francisco on Highway 1 takes you to the dive scene in the world-famous city of Monterey. Here, there are plenty of dive boats and the opportunity to dive directly from the shore all year round.

Probably the best dive location in California is in the Point Lobos State Reserve, where the number of divers is limited by law. The finest diving is to be had in late summer in the giant kelp, the world's longest aquatic plant. Crabs and starfish parade around this underwater jungle, and you are also likely to come across feeding nudibranchs, anemones, and kelpfishes. It is fascinating to watch the acrobatic performances of sea lions and seals as they hunt and play.

Farther south, at Catalina Island, you may with a bit of luck see blue sharks. Flamboyant garibaldi damselfish live in the kelp, which grows up to 100 ft/30 m high in the waters around the island. Off the coast of San Diego, divers can observe a variety of sharks from cages in open water.

Above left: Fireworks-like jewel anemones.

Above right: Kelp, a form of brown algae.

Left: Blue sharks have large eyes and a long snout.

75 FACTS

- **Depth:** 5–130 ft/2–40 m
- **Visibility:** 3–65 ft/1–20 m
- **Water temperature:** 52–72°F/ 11–22°C
- **Best time of year:** July–Oct
- **Level of difficulty:** ■–■■■■■
- **Diversity of coral species:** ■■
- **Diversity of fish species:** ■■■
- **Big fish:** ■■■
- **Wrecks:** ■■
- **Caves:** ■■■
- **Walls:** ■■■■
- **Snorkeling:** ■■■

PACIFIC: MEXICO

Baja California

BETWEEN THE PENINSULA OF BAJA CALIFORNIA AND THE MEXICAN MAINLAND LIES THE FISH-RICH GULF OF CALIFORNIA. DIVERS FROM ALL OVER THE WORLD ARE LURED HERE BY THE ATTRACTION OF MANTA RAYS, WHALES, SHARKS, AND SEA LIONS.

Baja California is the name given to the peninsula as a whole and to the northernmost federal state of Mexico located on it, as well as to the dive region in general. This includes the Gulf of California, also known as the Sea of Cortez, which in places is up to 10,000 ft/3,000 m deep. It covers an area with a length of about 700 miles/1,150 km and a width of just under 100 miles/160 km, from the estuary mouth delta of the Colorado River in the north as far as Cabo San Lucas in the south. In the Gulf, currents from the deep sea mix with the nutrient-rich supply of water from the inflowing Colorado, so there is a surplus of food, which has given rise to a great diversity of marine life.

La Paz, capital of the federal state of Baja California Sur, together with its bay in the south of the peninsula, is the recreational diving center of the region. One of the dive resorts, which lies in an idyllic location in Pichilinque Bay, slightly off the beaten track, has its own decompression chamber. From here you can reach the top sites around the islands of Espiritu Santo, Los Islotes, and Cerralvo in about one-and-a-half to two hours by boat. Around these islands, seamounts—underwater mountains—rise up from the ocean floor to within 30 to 65 ft/10 to 20 m of the surface. They are meeting places for a number of deep-sea fishes.

Sea lions can be seen near the dive resort at San Rafaelos Lighthouse. A further twenty-minute boat ride takes you to where you can explore the wreck of

76 FACTS

- Depth: 3–130 ft/1–40 m
- Visibility: 15–100 ft/5–30 m
- Water temperature: 64–82°F/18–28°C
- Best time of year: July–Nov
- Level of difficulty: ■–■■■■■
- Diversity of coral species: ■■■
- Diversity of fish species: ■■■■
- Big fish: ■■■■■
- Wrecks: ■■■
- Caves: ■■■
- Walls: ■■■■
- Snorkeling: ■■■■

the *Salvatierra*. This ferry ran aground on the Swanee Reef in 1976 and today forms a desirable habitat for fish. The Cortez and king angelfishes are particularly photogenic, as are the boulders at the Old Sea Lions Colony, which are overgrown with sea fans.

To the north of the island of Cerralvo lies La Reina: giant hawkfishes, manta rays, and sea lions love this "regal" site, at which you can also see the scattered remnants of a wreck.

About 30 miles/50 km north of La Paz, you come across Los Islotes, two small rocky islets off the coast of Isla La Partida. Their trademark feature is the 200 or so friendly sea lions, which you can get a great view of all year round. Also living around the island are barracudas, moray eels, surgeonfish, doctorfish, damselfish, and snappers.

The site of El Bajo, located farther to the northeast, is famous for its schools of hammerhead sharks, which circle in the deep open waters off the reef. Even orcas, whales, and great white sharks have been sighted here from time to time. The months from September to November promise similarly gargantuan encounters with whale sharks and manta rays in the bay off La Paz.

Opposite page: Encounters with the largest fishes, the whale sharks, provide moments of sheer pleasure for divers.

Above: Sea lions are speedy but obliging models.

Left: Cortez angelfish with beautiful markings.

PACIFIC: MEXICO

Socorro Islands

THIS SMALL ISLAND GROUP IN THE PACIFIC, ABOUT 250 MILES/400 KM SOUTH OF THE PENINSULA OF BAJA CALIFORNIA, HOLDS OUT THE PROMISE OF ENCOUNTERS WITH LARGE NUMBERS OF SHARKS AND INTERACTIVE DIVING WITH GIANT MANTA RAYS.

The four volcanic islands of Socorro, San Benedicto, Roca Partida, and Clarión form the archipelago of the Socorro Islands, which are also known as the Revillagigedo Islands. These exposed islands can be reached by cruise boats, which start out from Cabo San Lucas at the southern tip of Baja California. The crossing, which is usually quite choppy, takes about 22 hours. Since Clarión lies almost 250 miles/400 km farther than the main island of Socorro, it is seldom visited by dive boats.

The inhospitable-looking islands are uninhabited and in 1994 were declared a biosphere reserve by UNESCO. The Mexican navy has among other things been monitoring the fishing ban, which has been in force since 2002 following a massacre of big fish.

San Benedicto has become internationally renowned for its giant manta rays, whose "wings" can have a span of up to 20 ft/6 m. These friendly giants, which seem to seek divers' attention, are encountered around Submarine Canyon, which is located on the eastern side of the island. This site starts at a depth of 50 ft/15 m below the surface and plunges to a depth of about 6,500 ft/2,000 m.

The Boiler, a seamount that rises up from a depth of 165 ft/50 m, is breathtaking. Interactive diving with manta rays is possible here: these impressive giants actually enjoy being held and stroked, after which they remain still for a while, as if hypnotized. Touching

manta rays is generally prohibited worldwide and is allowed here only after divers have been given a detailed briefing on the correct procedure. Gloves, knives, and lamps are taboo, as is holding on to the wingtips or the tail. Caution is needed with the remoras, which use suction to hold firmly onto manta rays, as they are likely to bite.

There is still plenty more to see at both spots. Whitetip sharks doze in caves alongside crawfish, smaller groupers lie in wait, and rays bury themselves in the sand. Orange angelfishes and colorful wrasses provide a dash of color on the reef.

Roca Partida lies completely unprotected in the Pacific and can therefore be dived only when the weather permits. The larger residents of the Pacific congregate around the rocky crags of this superlative site. There are hundreds of black jacks in tightly packed formation. Galapagos, silky, and silvertip sharks swim around, and a little deeper a school of hammerheads. At Papos Reef near Socorro, sharks mingle with trevally, grunts, and butterflyfish.

Opposite page: Socorro is famous for its manta rays.

Above: A female wrasse off the coast of San Benedicto.

Left: A manta ray approaching a diver in order to be stroked.

77 FACTS

- **Depth:** 30–130 ft/10–40 m
- **Visibility:** 15–115 ft/5–35 m
- **Water temperature:** 70–82°F/ 21–28°C
- **Best time of year:** Nov–May
- **Level of difficulty:** ■–■■■■■
- **Diversity of coral species:** ■■
- **Diversity of fish species:** ■■■■
- **Big fish:** ■■■■■
- **Wrecks:** ■
- **Caves:** ■■■
- **Walls:** ■■■■■
- **Snorkeling:** ■■

PACIFIC: COSTA RICA

Cocos Island

THOSE WISHING TO DESCEND INTO THE UNDERWATER WORLD AROUND COCOS ISLAND HAVE TO PUT UP WITH A LONG JOURNEY. HOWEVER, SCHOOLS OF HAMMERHEAD AND WHITETIP SHARKS AND AN INCREDIBLE ABUNDANCE OF FISH MAKE IT WORTHWHILE.

Lying isolated in the middle of the Pacific, about 300 miles/500 km from Costa Rica, the uninhabited Cocos Island, which measures just 9 square miles/24 square km, is a mystical place which acquired fame as Treasure Island. A number of expeditions have headed into the dense rain forest, which extends up to an altitude of 2,080 ft/ 634 m, but none of the pirate treasure allegedly hidden there has so far been found.

The real treasure of the volcanic island is its natural wilderness, with more than 200 waterfalls, gorges, and mountains, and its fascinating underwater scenery. It was made a protected site as long ago as 1978 and a UNESCO World Heritage Site in 1997.

Cocos Island is a difficult-to-reach dream destination for experienced divers. Only a small number of cruise boats come here, and they are usually booked up early. About 36 hours are needed for the often rough crossing from the port of departure, Puntarenas in Costa Rica. However, those willing to endure this are more than royally rewarded. More than a dozen spots offer the ultimate in diving experiences.

The guarantee of seeing sharks draws divers here from all over the world. The dives are unforgettable and are unrivalled in terms of the excitement they offer—only on Galapagos can you experience something similar. Dozens of hammerhead sharks move quietly past you and can be watched as they allow themselves to be cleaned of parasites at

78 FACTS

- ❖ **Depth:** 10–130 ft/3–40 m
- ❖ **Visibility:** 50–100 ft/15–30 m
- ❖ **Water temperature:** 70–82°F/21–28°C
- ❖ **Best time of year:** Nov–May
- ❖ **Level of difficulty:** ■■■–■■■■■
- ❖ **Diversity of coral species:** ■■
- ❖ **Diversity of fish species:** ■■■■
- ❖ **Big fish:** ■■■■■
- ❖ **Wrecks:** ■
- ❖ **Caves:** ■■
- ❖ **Walls:** ■■■■■
- ❖ **Snorkeling:** ■■■

cleaning stations. Added to these are the many whitetip sharks, which are nowhere else to be encountered in such numbers. During the day, they lie quietly on the bottom, but during night dives you can observe them in action on a scarcely imaginable scale. The island of Malpelo, which lies approximately 250 miles/400 km to the southwest of Cocos Island and belongs to Colombia, is similarly famous for the large number of hammerhead sharks at its diving grounds. You can get there from Costa Rica.

Being able to observe large predators in a feeding frenzy is an experience for any diver, not just for underwater photographers and filmmakers. If you are lucky, you may witness thousands of small sardines forming bait balls near the surface of the water when they are being hunted by tuna or trevally. The latter dart wildly into the swirling protective ball. This spectacle also attracts a variety of sharks, dolphins, wahoos and birds, whose special hunting techniques can then also be observed.

The latest craze is to make a descent from the Undersea Hunter Group's mother vessel *Argos* in the small submersible *DeepSee*, in operation since 2008, down to depths of 1,000 ft/300 m.

Opposite page: A school of hammerhead sharks.

Above: A hungry family of moray eels.

Left: An encounter with the bizarre walking batfish.

Galapagos Islands

A FASCINATING RANGE OF FISH LIFE IS ATTRACTED TO THE AREA AROUND THE REMOTE GALAPAGOS ARCHIPELAGO BY ITS MANY CURRENTS AND NUTRIENT-RICH WATERS. IT IS A TOP DIVING DESTINATION FOR ENCOUNTERS WITH WHALES, SHARKS, RAYS, AND SEA LIONS.

The "Enchanted Isles" lie approximately 600 miles/1,000 km off the coast of Ecuador on mainland South America. The 13 main islands and many smaller islands are inhabited by a primitive and in part endemic fauna: primeval-looking marine iguanas, land iguanas, giant tortoises, cormorants, albatrosses, frigate birds, blue-footed boobies, and the small finches that were named after Charles Darwin can all be observed during shore excursions.

The region has been protected since 1959, and today both land and water are included within a UNESCO World Heritage Site. By law, a government-certified guide must accompany all excursions, including dive cruises.

The dive sites around the main islands are visited by both live-aboards and day boats from various dive centers. The sites are extraordinary, a veritable melting pot of marine life forms, but they are not easy to dive. Thermoclines, currents, swells, and visibility levels all vary daily, so experience is a must. The underwater scenery is dominated by fairly dark lava rocks—you will search in vain for colorful tropical corals.

One of the best-known spots is Gordon Rocks on the east coast of the island of Santa Cruz, where you dive in an old crater. This giant aquarium has a lot to offer: moray eels, various rays, hammerhead and Galapagos sharks, turtles, sea lions, and numerous reef fishes. At Pinnacle Rock, off the coast of the small island of Bartolomé, you will discover crustaceans between crevices and in caves, rays and large shoals of fish in the open water, and dozing whitetip sharks on the bottom. Snorkeling with the agile Galapagos penguins between dives is a unique experience.

Farther north, off the east coast of the island of Santiago, Cousins Rock rises about 30 ft/10 m out of the water. Below it, endemic black corals grow on a fantastic wall, and in the immediate vicinity you will find many invertebrates such as mollusks, echinoderms, worms, and perhaps even sea horses, which here can be 10 in/25 cm long or more. Hammerhead sharks, barracudas, eagle rays, and even manta rays can be viewed up close, and curious sea lions dart around in the waters above.

Further exciting dives are to be had at various sites off the islands of Floreana, Seymour, Santa Fe, Mosquera, Daphne, and the Plazas. Some of the best dive sites lie around the uninhabited islands of Wolf and Darwin, which are situated right in the northwest of the archipelago, and spot no. 80 is devoted to these.

Opposite page: Starfish migration on the sea bed.

Below left: A ray above black corals.

Below right: Colorful angelfish.

79 FACTS

- **Depth:** 3–130 ft/1–40 m
- **Visibility:** 15–80 ft/5–25 m
- **Water temperature:**
  Jan–June: 75–84°F/24–29°C
  July–Dec: 61–73°F/16–23°C
- **Best time of year:** Aug–Nov
- **Level of difficulty:** ■■■–■■■■■
- **Diversity of coral species:** ■■
- **Diversity of fish species:** ■■■■
- **Big fish:** ■■■■■
- **Wrecks:** –
- **Caves:** ■■
- **Walls:** ■■■■■
- **Snorkeling:** ■■

PACIFIC: ECUADOR

Wolf & Darwin

THE TWO NORTHERNMOST GALAPAGOS ISLANDS ARE AMONG THE WORLD'S TOP DIVING DESTINATIONS. THEY ARE SPECIALLY PROTECTED SITES AND ARE VISITED BY ONLY A SMALL NUMBER OF SAFARI BOATS.

Following the discovery of the Galapagos Islands by the Spanish Bishop Tomás de Berlanga in 1535, Charles Darwin was the next visitor of any note. He interrupted his research voyage on the *Beagle* for a few weeks here in 1835. The isolated islands formed an ideal ecological field study area that provided him with findings that later formed the basis of his theory of evolution.

This small but world-famous area was placed on UNESCO's Red List in 2007, which cited as a reason the "increasing tourism, which is introducing more and more alien species." Since then, far-reaching and not fully understandable rules and regulations have been put in place by the park administration, particularly for divers. Especially hard hit by these have been the two top dive sites around the islands of Wolf and Darwin right in the north of the archipelago. At the present time, only five cruise boats are allowed to visit these two islands. The approximately 160-mile-long/ 260-km-long tour heads out in a northwesterly direction from Puerto Ayora on Santa Cruz.

The cliffs on Wolf, where boats anchor to the north, are steep. A dinghy takes you to the southeastern tip, where the currents divide and hammerheads circle. The more calmly you behave, the closer these elegant hunters will come to you. Large numbers of green moray eels, large hawkfishes and groupers, turtles, and creolefishes live among the black volcanic rocks.

80 FACTS

- **Depth:** 3–130 ft/1–40 m
- **Visibility:** 15–80 ft/5–25 m
- **Water temperature:**
  Jan–July: 75–84°F/24–29°C
  July–Dec: 61–73°F/16–23°C
- **Best time of year:** Aug–Nov
- **Level of difficulty:** ■■■–■■■■■
- **Diversity of coral species:** ■■
- **Diversity of fish species:** ■■■■
- **Big fish:** ■■■■■
- **Wrecks:** –
- **Caves:** ■■
- **Walls:** ■■■■■
- **Snorkeling:** ■■

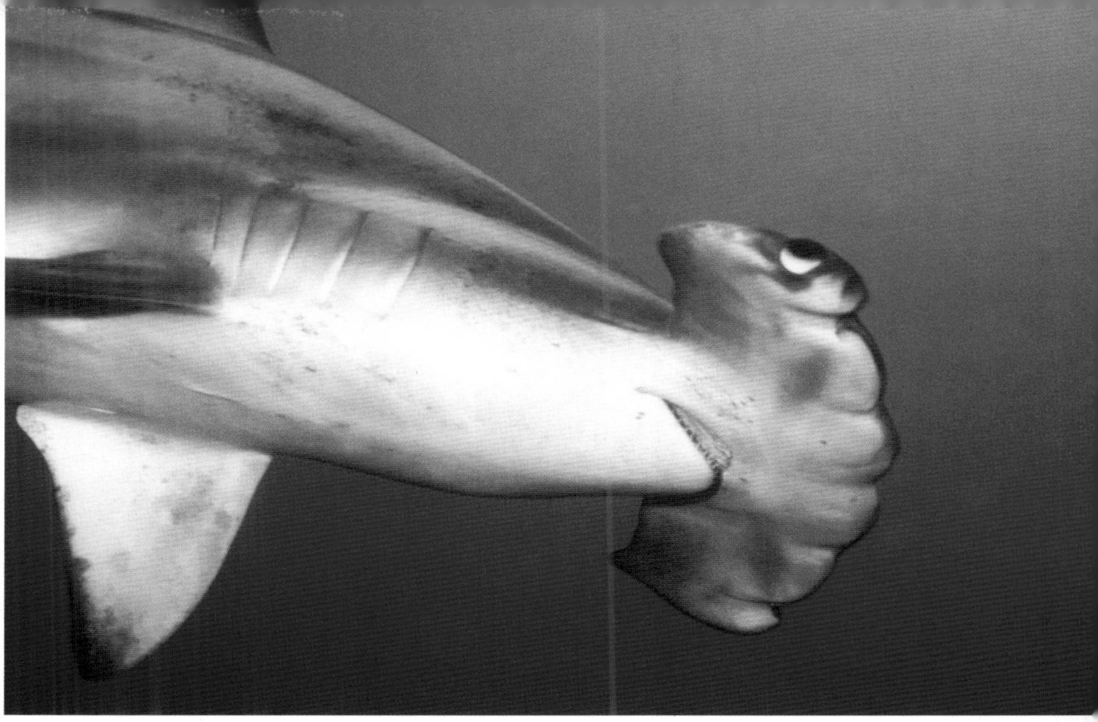

You can get a sense of nature's changing moods here during a single dive: temperature differences of 18°F/10°C and fluctuations in visibility between 15 and 65 ft/5–20 m may well occur, as can sudden changes in the current. The northeast trade winds and the Panama current generally bring higher water temperatures in the first half of the year. From July onward, the southeast trade winds and the Humboldt current cool the water down to between 61°F and 73°F (16–23°C).

Darwin Island lies just under 25 miles/40 km from Wolf. At the famous "Arch," thousands of bonitos swim around, sticking to their territory in densely packed formation. Hammerheads are also a permanent feature; sometimes there may be thirty of them, and sometimes more than three hundred. A few sea lions streak about acrobatically, often biting whitetip sharks' fins playfully. Rays are also at home here, and with luck on your side you may even see mantas or—during the months from August to November—a whale shark during your safety stop.

Opposite page: Sea lions are true underwater acrobats.

Top: A hammerhead shark at the southeast tip of Wolf Island.

Center: In the middle of a shoal of trevally.

Bottom: A rock crab in the intertidal zone.

This offshoot of the Atlantic is enclosed by the Bahamas in the north, the Lesser Antilles in the east, and the northern part of South America and the Central American isthmus in the west. This tropical dive region features magnificent reefs with gorgonian sea fans, sponges, and numerous fishes, as well as walls, wrecks, and caves. Spectacular encounters with sharks and dolphins are possible.

CARIBBEAN SEA

CARIBBEAN: GRENADA

Grenada

THIS CARIBBEAN ISLAND INVITES YOU TO VISIT FOR EASY DIVING IN ITS CLEAR, WARM, AND FISH-RICH WATERS. OFF THE COAST, THERE ARE NUMEROUS WRECKS, INTACT CORAL REEFS, AND AN UNDERWATER SCULPTURE PARK.

The state of Grenada, which is a member of the Commonwealth of Nations, comprises Grenada itself, known as the Spice Island, together with the neighboring islands of Carriacou (see spot no. 82) and Petit Martinique. It lies approximately 110 miles/180 km north of Venezuela and forms part of the Lesser Antilles.

Since Grenada was discovered by Columbus in 1498, it has been shaped by history. Its best-known export success is nutmeg, but tourism is the major factor in the economy. Its many dream beaches and the diverse range of activity holidays lure more than 400,000 tourists each year, including quite a number of divers. A few dive centers have been established around the southwestern corner of the island, where about a dozen dive sites are located. Nutrient-rich water and currents attract large numbers of fish. Many of the dives can also be accomplished by beginners.

Grenada's showpiece wreck, the *Bianca C*, on the other hand, is reserved for experienced divers only. The 650-ft-long/200-m-long cruise ship, also known as the "Titanic of the Caribbean," sits upright in 170 ft/52 m of water on Wibbles Reef. The dive here is a free-fall descent through currents down to the upper deck at a depth of 100 ft/30 m. The wreck has created an oasis and a place for flora and fauna to multiply, and always has a surprise in store.

Sites suitable for novices include the *Quarter* wreck (at a depth of 30 ft/10 m) and the *Veronica*

81 **FACTS**

- **Depth:** 30–130 ft/10–40 m
- **Visibility:** 50–165 ft/15–50 m
- **Water temperature:** 75–84°F/24–29°C
- **Best time of year:** Nov–May
- **Level of difficulty:** ■–■■■■■
- **Diversity of coral species:** ■■■■
- **Diversity of fish species:** ■■■■
- **Big fish:** ■■■
- **Wrecks:** ■■■■■
- **Caves:** ■
- **Walls:** ■■
- **Snorkeling:** ■■■

(50 ft/15 m). The *Shakem* and *Rum Runner* wrecks both lie in about 100 ft/30 m of water and are worthwhile dives for advanced divers. The *HEMA I* (at a depth of 110 ft/33 m), which sank as recently as 2005, has become home to a number of nurse sharks that previously lived on the *San Juan* (at 90 ft/28 m) and the *King Mitch* (at 125 ft/38 m). These three wrecks are not easy and, because of the currents, cannot always be dived. Eagle rays, turtles, and stingrays are regular visitors.

Splendid and typically Caribbean coral gardens such as Tropicana, Japanese Gardens, and Japanese Valleys lie on Boss Reef offshore from the well-known beach of Grand Anse in the southwest. Located farther to the north is a protected marine park containing the dive sites Flamingo Bay, Happy Hill, and Moliniere Bay. These beautiful coral sites are relatively flat and thus also ideal for snorkelers.

On the rougher Atlantic side, there is a nurse shark nursery on Shark Reef, where you will also see an occasional manta flying past. Lobster Point was named after its large numbers of lobsters and Stingray City after its rays.

In the past few years, considerable attention has been given to the underwater sculpture park at Moliniere Bay on the west coast, where the 65 sculptures by artist Jason Taylor can be easily viewed by snorkelers.

Opposite page: A nurse shark seeking protection on the wreck of the *San Juan*.

Top: Superb soft-coral gardens are to be found even in shallow waters.

Center: Looking through a porthole on the *King Mitch*.

Bottom: A fight between hermit crabs.

Carriacou

IF YOU WANT THE PRISTINE, PEACEFUL CARIBBEAN AND EXTENSIVE GARDENS OF HARD AND SOFT CORALS, YOU WILL FIND WHAT YOU ARE LOOKING FOR AT THE DIVE SITES AROUND CARRIACOU. THIS ISLAND FORMS PART OF THE GRENADINES AND IS STILL A WELL-KEPT SECRET.

Carriacou, Grenada's small neighbor, can be reached from there by high-speed ferry or small plane. Most of the inhabitants make their living from agriculture; the hectic pace of modern living is an alien concept, and tourism plays a minimal role. There are only small guesthouses, and all diving is done from boats. The name Carriacou translates as "land of the reefs," and this mountainous island is indeed surrounded by impressive and intact coral reefs. With its dive sites close by, it is a little paradise for divers and snorkelers.

Unlike most Caribbean destinations, but like Grenada, Carriacou lies outside the hurricane belt, so you can also dive here between June and November, when the rest of the Caribbean regularly experiences hurricanes.

Tall soft-coral forests and impressive black coral fans, various hard corals, and giant sponges are common here. There is also a fascinating range of marine fauna. From small nudibranchs and crabs to large spiny lobsters, from tiny blennies to majestic barracudas and large sharks, many of the species that live in the Caribbean are represented. At between 25 and 80 ft/ 8–25 m below the surface, conditions are ideal for diving, and there is seldom a need to go much deeper.

Most dive sites lie to the west of the island, offshore from the small capital of Hillsborough. Divers Surprise is a treat for macro lovers, and Western Adventure off Sandy Island, where larger fish are often present, is suitable for drift dives.

It is astonishing that despite the many reefs there are virtually no wrecks. Near the diminutive island of Mabouya, two old tugboats have been sunk to create artificial reefs. Off the island's coast you can also dive among virtually untouched coral forests in the World of Dreams, and large nurse sharks doze during the day at the adjacent site of Sharky's Hideaway. At Magic Garden, there is constant bubbling from the sand due to volcanic activity, making it a real paradise for nudibranchs.

The nearby site of Sister Rocks provides first-class dives with soft corals, gorgonian sea fans, sponges, trumpetfish, spiny lobsters, snappers, turtles, and trevally. At Chinatown, off the coast of the southern island of Frigate, the coral formations are reminiscent of pagodas, and at Tobago Keys eagle rays and reef sharks can be encountered.

Not far from the deep and still intact submerged volcano Kick'em Jenny, a superior-class diving area beckons: this is the Isle de Rhonde, which you can access either from Carriacou or from Grenada. Whip corals as well as elephant ear, vase and giant barrel sponges grow on the deep wall here.

Opposite page: Pillar corals at the Pagoda City dive site.

Above right: A portrait of a small pipefish.

Below right: A fine specimen of a spiny lobster.

82 FACTS

- **Depth:** 25–130 ft/8–40 m
- **Visibility:** 50–200 ft/15–60 m
- **Water temperature:** 77–84°F/ 25–29°C
- **Best time of year:** Nov–May
- **Level of difficulty:** ■–■■■■■
- **Diversity of coral species:** ■■■■
- **Diversity of fish species:** ■■■■
- **Big fish:** ■■■
- **Wrecks:** ■■■
- **Caves:** ■
- **Walls:** ■■■
- **Snorkeling:** ■■■■

CARIBBEAN: NETHERLANDS ANTILLES

Bonaire

THIS ISLAND IS REFERRED TO BY ITS INHABITANTS AS A DIVERS' PARADISE. ITS FANTASTIC UNDERWATER ENVIRONMENT AND ITS MANY DIVE SITES, WHICH CAN ALL BE DIVED INDEPENDENTLY FROM THE SHORE, ARE TRULY CAPTIVATING.

Bonaire belongs geographically to the Lesser Antilles and politically to the Netherlands Antilles. It is a highly acclaimed and well-known dive location. The island lies about 50 miles/80 km off the coast of Venezuela, is surrounded by a fringing reef, and is not prone to the influence of seasonal hurricanes.

The barren, boomerang-shaped coral-limestone island of Bonaire measures 24 miles/39 km in length and 3–5 miles/5–11 km in width. Around its highest point of 787 ft/240 m above sea level in the north is the Washington Slagbaai National Park, which covers more than 15 acres (6 ha) and features giant cacti and 200 bird species. Further attractions include the Pekelmeer with its salt pans and large number of flamingos, the former slave settlement at Witte Pan, and the offshore island of Klein Bonaire.

However, the island's greatest treasures are to be found underwater. The first to recognize this was the oceanographer Hans Hass, who enthused about this divers' paradise in his books at a time when the sport of recreational diving did not even exist. Bonaire went on the offensive to protect the underwater world very early on, serving as a model for others to follow: he worked to ban the sale of turtle products, the practice of harpooning, and the collection of corals and shellfish. As long ago as 1979, the government decided to declare the coastal area around the island down to a depth of 200 ft/60 m a protected marine park.

83 FACTS

- **Depth:** 30–130 ft/10–40 m
- **Visibility:** 50–180 ft/15–55 m
- **Water temperature:** 77–84°F/25–29°C
- **Best time of year:** All year round
- **Level of difficulty:** ■–■■■
- **Diversity of coral species:** ■■■■
- **Diversity of fish species:** ■■■■
- **Big fish:** ■■■
- **Wrecks:** ■■
- **Caves:** ■
- **Walls:** ■■■
- **Snorkeling:** ■■■

Today, there are many resorts and centers hiring out diving equipment. A special feature of diving on Bonaire is that, provided you follow detailed instructions and comply with the park rules, you can dive on the superb fringing reef completely independently from the shore. With a car, you can drive to the western lee side and seek out the best entry point for one of the sixty listed dive sites (for example, 1,000 Steps, Angel City, Bari Reef...), which are all marked by yellow-painted rocks along the coastal road.

In these turquoise waters, the tropical underwater landscapes, ranging from gentle slopes to steep walls, featuring spectacular flora and fauna and the occasional wreck, will cast their spell over you. Besides the many fishes, the pink-colored sea fans, soft corals, and many different sponges delight more than 50,000 dive tourists a year. The dive centers also organize boat tours to Klein Bonaire, where there are an equal number of worthwhile diving spots.

Opposite page: A shrimp in an anemone.

Above: A colorful sap-sucking slug on a sponge.

Left: A curious tiny blenny peers out of its coral castle.

CARIBBEAN: HONDURAS

Roatan

THE MAIN ISLAND OF THE ISLAS DE LA BAHIA OFF THE NORTHERN COAST OF HONDURAS IS SURROUNDED BY TOP DIVE SITES. HERE YOU WILL FIND SUBLIME UNDERWATER LANDSCAPES, AN IMMENSE ARRAY OF FISHES, AND DOLPHINS YOU CAN DIVE WITH.

Honduras, on the isthmus of Central America, has long been a draw for American divers and connoisseurs of the Caribbean, though islands like Guanaja, Barbareta, Utila, the Cayos Cochinos, or Roatan mean little to the majority of the international diving community. A trip here is worthwhile not only because of the impressive unspoiled natural environment and the Mayan ruins of Copan on the mainland, but also because of the diving grounds around the offshore islands.

The Islas de la Bahia, also known as the Bay Islands, form part of the world's second-largest barrier reef, situated on an undersea mountain chain about 30 miles/50 km from the mainland. Roatan is the largest of the islands, and is 30 miles/49 km long, but only 3 miles/5 km wide.

Dive tourists are very well catered for, with a whole series of resorts and dive shops. Diving is frequently organized along American lines, in fairly large groups and in a highly disciplined fashion, which is something individual divers sometimes have problems with. You should therefore find out in advance how the individual dive shops operate. Tourism is centered in the west of the island, and things are quieter in the southeast. Dive cruises around Roatan and the beautiful neighboring islands are also available.

The reefs on the north side initially fall off gradually down to 30–40 ft/10–12 m and then drop

84 FACTS

- **Depth:** 20–130 ft/6–40 m
- **Visibility:** 50–130 ft/15–40 m
- **Water temperature:** 77–84°F/ 25–29°C
- **Best time of year:** Dec–June
- **Level of difficulty:** ■–■■■
- **Diversity of coral species:** ■■■■
- **Diversity of fish species:** ■■■■
- **Big fish:** ■■■
- **Wrecks:** ■■■
- **Caves:** ■■■
- **Walls:** ■■■■
- **Snorkeling:** ■■■ (Snorkeling with dolphins at Anthony's Key Resort ■■■■■)

away steeply to between 100 and 130 ft/30–40 m. On the south side, the 130 to 165-ft-deep (40 to 50-m-deep) drop-offs begin just 15 ft/5 m down.

Resting on the sandy bottom in 65 ft/20 m of water at French Harbor on the south coast is the wreck of the *Prince Albert*, which provides numerous hiding places for a number of fish. As soon as the dive boat anchors at the dive site Fishsoup, the water will seethe with large quantities of fish. The reason for this is that they are regularly fed by the dive guides. Wonderful displays of light can be enjoyed at a break in the reef at Calvin's Crack, and you can see photogenic chasms, giant gorgonian sea fans, and sponges at Church Wall. One of the most beautiful sites is Mary's Place, with an imposing and varied landscape that includes canyons. Also popular are Herbie's Place at the southwestern corner and Herbie's Fantasy on the western side.

More than two dozen worthwhile dive spots are located in close proximity to Anthony's Key Resort, which belongs to the island's dive pioneer. The resort's comfortable over-water bungalows stand on the reef off a small island on the north coast, where a marine park guarantees plenty of fish. The resort's specialities are close-up dolphin encounters in the resort's own pool and a dive spot with gray reef sharks.

Opposite page: A colorful creole wrasse.

Above: A cheerful boxfish.

Right: A pair of gray angelfish.

CARIBBEAN: MEXICO

Banco Chinchorro

VIRTUALLY UNKNOWN AND UNSPOILED, THE CARIBBEAN ATOLL OF BANCO CHINCHORRO LIES BETWEEN THE TOURIST HOTSPOTS OF COZUMEL AND BELIZE. IT BOASTS GIANT SPONGES, A PRODIGIOUS VARIETY OF CORALS, AND A LARGE SHIPS' GRAVEYARD.

This atoll lies off Mexico's Yucatán Peninsula, on a level with the Costa Maya. It can only be reached by dive boat from the fishing villages of Majahual and Xcalak.

The Banco Chinchorro, which measures about 28 by 9 miles/45 by 15 km, has been designated a biosphere reserve by UNESCO and an archaeological marine protected area by the Mexican government. The only inhabitants are about 200 fishermen who live in stilt houses off the coast of the largest of the three islands in the atoll's lagoon. There are plans to ban fishing completely in the future.

A submerged valley 3,300 ft/1,000 m deep and 18 miles/30 km wide separates Banco Chinchorro from the mainland. Dive centers need a permit to head out to the reefs. Day trips including three dives are available; the main problem is usually the boat journey over quite often rough seas to get there, which takes about two hours.

More than a dozen protected top diving spots are located on the western side. Some of these are smallish drop-offs, others are sandy 45-degree slopes in clear water. Areas of 3-ft-tall (1-m-tall) gorgonians and other sea fans alternate with Caribbean sponges.

At the dive spot Punta Isabel, corals and sponges dominate and there tend to be fewer fish. At Theresa, on the other hand, you will be rewarded with sightings of rare cobias (which look similar to sharks), blue fusiliers, and various species of sea bass. There are also yellow vase sponges of gigantic dimensions here. Los Faros, at a depth of 65–80 ft/20–25 m, is a colorful, unspoiled site with purple vase sponges, orange elephant ear sponges, and giant barrel sponges. Groupers and nurse sharks love the strong currents of Tinas Reef at the southern tip, where grunts and snappers hide in small caves when there is danger.

At the Forty Cannon Galleon dive site, a wreck from the seventeenth century lies in just 13–26 ft/4–8 m of water. The many cannons are so densely colonized with corals that they can scarcely be recognized any longer. Further remnants of innumerable wrecks dating from the sixteenth to the twentieth centuries can be found on the rough eastern side of the atoll. For archaeological reasons, only snorkeling is permitted at these sites. On the reef directly facing Xcalak, you can dive in caves and crevices at Chiminea, and in summer you will encounter hundreds of tarpons at La Poza.

Opposite page: A giant tube sponge.

Above right: Old cannons can still be found on the Banco Chinchorro.

Below right: A diver in a chimney.

85 FACTS

- **Depth:** 15–115 ft/5–35 m
- **Visibility:** 30–115 ft/10–35 m
- **Water temperature:** 75–84°F/24–29°C
- **Best time of year:** May–Nov
- **Level of difficulty:** ■–■■■
- **Diversity of coral species:** ■■■■
- **Diversity of fish species:** ■■■
- **Big fish:** ■■■
- **Wrecks:** ■■■ (Only snorkeling is allowed.)
- **Caves:** ■■
- **Walls:** ■■
- **Snorkeling:** ■■■■

CARIBBEAN: BELIZE

Belize

BELIZE IS ONE OF THE CARIBBEAN'S MOST VISITED DIVE DESTINATIONS. ON ITS THREE ATOLLS AND THE WORLD'S SECOND-LARGEST BARRIER REEF, DIVERS WILL FIND COUNTLESS BREATHTAKING DIVE SITES WITH WALLS AND AN EXTREMELY DIVERSE RANGE OF FISH LIFE.

This small Central American state to the south of Mexico and east of Guatemala has been independent since 1981. Virgin rainforests containing rare animals and plants, Mayan temples, gorgeous sandy beaches, secluded islands, and coral reefs make the country a real attraction, and not just for divers.

Two major diving regions can be distinguished: the approximately 185-mile-long/ 300-km-long Belize Barrier Reef, which constitutes the largest barrier reef in the northern hemisphere and the second-largest in the world, and three atolls located farther to the east.

The Belize Barrier Reef accommodates several national and marine parks and has been designated a UNESCO World Heritage Site. It includes many islands and small sandbanks known as cayes. Most of the smaller cayes are uninhabited, while some have resorts on them. The following (from north to south) are some of the best-known islands and places with numerous dive sites: Ambergris Caye, Hol Chan Marine Reserve, Caulkner Caye, Long Caye, Alligator Caye, Tobacco Caye, Queens Caye, and Hunting Caye. There are daily trips to these sites from the dive resorts.

Farther to the east in the Caribbean Sea lie three separate atolls: Turneffe Atoll, Glover's Reef, and Lighthouse Reef, the latter extending along a different submarine ridge from the first two. Between the two ridges there is a deep trench, and thrilling big-fish encounters are possible. Hard corals and gorgonian sea

86 FACTS

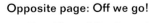

- Depth: 15–130 ft/5–40 m
- Visibility: 50–165 ft/15–50 m
- Water temperature: 75–84°F/24–29°C
- Best time of year: Nov–May
- Level of difficulty: ■–■■■
- Diversity of coral species: ■■■■
- Diversity of fish species: ■■■■
- Big fish: ■■■
- Wrecks: ■■
- Caves: ■■■■
- Walls: ■■■■■
- Snorkeling: ■■■■■

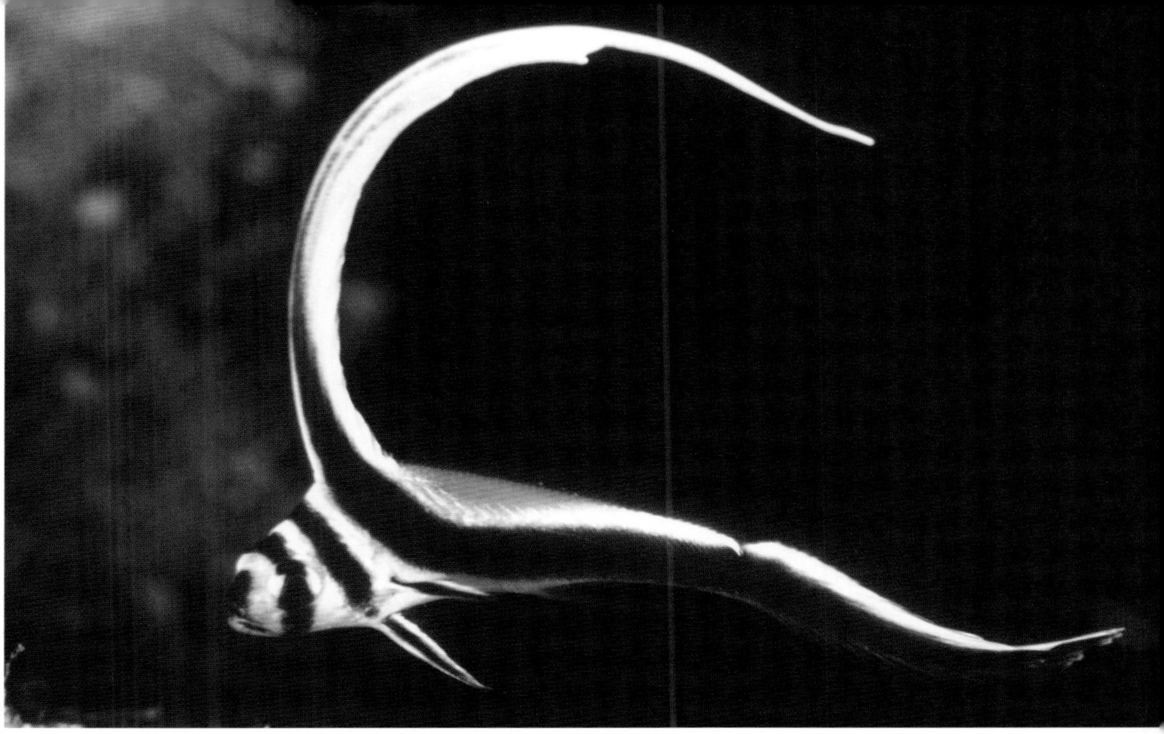

fans grow everywhere: on walls, between canyons, and on gentle slopes. The waters abound with more than 400 fish species, from small sea bass to large sharks. The various nudibranchs, shellfish, and crabs, together with the many sponges, make the reefs a real El Dorado for divers.

The Lighthouse Reef is the most beautiful reef, both above and below water. One of its many attractive dive sites is the famous Blue Hole (see spot no. 87). Not far from the bird paradise of Half Moon Caye lie further dive spots with fantastic coral gardens and an immense wealth of fish.

Those who wish to dive the best sites on the atolls in a more leisurely and extended way than is possible on the one- or two-day tours should opt for a week-long live-aboard trip. These are offered by several operators and depart from the harbor in Belize City. Based on the American model, up to five dives a day are organized, so you can stay in the water from early morning until after sunset, apart from any necessary breaks.

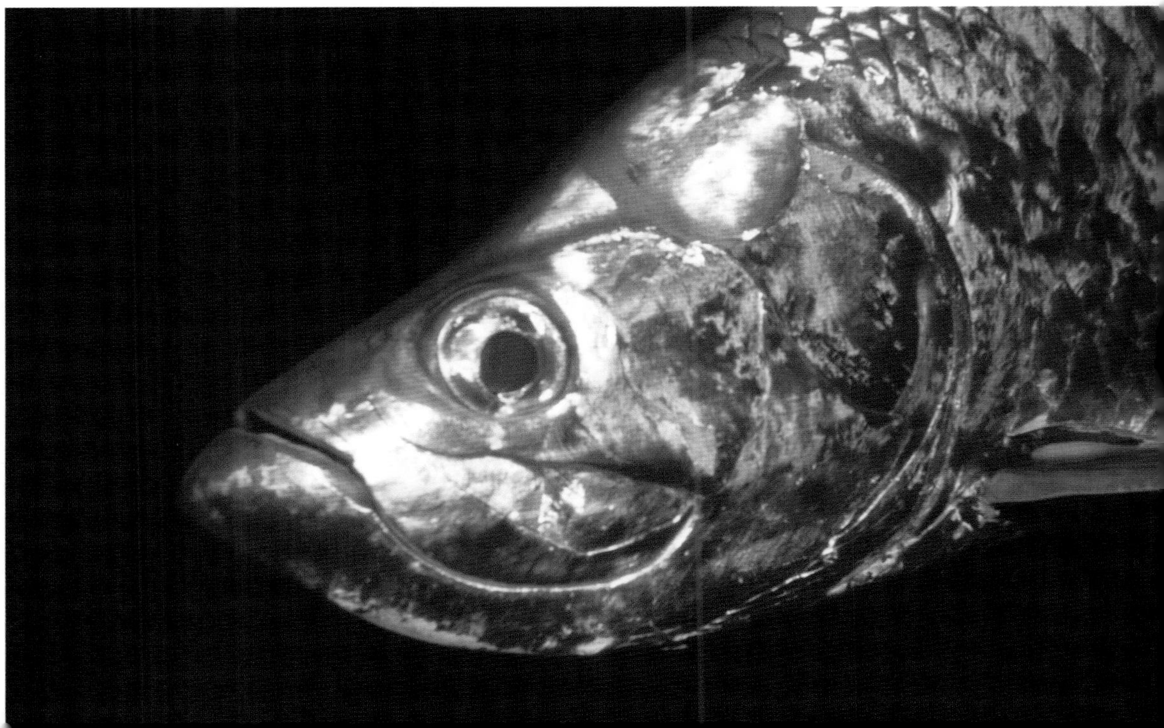

Opposite page: Off we go!

Top: The oddly shaped jackknife fish.

Center: The indigo hamlet belongs to the family of serranids (sea basses and groupers).

Bottom: A shining silver tarpon.

Blue Hole

THIS DEEP CIRCULAR HOLE WITH ITS LONG STALACTITES OFFERS A SPECIAL KIND OF DIVING EXPERIENCE AND A PURE ADRENALINE RUSH. THE BLUE HOLE ON LIGHTHOUSE REEF OFF THE COAST OF BELIZE IS A LEGENDARY SITE WITH CULT STATUS.

The Blue Hole is to American divers what Ras Mohammed is to Europeans—if you dive in Belize, then "Blue Hole" has to appear in your logbook. Cousteau's expedition in 1972 and his subsequent film made this deep blue site famous the world over.

After a labyrinthine journey through the reefs, you anchor about 100 yd/100 m from the site and snorkel to its edge. You start by diving down slowly to 25 ft/8 m, and then comes the abyss: there is a sheer vertical drop with virtually no vegetation. After 100 ft/30 m things become clearer, and the first stalactites appear under overhangs. Below a depth of 150 ft/45 m it becomes truly awesome, with 3-ft-thick (1-m-thick) limestone columns hanging down that measure from 20 to 23 ft/6 to 7 m in length.

The marine crater measures 440 yd/400 m in diameter and is about 460 ft/140 m deep. It was formed—probably as a result of an earthquake millions of years ago—when the roof collapsed into a large cave in the middle of the underground cave system, which was originally filled with air.

It is the atmosphere at Blue Hole that attracts divers. Only seldom does a shark, a turtle, or a school of trevally lose its way and end up in this mystical place.

87 FACTS

- **Depth:** 10–165 ft/3–50 m
- **Visibility:** 50–130 ft/15–40 m
- **Water temperature:** 75–84°F/24–29°C
- **Best time of year:** Nov–May
- **Level of difficulty:** ■■■–■■■■■
- **Diversity of coral species:** ■
- **Diversity of fish species:** ■
- **Big fish:** ■
- **Wrecks:** –
- **Caves:** ■■■■■
- **Walls:** ■■■■■
- **Snorkeling:** ■■

Below left: A bird's-eye view of the Blue Hole.

Below right: A giant stalactite in Belize's Blue Hole.

CARIBBEAN: US

Florida Keys

THIS CHAIN OF ISLANDS IN SOUTHERN FLORIDA IS AMERICA'S DIVING MECCA. INTERESTING MARINE PARKS AND EASY-TO-DIVE, SPECIES-RICH REEFS AND WRECKS ARE THE REASONS WHY.

Highway no. 1 links the islands in this approximately 135-mile-long/220-km-long chain, which lies between the Gulf of Mexico and the Caribbean Sea. Off the islands' shores stretch the only coral reefs in the US, and the flawlessly organized day excursions, on which two dives per boat trip are the norm everywhere, consequently attract large numbers.

The dive sites and dive shops are mainly concentrated (from north to south) on the islands of Key Largo, Islamorada, Marathon, and the Lower Keys, including Key West. Diving always takes place on the Caribbean side, where all the reefs begin about 5 miles/8 km away from the islands.

The most dived location is the John Pennekamp Coral Reef State Park off Key Largo, with its forty dive spots. The most well-known site here is the 10-ft-tall/3-m-tall bronze statue of Christ, which is a copy of a statue near Genoa.

There are wrecks, a wealth of colorful fish, stately barracudas, and sea bass, as well as remarkable elkhorn and brain coral gardens at many sites.

Above left: The eyes of the common spider conch.

Above right: A spotted grouper.

Left: An elegant queen triggerfish.

88 **FACTS**

- **Depth:** 15–115 ft/5–35 m
- **Visibility:** 30–115 ft/10–35 m
- **Water temperature:** 68–90°F/20–32°C
- **Best time of year:** Oct–May
- **Level of difficulty:** ■–■■■
- **Diversity of coral species:** ■■■
- **Diversity of fish species:** ■■■■
- **Big fish:** ■■■
- **Wrecks:** ■■■■
- **Caves:** ■■
- **Walls:** ■
- **Snorkeling:** ■■■

CARIBBEAN: BAHAMAS

Bahamas

THE BAHAMAS OFFER ALMOST PERFECT CONDITIONS AND OPPORTUNITIES FOR DIVERS: WARM, CLEAR WATER, AN ABUNDANCE OF CORAL AND FISH, CAVES, WRECKS, ENCOUNTERS WITH SHARKS AND DOLPHINS, AND AN EXCELLENT INFRASTRUCTURE.

More than 700 islands and innumerable small cayes make up the archipelago, which stretches some 550 miles/almost 900 km from the east coast of Florida to the northeast of Cuba.

Up until 1973, the country was ruled from the United Kingdom, and since that year it has been a sovereign member of the Commonwealth of Nations.

Columbus gave the islands the name of "Baja Mar," which translates as "shallow sea." However, this is only to be found on the calmer and clearer Caribbean side, which people often compare to a colossal aquarium. The Atlantic side is rougher and deeper, but in return holds out the promise of more big fish.

Only thirty islands in the Bahamas are inhabited, and of these New Providence and Grand Bahama are the largest. They each have an international airport, and a few of the other islands, which are grouped together under the name Out Islands, also have small airfields. According to official figures, more than thirty dive destinations comprising more than a thousand dive sites now beckon in the Bahamas. The dive shops, resorts, and live-aboards conform to high international standards.

It is easy to see why enthusiasts have been coming here from all over the world since the early days of dive tourism: The water is clear and warm, and there are wonderfully overgrown submarine landscapes in shallow waters as well as on steeply

89 FACTS

- **Depth:** 15–130 ft/5–40 m
- **Visibility:** 50–165 ft/15–50 m
- **Water temperature:** 75–84°F/24–29°C
- **Best time of year:** Nov–June
- **Level of difficulty:** ■–■■■
- **Diversity of coral species:** ■■■■
- **Diversity of fish species:** ■■■■
- **Big fish:** ■■■■■
- **Wrecks:** ■■■■
- **Caves:** ■■■■■
- **Walls:** ■■■■■
- **Snorkeling:** ■■■■

descending drop-offs. In addition, there are a number of cave systems, deep blue holes, and numerous exciting wrecks.

The 2,000 reefs and sandbanks were formerly an ideal hiding place for pirates—and today they remain a paradise for treasure divers.

Stuart Cove's dive center on New Providence is world-famous, offering a number of adventures: scooter diving, trips in mini-submersibles, shark feeding under strict safety instructions, and diving on famous wrecks.

The UNEXSO project's curious dolphins and impressive gray reef sharks have for many years been one of Grand Bahama's most spectacular attractions. The circus-standard choreographed performances by the animals are usually fully booked. Besides these, special shark safaris are offered in which you can get close to tiger sharks, lemon sharks, and bull sharks. These spectacles have both supporters and opponents. Some are critical and foresee accidents, while others believe that the dives and films will change the image that most people have of these elegant predators and will reveal that humankind is the danger and that the shark is not a bloodthirsty monster.

Opposite page: In close contact with a dolphin.

Above: A magnificently colored king angelfish.

Left: Gray reef sharks off Grand Bahama.

Turks & Caicos Islands

THIS COUNTRY, WHICH COMPRISES TWO ISLAND GROUPS, LIES BETWEEN THE ATLANTIC AND THE CARIBBEAN. FROM JANUARY TO MARCH, YOU CAN SNORKEL WITH HUMPBACK WHALES. THERE ARE BIG FISH HERE AND, MOST IMPORTANTLY, SUNSHINE ALL YEAR ROUND.

This island state lies north of the Dominican Republic and southeast of the Bahamas. There are more than forty islands and cayes, barely a quarter of which are inhabited. They have been under Spanish, French, and British rule, and they once belonged to the Bahamas and for a long period to Jamaica. The state is a British overseas territory, with the US dollar as its currency.

Tourism is vibrant and booming and is the principal source of revenue, with the number of flights from the US increasing steadily. Tourists are wooed by twelve months of sunshine, white powder beaches, and pristine Caribbean waters, with the added attraction for divers of "Big Blue Unlimited" and big fish: between January and March, the humpback whales pass by, coming from the Arctic Ocean and heading for the Silver Banks or Mouchoir Banks to give birth to their young there. There are only a few places in the world where snorkeling with these giants is both possible and permitted.

Almost all the archipelago's dive sites can be reached on day boats or dived during one-week live-aboard tours on cruisers. Most of the dive sites are located on walls off the protected sides of the islands. The best are to be found in Northwest Point Marine Park off the coast of the western island of Providenciales, in West Caicos National Park, and off the islands of South Caicos and French Caye. The reefs off Grand Turk and Salt Caye are visited less often.

In Northwest Point Marine Park, there is first-class wall-diving on a reef more than 3 miles/5 km in length. The dive site Thunderdome, a hemispherical steel grid that was originally constructed for a French television show, is popular. At Black Coral Forest, black corals project from the wall, while The Crack is home to anemones and sponges.

Most of the sites off West Caicos lie in the 6-mile-long/10-km-long Marine Park. A host of horse-eye jacks welcomes divers at Rock Garden Interlude, while gray sharks swim around at White Face and Highway to Heaven. All kinds of sponges grow at the dive spot known as Land of the Giants, but there are even more to be seen at Tons of Sponge.

The most spectacular dive sites are those off French Caye, 15 miles/24 km southeast of West Caicos. Here, nurse sharks give birth to their young in summer. The G-Spot is famed for black corals and sharks, Double D for eagle rays. West Sand Spit, situated to the south, is seldom visited. It is an unspoiled coral garden with schools of yellow sea bream, colorful angelfish, large Nassau groupers, and small sharks.

Opposite page: A sea squirt colony between black corals.

Below left: A huge vase sponge.

Below right: A view through the steel grid encrusted with sponges at Thunderdome.

90 FACTS

- **Depth:** 10–130 ft/3–40 m
- **Visibility:** 50–130 ft/15–40 m
- **Water temperature:** 75–86°F/24–30°C
- **Best time of year:** Nov–June
- **Level of difficulty:** ■–■■■
- **Diversity of coral species:** ■■■■
- **Diversity of fish species:** ■■■■
- **Big fish:** ■■■■■
- **Wrecks:** ■■
- **Caves:** ■■■
- **Walls:** ■■■■■
- **Snorkeling:** ■■■■

CARIBBEAN: CUBA

Southwest Cuba

THE NORTH COAST OF CUBA BORDERS ON THE ATLANTIC, THE SOUTH COAST ON THE CARIBBEAN SEA. THERE ARE INTERESTING DIVE LOCATIONS RIGHT AROUND THE ISLAND, BUT THE SOUTHWEST STANDS OUT, AS THIS IS WHERE THE CARIBBEAN SHOWS ITSELF AT ITS BEST UNDER THE WATER.

Cuba is the largest Caribbean island and has a coastline totaling about 3,600 miles/5,800 km and containing almost 300 beaches. Although it is only about 90 miles/140 km from the US coast and only 130 miles/210 km from Mexico, Cuba is a largely isolated country. However, it appears to be only a matter of time before this changes. This socialist state is a fascinating country, with the best diving spots of the entire Caribbean. Unfortunately, though, the planned economy does not particularly promote dive tourism, so in comparison to other dive destinations only limited development is taking place.

The best dive locations lie toward the Yucatán Basin and Cayman Ridge. Off the coast of Cuba, the best sites are around the western tip, at Cabo San Antonio and Maria La Gorda. To these can be added the areas around the islands of the Canarreos Archipelago, Cayo Largo, and Isla de la Juventud, as well as the island group of Jardines de la Reina (see spot no. 92).

Maria La Gorda lies on the western peninsula of Guanahacabibes, in the middle of a large national park and UNESCO biosphere reserve. The dive sites here are among Cuba's best, with a well-preserved underwater environment. There are a number of different caves, and on some reefs you can see the remnants of sunken galleys, including anchors and cannons.

There is a lot of virgin diving territory to explore at Cabo San Antonio, at the westernmost tip of the island. All the dive sites lie in the current-prone Yucatán Channel and feature blue holes, some of the larger marine inhabitants, and spectacular drift dives along drop-offs.

Cayo Largo is the easternmost island of the Canarreos Archipelago and has already established a reputation for itself among divers. Off the coast of the 17-mile-long/27-km-long former smugglers' island lie more than 40 dive spots, two of which carry the name Aquario: here you are sure to encounter grunts, snappers, barracudas, sea bass, moray eels, rays, tarpons, sharks, spiny lobsters, angelfish, and turtles. Caribbean fishes of all kinds are also to be found about 90 miles/150 km farther westward off the Isla de la Juventud. The largest of Cuba's lesser islands is alleged to have inspired Robert Louis Stevenson to write his novel *Treasure Island*. From the Colony marina, superlative dive sites with canyons, caverns, and labyrinths can be reached in about an hour and a half by boat. There is always the possibility of encountering big fish off luxuriantly overgrown drop-offs. The site has been a marine protected area since 1980.

Opposite page: A curious grouper checking out a diver.

Above: The dive site El Salon de Maria at Maria La Gorda.

Below: A young blueface angelfish cleaning a grunt.

91 FACTS

- **Depth:** 10–130 ft/3–40 m
- **Visibility:** 30–165 ft/10–50 m
- **Water temperature:** 75–86°F/ 24–30°C
- **Best time of year:** Nov–June
- **Level of difficulty:** ■–■■■
- **Diversity of coral species:** ■■■■■
- **Diversity of fish species:** ■■■■■
- **Big fish:** ■■■■■
- **Wrecks:** ■■■
- **Caves:** ■■■■
- **Walls:** ■■■■■
- **Snorkeling:** ■■■■

Jardines de la Reina

THIS ARCHIPELAGO OFF THE SOUTH COAST OF CUBA WAS DISCOVERED AND NAMED BY CHRISTOPHER COLUMBUS. THE REGION INCLUDES ABOUT 600 CORAL ISLANDS AND IS CONSIDERED TO BE CUBA'S BEST DIVE LOCATION. IT IS HOME TO BIG FISH OF ALL KINDS.

As a sailor in the services of the Spanish, Columbus was the first to come to this island paradise, where he immediately recognized the diversity of the flora and fauna, so he named the archipelago "The Queen's Gardens" in honor of the Spanish queen Isabella.

Today, the Parque Nacional Jardines de la Reina, which covers about 850 square miles/2,200 square km, is one of the largest conservation areas in Cuba. However, nature's abundance on the islands is in evidence not only on land, but also underwater, so an area measuring 100 by 22 miles/160 by 36 km has been designated a marine park. The fish population has been rising steadily since commercial fishing was banned in 1996. Due to the many species of sharks, groupers, barracudas, and tarpons, as well as the schools of fish found here, it is often called the Caribbean's "Big Fish Paradise."

The number of divers is limited to 400 visitors annually. The only dive center in this underwater paradise is a floating hotel complex anchored between mangroves, with a dive shop and space for fourteen guests. Anyone wishing to travel here has to allow more than three hours for the 55-mile-long/90-km-long boat ride from the town of Jucaro on Cuba across the Golfo de Ana Maria. In addition, there are currently three safari boats that visit the famous diving area.

The fifty listed dive spots lie in a 40-mile-long/70-km-long area and are marked with buoys. There will doubtless be a couple of dozen silky sharks welcoming you at the Pippin dive site. When you jump into the water, be careful not to hit these fascinating predators. At one time, they were lured with feed for research purposes, as some of them had to be caught for relocating and the scientists didn't want to injure them in the process. The shark catchers discovered zones on their bodies which, when massaged, send the shark into a state of paralysis, also termed tonic immobility. The guides now occasionally play with them as you would with a young trained dog. Divers, however, are absolutely banned from doing this.

Close to the surface live enormous groupers, and in the canyons lurk magnificent tarpon and barracuda. Large numbers of fat reef sharks besiege the dive site Black Coral, while La Cana is a gorgeous picture-book coral garden full of fishes. The groupers living at Meseta de los Meros, which weigh up to 440 lb/200 kg, exhibit no fear of divers. Everywhere there are large turtles, tame lizards, and the occasional crocodile.

Opposite page: A shark whisperer putting a shark in a trance.

Below: The giant groupers at Meseta de los Meros display no shyness whatsoever.

92 FACTS

- **Depth:** 10–130 ft/3–40 m
- **Visibility:** 65–165 ft/20–50 m
- **Water temperature:** 75–86°F/24–30°C
- **Best time of year:** Nov–June
- **Level of difficulty:** ■–■■■
- **Diversity of coral species:** ■■■■■
- **Diversity of fish species:** ■■■■■
- **Big fish:** ■■■■■
- **Wrecks:** ■■■
- **Caves:** ■■■■
- **Walls:** ■■■■■
- **Snorkeling:** ■■■

CARIBBEAN: CAYMAN ISLANDS

Cayman Islands

IN THE MIDDLE OF THE CARIBBEAN LIES WHAT IS NOT ONLY THE WORLD'S FIFTH-LARGEST FINANCIAL CENTER, BUT ALSO ONE OF THE MOST BEAUTIFUL DIVING AREAS IN THE CARIBBEAN SEA—WITH WRECKS, WALLS, GENTLY SLOPING REEFS, CANYONS, AND FRIENDLY STINGRAYS.

Columbus discovered these islands and named them "Las Tortugas" after sea turtles; the indigenous people later gave them the name "Las Caymanas" after the lizards. The European great powers engaged in fierce sea battles here over the treasures from the plundered cultural sites of Central America, and rumors of Captain Blackbeard's pirate treasure still circulate.

Nowadays, the threads of the world of international finance and commerce come together in this small three-island state south of Cuba and northwest of Jamaica. No wonder, for the British Crown Colony is still a tax haven today. However, the islands' real wealth is the Caribbean Sea around them—it is excellent for swimming, windsurfing, sailing, fishing, and diving, although not exactly cheap.

Grand Cayman is, as the name suggests, the largest of the three islands. It is deemed to be one of the birthplaces of scuba diving and offers many opportunities for diving both from the shore and from boats.

There are well-known dive spots off the busy Seven-Mile Beach at West End, north of the capital George Town. Easy-to-dive sites, whose names speak for themselves, include Aquarium, Bonnie's Arch, the *Balbao* wreck, and the *Oro Verde* wreck. For experienced divers, there is also a variety of different drop-offs on the western side. Off the south coast, there are a number of relatively flat spots with coral

93 FACTS

- **Depth:** 12–130 ft/4–40 m
- **Visibility:** 50–130 ft/15–40 m
- **Water temperature:** 79–86°F/26–30°C
- **Best time of year:** Nov–June
- **Level of difficulty:** ■–■■■
- **Diversity of coral species:** ■■■■
- **Diversity of fish species:** ■■■■■
- **Big fish:** ■■■■
- **Wrecks:** ■■■■
- **Caves:** ■■■
- **Walls:** ■■■■■
- **Snorkeling:** ■■■■■

gardens such as Tarpon Alley, South Sound Garden, and Red Bay Gardens.

Several dozen sites are located on the northern and eastern sides, though these are not in the immediate vicinity of most of the dive shops. You must also bear in mind that this section of the coast is unprotected and lies at the mercy of the waves. The best-known spots besides the Turtle Farm in the northwest are Mini Wall, North Sound Reef, Grand Canyon, North Wall, and East Side Reefs.

Stingray City in the large protected bay of North Sound, in which for many years about 200 stingrays have gathered at various places to be fed by hand, is world-famous. Although these creatures have become very accustomed to humans, caution is still advised.

Things are much more sedate on the neighboring islands. Top-quality diving is possible off Little Cayman's west coast at Bloody Bay Wall, with its large sponges, corals, groupers, and turtles. What must be a unique experience in the Western hemisphere is a dive on a Russian warship. The 331-ft-long/101-m-long wreck was sunk in 1996 after being bought from the Cubans.

Opposite page: In the middle of a shoal of glassfish in a cave.

Above: Impressive elkhorn coral.

Right: Barracudas are the reef police.

Fresh water, the foundation on which our lives are built, accounts for a minute proportion of the water on our earth, and fresh waters attract a correspondingly small amount of attention from divers. Yet there are sublime freshwater dive spots all over the world, and once you have gazed into magical mountain lakes, crystal-clear springs, spectacular caves, and lakes, rivers, and mountain streams rich in fish, you will be spellbound.

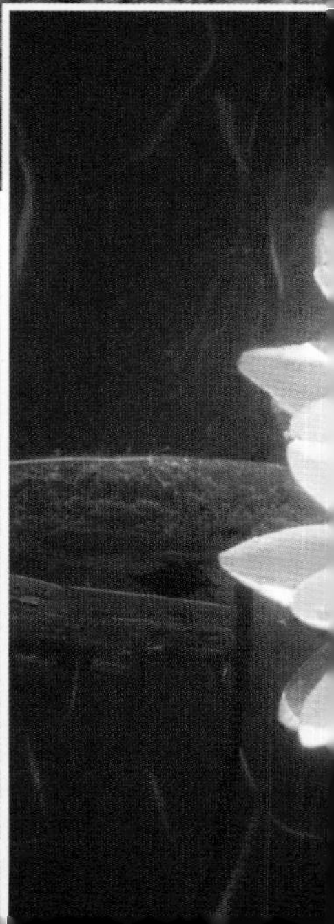

FRESH WATER

Crystal River

IN THE WINTER, MANATEES, ALSO KNOWN AS SEA COWS, TAKE UP RESIDENCE IN KINGS BAY AT CRYSTAL RIVER IN NORTHWEST FLORIDA. NOWHERE ELSE IN THE WORLD CAN DIVERS HAVE CLOSER CONTACT WITH A MARINE CREATURE THAN HERE.

The city of Crystal River on the Florida coast can be reached in just under two hours' drive from Orlando. The river of the same name has its source in Kings Bay. Warm springs ensure that the water temperatures stay fairly constant throughout the year at between 72 and 79°F/22 and 26°C. So in the winter months, when the Gulf of Mexico cools down, large numbers of manatees seek out its warmer waters in order to overwinter there.

There are more than 20 different rivers and springs in Florida to which these warm-blooded herbivores retire in the winter. The bay near Crystal River is the only area in which snorkelers are allowed to get close to them in the wild. These gentle sirenians, weighing up to 1,325 lb/600 kg, are fond not only of the temperatures in the conservation area but also of the seagrass and weed that grows there, of which they need—depending on their bodyweight—about 220 lb/100 kg a day.

A number of dive shops in Crystal River offer guided snorkeling tours to this unique attraction. If you want to try it on your own, you can also hire a boat, but it is not at all easy to find the mammals in the many branches of the bay. The colder it is outside, the better are the opportunities for close encounters with the manatees.

If you want to get a good look at these placid giants with their small button eyes, you have to head out at dawn. There is considerable congestion due to the numbers of people wanting to see these popular, ponderous animals, and if there is too much hustle and bustle they withdraw into the marked protection zones. Special rangers watch to ensure that no one intrudes, and anyone infringing the laws will face a severe fine. These "elephants of the sea" normally exhibit no shyness at all, quite the opposite, in fact, they often seek out contact with humans, which is a really fantastic experience.

The population worldwide is put at approximately 3,000 individuals, about 350 of which overwinter in Kings Bay. Manatees have no natural enemies, the principal danger for them being collisions with boats and injuries from propellers, as they continually have to come to the surface in order to breathe. They have been protected in the US since 1967, and various organizations run elaborate protection programs.

Since diving with the manatees takes place only in the mornings, afterwards you can dive down into one of the clearest rivers in the world, the Rainbow River, where the visibility can be up to 200 ft/60 m, in nearby Dunnellon.

Opposite page, top: Love among the manatees: sea cows in Crystal River.

Opposite page, bottom: A pair of manatees chilling out.

Below: Snorkeling in the crystal-clear Rainbow River.

94 FACTS

- **Depth:** 3–15 ft/1–5 m (With the manatees, only snorkeling is allowed.)
- **Visibility:** 10–130 ft/3–40 m
- **Water temperature:** in winter 72°F/22°C
- **Best time of year:** Nov–Mar
- **Level of difficulty:** ■
- **Diversity of coral species:** –
- **Diversity of fish species:** ■■
- **Big fish:** ■
- **Wrecks:** –
- **Caves:** ■■ (in the Kings Spring)
- **Walls:** –
- **Snorkeling:** ■■■■■

FRESH WATER: US

Ginnie Springs

SEVERAL OF THE MANY SPRINGS OF CENTRAL AND NORTHERN FLORIDA LIE AT GINNIE SPRINGS. THEY HAVE LONG BEEN A POPULAR LOCATION, AS HERE YOU CAN SNORKEL, SCUBA, AND EVEN CAVE-DIVE IN IDEAL WARM-WATER CONDITIONS.

Wherever you look in central or northern Florida, you will find springs, rivers, ponds, and lakes. Many millions of years ago, the whole of Florida lay under water, until the sea level fell and dry land took over. The latter lies only slightly above sea level, and the water table is generally just below the surface. The bedrock in karst areas consists of limestone, and in numerous collapsed caves water collects in dolines (sinkholes). There are many springs at which filtered groundwater bubbles out with immense force.

Ginnie Springs, near High Springs, is a well-known divers' paradise. There is a leisure park with a spacious campsite and a dive center with attached shop. Every day, the seven springs in the 200-acre/80-ha site supply hundreds of millions of gallons of very clear, warm water measuring a constant 72°F/22°C.

The spring pool at Ginnie Springs measures about 100 ft/30 m in diameter and is 15 ft/5 m deep. The banks are wonderfully overgrown with all kinds of plants. You may see the odd turtle, eel, lungfish, or crab, and colorful pumpkinseed sunfish dart around everywhere. A broad entrance at the bottom of the spring leads to the main attraction, the large cave. It is ideal for experienced divers and budding cave divers alike, as some daylight still enters the upper section. The maximum depth in this Ball Room is 50 ft/15 m, and the tunnel that leads on into the depths of the earth has been grated for safety reasons.

95 FACTS

- **Depth:** 3–50 ft/1–15 m
- **Visibility:** 23 ft/7 m in the river, more than 130 ft/40 m in the springs
- **Water temperature:** 72°F/22°C
- **Best time of year:** All year round
- **Level of difficulty:** ■–■■■
- **Diversity of coral species:** –
- **Diversity of fish species:** ■■■
- **Big fish:** ■
- **Wrecks:** –
- **Caves:** ■■■■■
- **Walls:** –
- **Snorkeling:** ■■■■■

The spring pool leads into the Santa Fe River via a 150-ft-long/45-m-long outflow. At its mouth, the mixing of the clear spring water with the yellowish river water, together with the impressive alligator gars lurking there, makes for atmospheric scenes that are highly photogenic.

The springs and caves of Devil's Ear and Devil's Eye may be visited only by licensed cave divers. A river dive from the mouth of the spring as far as Ginnie Springs is very interesting, and divers often search for fossilized shark teeth on the river bottom. July Spring, Deer Spring and Twin Spring are other springs in the area that resemble huge aquariums.

There is also wonderful snorkeling in the nearby Ichetucknee River. Besides the many fish, you may, if you are lucky, come across an alligator.

Opposite page: An alligator gar in the evening sun in Santa Fe River.

Above: A heavenly body of water, the spring pool at Ginnie Springs.

Left: Divers in front of the entrance to the Devil's Eye cave system.

FRESH WATER: MEXICO

Cenotes

BENEATH THE MEXICAN PENINSULA OF YUCATÁN LIES AN ENORMOUS AND UNIQUE LABYRINTH OF WATER. THROUGH THE CENOTES YOU CAN ENTER FASCINATING CAVERNS, CAVES, AND UNDERGROUND RIVER PASSAGES.

The Mayas gave the name cenotes to these underground chambers filled with fresh water. For them, these were the entrances to the underworld and therefore places for spiritual activities and sacrificial sites. The caves were formed about 1.5 million years ago, after the polar regions expanded during the ice age, the sea level fell, and the reefs that had been built by tiny coral polyps now lay above water. Through the action of rain and earth movements, the coral reef was then gradually hollowed out and, drop by drop, unique forms took shape in the caverns. When the polar ice caps melted again, many former areas of land were inundated. The labyrinth of Yucatán has lain underwater ever since, and everywhere there are holes in the ground containing collapsed karst cave ceilings, shafts, water basins, pools, lake, and lagoons—the cenotes.

Many cenotes are connected to one another by underground passages. In January 2007, cave explorers were able to discover entirely new passages, and in doing so reveal the world's longest contiguous water-filled system—a 167,977-yd-long/153,599-m-long paradise for cave divers.

Some cenotes lie so well concealed in the jungle that they can only be reached by elaborate expeditions. Some of the fabulous watery paradises around Playa del Carmen on the northeast coast and in the vicinity of Tulum farther to the south are easy to reach, and various dive centers offer guided tours to these. It should be noted that without specialist cave training, only the so-called daylight zone can be explored.

The best-known caves lie to the south of Playa del Carmen. At Chac-Mool you can enjoy the spectacular atmosphere produced by shafts of sunlight falling on the cenote. Not far from here lie the cenotes of Ponderosa and Taj Mahal, which are also ideal for snorkeling, as neither exceeds 45 ft/14 m in depth.

Dos Ojos, to the northeast of Tulum, was named after its two entrances, which look like eyes. Even at the entrance, you can marvel at wonderful stalactites and stalagmites. Most caves charge an entrance fee, including Gran Cenote near Tulum, one of the region's most beautiful caverns, which is also ideal for snorkelers. Calavera has a very mystical, enjoyable atmosphere, while large numbers of fish have colonized the Actun Ha cenote, and the beautifully overgrown Cristal cenote offers virtually unlimited visibility. Hidden in the middle of the jungle is the sensational Tuhx Cubaxa, deep in the interior of which mastodon teeth have been found.

Opposite page: Entrance to the Temple of Doom.

Top: Bones of a mastodon, about 12,000 years old.

Center: The Grand Cenote's entrance area is also excellent for snorkeling.

Bottom: The spring pool and entrance at Dos Ojos cave.

96 FACTS

- **Depth:** 3–52 ft/1–16 m (Cenote Angelitaca: 200 ft/60 m)
- **Visibility:** 65–260 ft/20–80 m
- **Water temperature:** 73–79°F/23–26°C
- **Best time of year:** Dec–May
- **Level of difficulty:** ■–■■■■■
- **Diversity of coral species:** –
- **Diversity of fish species:** ■■■
- **Big fish:** –
- **Wrecks:** –
- **Caves:** ■■■■■
- **Walls:** –
- **Snorkeling:** ■■■■■

FRESH WATER: NEW ZEALAND

Waikoropupu Springs

IN THE NORTH OF NEW ZEALAND'S SOUTH ISLAND LIES THE COUNTRY'S LARGEST AND MOST POPULAR FRESHWATER SPRING. WITH A VISIBILITY OF EXACTLY 203 FT/62 M, IT IS CONSIDERED TO BE ONE OF THE CLEAREST BODIES OF WATER IN THE WORLD.

The Maoris, the original inhabitants of New Zealand, have been troubled for some time now: Huriawa, the guardian spirit of the water, is being disturbed in her tranquility by tourists. She resides in and watches over Waikoropupu Springs, the most precious of all waters. However, because this clear spring is a real tourist attraction, it is now advertised in every guidebook, and this place sacred to the Maoris is consequently being besieged by visitors.

No one traveling to New Zealand would want to miss this crystal of blue and turquoise water set against the countless green tones of the underwater flora. Visiting it has only been possible since the area was declared a protected national park in 1977, as it was previously in private ownership. In the high season, you now have to queue in order to be able to spend a maximum of 15 minutes gazing around below the water's surface. The regulations are strict: The number of people and dive time are limited, and every guest has to enter his or her name in a book at the entrance. How long things will remain like this, no one knows, as the Maoris want to establish a ban on diving in the springs.

The water bubbles up from the main spring under great pressure from a 23-ft-deep/7-m-deep split in the rock. Between 250 and 750 cubic ft/7 and 21 cubic m of water, which comes from the Takaka River 10 miles/16 km away, is discharged every second. After the water has trickled underground, however, 10 years

might pass before it emerges again here. The extreme clarity is produced by natural filters and an artesian tunnel system.

The main spring pool measures exactly 138 ft/42 m in diameter, and using mirrors and laser technology, it has been possible to measure a horizontal visibility of 203 ft/62 m. The temperature is a constant 53°F/11.7°C all year round.

A variety of mosses thrives on the bottom alongside aquatic forget-me-not. Watercress reaches up to the surface and rushes grow at the edge, and there are even some red grasses. A few freshwater crabs live hidden in cracks, but fishes are seldom seen. If you stay quite still, the underwater garden is reflected downward from the surface of the water, producing a fantastic scene.

A short way down from the spring there are further crystal-clear pools that are not quite as deep. The water bubbles constantly, small sand volcanoes swirl around, and it appears as if the sand were dancing wildly, which is why the Maoris give this unique biotope the name "Dancing Sands." Unfortunately, these springs are too small and inaccessible for divers, so the attraction may only be viewed from above.

Opposite page: A spring sinkhole.

Above: Diving here is like being in a greenhouse.

Left: Wonderful plants in crystal-clear water.

97 FACTS

- **Depth:** 3–23 ft/1–7 m
- **Visibility:** 203 ft/62 m
- **Water temperature:** 54°F/12°C
- **Best time of year:** Nov–May
- **Level of difficulty:** ■
- **Diversity of coral species:** –
- **Diversity of fish species:** ■
- **Big fish:** –
- **Wrecks:** –
- **Caves:** –
- **Walls:** –
- **Snorkeling:** ■■■■■

FRESH WATER: SWITZERLAND/GERMANY/FRANCE

The Rhine

THE HIGH RHINE AND THE UPPER RHINE, IN PARTICULAR, HAVE MANY THRILLING DIVE SITES TO OFFER. IN THE SOUTH BADEN REGION, THERE IS A FASCINATING AREA IN WHICH THE FULL RANGE OF FLORA AND FAUNA FOUND IN COLDER FRESH WATER IS REPRESENTED.

The Rhine, which originates in Switzerland and flows into the North Sea, has a length of 820 miles/1,320 km and is one of the world's most congested waterways. However, in the border region where Switzerland, France, and Germany meet, the river has a few surprises in store for divers.

Lake Constance, through which the Rhine flows, is a varied and challenging dive location with walls and wrecks. A number of dive centers have therefore been set up in this area. Excellent diving opportunities are available in the sections of the High and Upper Rhine that follow, between Schaffhausen and Strasbourg, and in the nearby spring pools.

Special rules apply to river diving. You have to obtain accurate information about entry and exit points, hazards, statutory regulations, and conservation areas. In addition, diving is not recommended following rainy days, as visibility levels are then severely impaired.

One very popular dive site is located at the toll bridge in Rheinau, where you can enter the water from both the German and the Swiss sides. Below the weir, you will see a variety of juvenile fish among the plant growth in the shallow waters downstream. Under the bridge, where depending on the water level it is between 13 and 20 ft/4 and 6 m deep, there are ideal hiding places between blocks of stone for perch and ruffe, fat eels, and heavy Wels catfish.

98 FACTS

- **Depth:** 3–30 ft/1–10 m
- **Visibility:** 10–100 ft/3–30 m
- **Water temperature:** 46–75°F/ 8–24°C
- **Best time of year:** Mar–Nov
- **Level of difficulty:** ■–■■■
- **Diversity of coral species:** –
- **Diversity of fish species:** ■■■■
- **Big fish:** ■■■
- **Wrecks:** ■■■ (Lake Constance)
- **Caves:** –
- **Walls:** ■
- **Snorkeling:** ■■■■■

At the deepest point behind the toll bridge, you can dive in 30–33 ft/9–10 m of water along a small rock wall where there are trees and branches decorated with algae.

A few miles downstream lies Ellikon. Here, you enter the river below the weir on the Swiss side. Caution is necessary on account of the water mill, and you must pay attention to the no-entry signs. While you drift with the current for about 50 minutes, you will come across a large number of eels as well as a few carp and fast-swimming grayling. Important information about the many other sites in the area can be obtained from the *Swiss Dive Guide*.

In southern Baden and Alsace, clear, nutrient-poor, cold water flows out of the ground at a constant 46°F/8°C in spring pools near the Old Rhine. The magnificent atmospheric scenes produced by the underwater flora could be watercolors. The blue waters are no more than 10 ft/3 m deep. They are jewels of nature and unique biotopes, many of which are protected sites. In among this fascinating world, stately pike lie in ambush for prey fish.

Opposite page: A huge pike—the freshwater equivalent of the barracuda.

Above: A diver in one of the Old Rhine springs.

Left: A broad-headed eel looking out from its hiding place.

FRESH WATER: SWITZERLAND

Verzasca & Maggia

SWITZERLAND PRESENTS A DIVERSE RANGE OF DIVING OPPORTUNITIES: LAKES, RIVERS, AND WILD MOUNTAIN STREAMS ALL HAVE SOMETHING SPECIAL TO OFFER. IN TICINO, RIVER-DIVING IN CRYSTAL-CLEAR ROCK GARDENS AND BENEATH WATERFALLS IS A REAL CHALLENGE.

Switzerland has lots to offer underwater. Quite apart from the freshwater divers' paradises of the Verzasca and Maggia rivers in Ticino, the country has 1,484 natural and 44 artificial lakes, as well as deep pools in mountain streams.

The two most beautiful valleys, which over millions of years have been shaped by water into a wild landscape, are the Verzasca and Maggia valleys above Lake Maggiore near Locarno. These rivers contain occasional quiet pools interspersed between wilder stretches. The many dive sites have been excellently signposted by the Swiss Diving Federation, but they get rather overcrowded on weekends during the peak season. Parking spaces are usually available in the vicinity.

When diving in a mountain torrent, divers will first often have to walk or even climb a little. So, in addition to adequate experience, fitness is called for and special rules must be adhered to. It is important that hazardous situations be assessed and identified in good time. Diving in torrential floods is a no-no, while taking a look at the latest weather report is a must. Before entering the water, the entire dive route should be inspected and the exit point memorized or well signposted.

Anyone diving or snorkeling in the two rivers will be amazed. Their charm lies in the transparency of the water, which is shot through with every possible tone of green and blue. About midday, wonderful moods are produced when the sun penetrates the narrow gorges and makes the rock crystals sparkle. Superb stripy patterns are produced in the submerged canyons and on the heavy, smoothly polished boulders made of quartz, granite, feldspar, and mica.

Caution is required at rapids and waterfalls, where brown trout appear almost to dance, but where diving can be perilous. Along quieter sections of the riverbanks you will come across gobies, frogs, and even newts. Reflections on the surface of the water from below form magical, surreal shapes, a dream for any photographer or filmmaker.

The best-known sites in the Verzasca Valley are at the Roman bridge, at Pozzo delle Posse, at Pozzo della Misura, and at the waterfall near Frasco. In the Maggia Valley, there are worthwhile dives at the village of Ponte Brolla, at a few sites upstream from the railway bridge, in the Wolf's Gorge, and in the higher reaches near Fusio.

Opposite page: Diving under the Roman bridge in the Verzasca Valley.

Top: A brown trout, typical of this wild region.

Center: Rapids in a mountain stream.

Bottom: A diver below a waterfall.

99 FACTS

- **Depth:** 3–46 ft/1–14 m
- **Visibility:** 30–100 ft/10–30 m
- **Water temperature:** 45–64°F/7–18°C
- **Best time of year:** June–Oct
- **Level of difficulty:** ■–■■■■■
- **Diversity of coral species:** –
- **Diversity of fish species:** ■■
- **Big fish:** –
- **Wrecks:** –
- **Caves:** ■■
- **Walls:** ■■
- **Snorkeling:** ■■■■

Fernsteinsee & Samaranger See

THESE TWO MOUNTAIN LAKES IN TIROL ARE AMONG THE TOP DIVE DESTINATIONS IN THE WHOLE ALPINE REGION. WITH STUNNING VISIBILITY AND A FABULOUS UNDERWATER LANDSCAPE, THEY WILL ENTHRALL EVEN DIVERS SPOILED BY DIVING IN TROPICAL WATERS.

An almost fairytale land underwater, the magnificent landscape of the Fern Pass, and a stay in a castle hotel await those wishing to dive in these two crystal-clear mountain lakes. As the numbers of divers coming here until recently exceeded the ecological capacity of the lakes, which are privately owned, now only hotel guests are allowed to dive in them.

The second requirement for diving here is a degree of experience. Accurate buoyancy control is vital, since stirred-up sediment would damage the underwater plants and destroy the delicate slime algae that coat the sunken trees and branches so strikingly. In the middle of Fernsteinsee, which measures about 500 yd/450 m in diameter, lies an island with a ruined castle and a hotel restaurant. Trout and char live in the turquoise green lake.

The smaller and colder Samaranger See is a fabulous body of incredibly transparent steel-blue water. Like oversized pick-up sticks, huge tree trunks lie scattered around on the lake bed and are covered with fantastic algae. If you dive in the middle of the lake, you will have a superb panoramic view of the entire shoreline.

100 FACTS

- **Depth:** 3–55 ft/1–17 m
- **Visibility:** 50–165 ft/15–50 m
- **Water temperature:** 39–64°F/4–18°C
- **Best time of year:** Apr–Oct
- **Level of difficulty:** ■
- **Diversity of coral species:** –
- **Diversity of fish species:** ■■
- **Big fish:** –
- **Wrecks:** –
- **Caves:** –
- **Walls:** –
- **Snorkeling:** ■■■■

Below left: Tree trunks scattered like pick-up sticks on the bottom of Samaranger See.

Below right: Algae like cotton wool.